Tamils and LTTE
in
Sri Lanka

Perspective and Prospects

Attention Authors

'We Convert Fighters into Writers'. That has been the motto of Manas Publications, since more than four decades. Our message to the world is that India can win the battle, not only by the bullet but also by the pen. There is no dearth of intellectuals in our country, but their knowledge is confined to them only. No sincere effort has been made by any other publisher to channelise their knowledge in national interest. That is why the talent of a large number of intellectuals, remains latent. An author transforms his knowledge, into a manuscript, and it is our job to spread his/her knowledge by converting it into a beautiful book.

For over four decades, Manas has been motivating the intellectuals by publishing their manuscripts and would like to publish your manuscript too. If you or your colleagues have any manuscript, ready for publication or are working on it, kindly contact us with detailed synopsis and the list of contents. We would transform your work, into a valuable publication. If you wish, we can also suggest you, the suitable subjects for writing books, related to your area of expertise. Manas is known for its publishing quality and commitments. We take utmost care in production and give wide publicity to the book, as well as its author, through our national and international distribution network.

Tamils and LTTE in Sri Lanka

Perspective and Prospects

Dr. Chandra Prakash Singh

Manas Publications
(We Convert Fighters into Writers)
New Delhi-110002 (INDIA)

MANAS PUBLICATIONS
(We Convert Fighters into Writers)
(Publishers, Distributors, Importers & Exporters)
4402/5-A, Ansari Road (Opp. HDFC Bank)
Darya Ganj, New Delhi-110 002 (India)
Off. 011-23260783, 23265523, Res. 011-23842660
Fax: 011-23272766
E-mail: manaspublications@gmail.com
manaspublications@yahoo.com
Website: www.manaspublications.in

ISBN 978-81-7049-401-0

₹ 995/-

Designed at Innovative Processors

Printed in India at
Printways, Delhi and
Published by Mrs Suman Lata for
Manas Publications, 4402/5-A, Ansari Road, (Opp. HDFC Bank),
Darya Ganj, New Delhi-110 002 (INDIA)

Dedicated to

Krishna Shankar Singh, Advocate

Contents

Preface

Sri Lanka is a multi-ethnic, multi-religious, multi-lingual and multi-cultural country. The ethnic Sinhalese and the ethnic Tamils have been in the country for at least 2500 years – the Tamils for probably much longer, given the proximity of Sri Lanka to South India from where the ethnic Tamils migrated. One of the major political problems facing Sri Lanka today, such as the complexities of Tamil problem, is commonly attributed to the colonial experience and plantation economy. Since Sri Lanka gained independence from Britain in 1948, relations between the majority Sinhalese and minority Tamil communities have been strained, and both sides used history to buttress their respective cases. Rising ethnic and political tensions, along with ethnic riots and pogroms in 1956, 1958, 1977, 1981 and 1983 led to the formation and strengthening of militant groups advocating independence for Tamils.

The purpose of this book is to show the origin and complexities of the Tamil problem in Sri Lanka. The origin of the Tamil problem cannot be understood unless the concept of Tamil nation is examined. Are the Sinhalese the only indigenous people or the first to arrive in the island? In other words, are the Tamils outsiders or later entrants? The concept that the Tamils have always constituted a nation has been disputed by the Sinhalese scholars, such as Professor K. M. de Silva, but renowned Sri Lankan historians and archaeologists like K. Indrapala, Sriyan Deraniyagala, Leslie Gunawardena and Sudarshan Senevirathe contend that Sri Lanka has been multi-ethnic and multi-cultural from pre-historic times. But with the exacerbation of the ethnic conflict, the chauvinists among the Sinhalese and the Tamils, two sides of the same coin, started projecting the two communities as antagonistic entities who were at war with one another for several centuries.

Actually it is the political outbidding of Sinhala politicians on Sinhala-Buddhist emotions and symbols against the Tamils that eventually produced a state-seeking violent Tamil resistance movement, which erased the country's stunningly beautiful global image as a tropical paradise and made the country one of the most dangerous places on the earth to live on.

The military defeat of LTTE on 18 May 2009 brought the Sri Lankan conflict to an end. There was and is a strong perception in Sri Lanka that this beautiful island would embrace peace because the LTTE has been militarily defeated. There are, however, roadblocks on the road to peace and tranquility. To enjoy the fruits of military victory, it is important that Sri Lanka consider Sri Lankan Tamils as partners in progress and not merely throw some crumbles at them. There is a great responsibility now to make sure that Sri Lanka's future is not defined by the way the war has ended – and that the questions of democracy, justice and accountability are addressed. While the militant leaders of a major terrorist group have been eliminated/neutralized, the seeds of militancy will remain as long as the basic grievances and deprivations of the Tamils are not addressed and effectively resolved. Hence a number of questions crop up here: who is the indigenous Sri Lankan? Are the Tamils outsiders or later entrants? What went wrong? Why did a land seen as a paradise slip so badly? What are the explicit and implicit dynamics of the Tamil problem? and last, but not the least, what are the prospects for the Tamils after the defeat of the Tigers? This book attempts to re-examine these questions to provide an exposition of the character and complexion of the Tamil problem in Sri Lanka. This book is an endeavour to discuss and analyse systematically the multi-dimensional facets of the history of Tamils in Sri Lanka. The interpretation is freed from misconceptions and inaccuracies. I have no intention of claiming objectivity, but I may say that I have tried to refrain from bending facts to meet by hook or crook my own values.

The approach of this book is historical to collect relevant facts and materials and the facts and materials thus collected have been analysed and scrutinized through historical and analytical methods to extend our understanding of the situation and problems of the Tamils from the ancient times, through colonial rule, and into an independent Sri Lanka.

Different official documents and records of Sri Lanka and India relating to the migration of Tamils in pre-independence era, their problem of citizenship, books and articles of primary source character, and newspaper reports have been the primary sources of information for this book. The secondary sources of information for it have been books by eminent authors, articles in reputed journals and feature articles in newspapers.

This book owes a great deal to the debate and discussion in the University Department of History, West Campus, P. G. Centre, Saharsa, over last two years, on and around the subject of the history of Tamils in Sri Lanka. It was this debate in the corridors of the department that first brought home to me the idea that such a volume needs to be written and produced as soon as possible in order to contribute, even if marginally, to the wider discussion on this very important concern in the field of Tamil history in Sri Lanka. It is, therefore, first of all the department as a whole – faculty and students – to whom I owe a debt of gratitude for providing the stimulus for the production of this volume.

I am grateful to Prof. Raj Kumar Singh, University Dept. of Political Science, West Campus, P.G. Centre, Saharsa, who helped and encouraged in many ways to get the book published. I express my sincere regards to Dr. Swatantra Kumar Singh who has been constant source of encouragement at every stage. I am deeply grateful to Prof. Prashant Dutta (Patna University), Prof. Damodar Singh (Magadh University), Prof. Ram Naresh

Singh (Department of Maithili), Prof. Kumar Jyotiwardhan (Dept. of Hindi), Dr. D.N. Singh (Dept. of Political Science), Prof. Arun Kumar Singh (B.H.U), Dr. Rajeev Sinha (Principal), Dr. Amitabh Tiwari, Dr. Udayan Mishra (Principal) for their co-operation and good wishes.

The good wishes and encouragement that I received from my father-in-law J.P. Singh, Advocate are acknowledged with gratitude. I owe a deep sense of gratitude to my eldest brother Krishna Shankar Singh, Advocate for his affection and keen interest in my academic progress. Elder brother Bal Krishna Singh deserves deep sense of gratitude for his good wishes. My sincere thanks are also due to Dr. Ashutosh Kumar Singh, Advocate; Seema Singh, Dr. Vipin Prakash Singh, Manish Kumar Singh, Advocate; Engineer Suryaveer Singh, Dr. Anamika Singh. I must acknowledge and extend a word of appreciation to my wife Meera Singh, sons Abhinandan and Abhyudaya Prakash in the completion of the book.

I also thank the authorities and staffs of the several libraries and institutions for providing facilities without which this book would not have been possible. Lastly I thank to my publisher Manas Publications, New Delhi, for bringing this book in its present form.

Chandra Prakash Singh

CHAPTER 1

Beginning of Tamils in Sri Lanka

Sri Lanka, known as Lanka – the "resplendent Island", is located about 30 kilometres off the Southern coast of India.[1] The Island of Sri Lanka is separated from the Indian subcontinent by the Gulf of Mannar and the Palk Strait. The natural beauty of Sri Lanka's tropical forests, beaches and landscape, as well as its rich cultural heritage, make it a world-famous tourist destination. The Island consists mostly of flat-to-rolling coastal plains, with mountains rising only in the south-central part. The climate of Sri Lanka can be described as tropical and warm. Its position between 5° and 10° North latitude endows the country with a warm climate moderated by ocean winds and considerable moisture. The Island is divided into two distinct climatic zones – the Dry Zone and the Wet Zone. The mountains and the south-western part of the country, known as the wet zone, receive ample rainfall at an average of 2,500 mm (98 in). Most of the east, south-east, and northern parts of the country comprise the dry zone which receives between 30 and 70 inches rainfall annually.[2]

Early History and Population

Sri Lanka is made of diverse populations, the two major constituents of which are the Sinhalese Buddhists and the

Tamil Hindus. The Sinhalese comprise the dominant ethnic group of Sri Lanka and comprise about 74 per cent of the population. The next largest ethnic group is the Tamils, at about 18 per cent of the population, in two groups (ethnic Tamils 12.5% and the plantation or the Indian Tamils 5.5%). The Moors and Malays, all Muslims make up a total of 7.4 per cent of the population.[3] The ethnic Sinhalese and the ethnic Tamils have been in the country for at least 2500 years – the Tamils for probably much longer, given the proximity of Sri Lanka to South India from where the ethnic Tamils migrated. The Plantation Tamils / the Indian Tamils are descendants of indentured labourers brought to the Island by the British in the mid 1850's to work in the tea plantation in the central hills.[4]

To add religious-linguistic dimensions to an already existing ethnic one, the Sinhalese are Buddhist, and the Tamils are primarily Hindu although there is a sizable Christian population of both Sinhalese and Tamils dating back to the Portuguese colonization of the Island in the early 1850's. The Sinhalese speak an Indo-Aryan language, Sinhalese, while the Tamils a Dravidian language, Tamil. The moors are mainly Tamil speaking but many are bilingual.

The chronicle records and archaeological discoveries of human beings and their events happened in areas known as Sri Lanka is called the history of Sri Lanka. The earliest archaeological evidence of human civilization in Sri Lanka appears at the site of the Balangoda Man. These Balangoda people arrived on the Island about 34,000 years ago and are identified as Mesolithic hunter gatherers who lived in caves. The hunter-gatherer people, known as the Wanniyala – Aetto or Veddas,[6] (who still live in the central, Uva and north-eastern parts of the Island), are probably direct descendants of the first inhabitants, that is, the Balangoda man. The indigenous Veddah population were conquered in the 5th century B. C. by the Sinhalese, who were originally from North India.

The valuable sources of knowledge for scholars probing the legends and historical heritage of Sri Lanka are the Pali chronicle, the Dipavamsa, Mahavamsa, Thupavamsa and the Kulavamsa as well as large collection of stone inscriptions, the Indian epigraphical records, the Burmese versions of the chronicle etc. Actually the first major legendary reference to the Island is found in the Indian epic, the Ramayana, thought to have been written around 500 B.C. The Ramayana probably reflects a poetic account of the early southward expansion of Brahmanic civilisation. However, the most valuable source of information for scholars probing the early Sri Lankan history is still the Mahavamsa (Great Genealogy or Dynasty), a chronicle compiled in Pali, the language of Theravada Buddhism, in the sixth century.

There is some debate among historians as to whether settlement by Indo-Aryan speakers preceded settlement by Dravidian-speaking Tamils. One theory states that there was not an organized Tamil presence in Sri Lanka until the invasions from what is now South India in the 10th century A.D.; another theory contends that Tamil people were the original inhabitants of the Island. Satchi Ponnambalam, who has written extensively on the Tamils, claims that the original inhabitants of the Islands were Tamils. He says that many of the monuments considered important by the Sinhalese were constructed by the Tamils.[7] On the other hand, the Sinhalese also believe that they were the first to settle Sri Lanka, and have contentious discussions with Tamils over who settled the land first. The Sinhala Commission Report echoes this view. According to the report, the Sinhalese were the lawful rulers and legal heirs to the Jaffna kingdom. This report further states that there is no evidence of a distinct Tamil Community or a Tamil Kingdom in the Jaffna peninsula before the 13th century.[8]

From above discussion, it is evident that like two types of climate, the Sinhalese and the Tamil people have two versions of their past.[9] So what is the reality? In fact, most historians tend to look at the past through a prism of the present. This invariably results in a jaundiced view and leads to distortion and falsification of history. "History", Eric Hobsbawm has pointed out, "is the raw material for nationalist, ethnic or fundamentalist ideologies as poppies are the raw material for heroin addiction."[10] In this chapter, an attempt will be made to unearth the reality of this complex and fascinating question – who preceded who into Sri Lanka?

The Sinhalese people trace their origin in the Island to the arrival of Prince Vijay from India around 500 B.C. and the Mahavamsa, the Sinhala chronicle of a later period (6th century A.D.), records that Prince Vijay arrived on the Island on the same day that the Buddha attained enlightenment in India.[11] Vijay is the legendary figure in the Mahavamsa. The legendary colonizer of Sri Lanka and primogenitor of the Sinhalese migrant group, Prince Vijay, a Kshatriya from North India arrived in Sri Lanka with 700 followers in 544 B.C. and established himself as ruler with the help of Kuveni, an aboriginal princess. Vijay married Kuveni. Although Kuveni had betrayed her own people by actively participating in the strategy of Vijay and had given birth to two of Vjiay's children, she was banished by the ruler, who then arranged a marriage with a princess from Madurai in south-eastern India, and made her the Queen.[12] Kuveni's offsprings are the folkloric ancestors of the present day Veddahs, an aboriginal people now living in scattered areas of eastern Sri Lanka.[13]

The trouble over this bit of history is that because the Mahavamsa is essentially a chronicle of the early Sinhalese-Buddhist royalty on the Island, it does not provide information on the Island's early ethnic distributions. There is, for instance, only scant evidence as to when the first Tamil settlements were established. In fact, the ancient Tamils from the time of their migration, most probably from the Indus Valley to the South of India did not keep chronological records of their history. All available evidence of their historical past had been gathered from anthropological evidence and other artifacts left behind. What is even more surprising, even at the climax of Tamil civilization – the Chola period – detailed records were not kept. Naturally, therefore, most of the history of the Sri Lankan Tamil people has been reconstructed from stone inscriptions.

Potsherds with early Tamil writing from the 2nd century B.C. have been found in excavations in Poonagari, Jaffna. They bore several inscriptions, including a clan name – Vela, a name related to Velir from ancient Tamil country.[14] Epigraphic evidence shows people identifying themselves as Damelas or Damedas (the Prakrit word for Tamil people) in Anuradhapura, the capital city of Rajarata, the middle kingdom, and other areas of Sri Lanka as early as the 2nd century B.C.[15] There is evidence from archaeological excavations conducted at Pourparippu in the north west of the Island in 1956 and 1957 of a culture which bears some resemblance to the South Indian Megalithic culture, the similarities are most obvious in the Adichchanallur site across the water in South India.[16]

Moreover, Tamil literary sources and excavations in the area of Tissamaharama in Southern Sri Lanka have unearthed locally issued coins, produced between the 2nd century B.C. and the 2nd century C.E., some of which carry local Tamil personal names written in early Tamil characters,[17] which suggest that local Tamil merchants were present and actively involved in trade along the Southern coast of Sri Lanka.[18] Therefore, there is strong archaeological evidence for the presence of Tamils in Sri Lanka.

In the above-mentioned context, it seems necessary to weigh the accuracy of the events mentioned in the Mahavamsa and Kulavamsa. These were written by Buddhist monks or debatably by nuns, and they attempt to convey a religious message using the events to illustrate the importance of the Buddhist religion, hence a very prejudiced version. There is evidence to suggest that these were written long after the events actually took place. Hence, these cannot be considered as accurate records of events. The description of the events had a hard religious coating and the history was modified to glorify those Kings who patronized and supported Buddhism and those who did not, were portrayed as bad kings and in the most unfavourable light possible. Historian K. M. de Silva expresses the same sentiments when he states: "The Mahavamsa and its continuation Kulavamsa were the work of Bhikus and naturally enough were permeated by a strong religious bias, and encrusted with miracle and invention. The central theme was the historic role of the Island as a bulwark of a Buddhist civilization, and in a deliberate attempt to underline this, it contrives to synchronise the advent of Vijay with the parinabban (the passing away) of Buddha.[19]

Thus we see that the Mahavamsa does not mention the presence of Tamils in ancient Sri Lanka. However, when we scratch the surface of the historical details and analysis encapsuled in the Mahavamsa, we find that it provides adequate clues to the presence of the Tamils in Sri Lanka from the ancient times probably well before the arrival of the Sinhalese race. Historical records establish that Tamil kingdoms in Modern India were closely involved in the Island's affairs from about the 2nd century B.C.[20] In Mahavamsa, there is evidence that in 177 B.C. two Tamil kings usurped the Sinhalese throne at Anuradhapura. Their combined twenty-two years rule marked that the first time Sri Lanka was ruled by Tamils. The two were subsequently murdered, and the Sinhalese royal dynasty was restored. In 145 B.C. a Tamil general named Elara took over the throne at Anuradhapura and ruled for a much longer period – forty four years.[21]

From the above observation, it is clear that the chronological context (largely) obtained in the form of radiometer dates, the techno-cultural elements and their region of origin, does not in any way agree with the descriptions of the peopling of Sri Lanka narrated in the middle historic chronicles of Sri Lanka.[22] While it is a fact that the majority of the people of Sri Lanka today are Sinhalese, yet it has to be accepted that a very large number of them are descendants of South Indian Tamils who had come to the Island throughout the ages as peaceful migrants or South Indian warriors of Sinhalese pretenders to the Island's throne/or as warriors of Pandyan and Chola invaders who settled here and were Sinhalised during course of time. In Sri Lanka, people of megalithic culture together with the pre-historic population, namely the Austric-language speakers, developed Sri Lankan civilization. Their exposure to the outside cultural and other influences would have been the contributory factor for the emergence of civilization in Sri Lanka around 250 B.C. Of these, introduction of Buddhism played a vital role in giving a Sinhala identity. As Susantha Goonetillake aptly writes: "Sinhalisation was fundamentally a cultural process associated with Buddhism and that migration even if it did take place was of a minor kind, so as not to have left a significant trace in the archaeological data or in demographic terms on population.[23] In short, Sinhalisation came after, and not before Buddhism.

The Pandya and Chola Annexation Syndrome

Thus, the Tamils had a continuous presence in the island from the ancient times. The Tamil threat to the Sinhalese Buddhist kingdoms had become very real in the fifth and sixth century A.D. Three Hindu Empires in South India – The Pandya, Pallava, and Chola – were becoming more assertive. The Sinhalese perception of this threat intensified because in India, Buddhism – vulnerable to pressure and absorption by Hinduism – had already receded. Tamil ethnic and religious consciousness also matured during this period. Tamil soldiers from what is now South India were brought to Anuradhapura between the 7th and 11th century A.D. in such large numbers that local chiefs and kings trying to establish legitimacy came to rely on them.[24]

The Kulavamsa mentions Tamil rule in Anuradhapura by the Pandyas for a period of 27 years. They are Pandu (429-434 A.D.) his son Parinata (434-437 A.D.) his brother Khudda Parinda (437-452 A.D.). There is no specific reference in the chronicles either to the faith of these rulers or the monasteries that benefited by their donations but inscriptions which record these benefactions to Buddhist monasteries afford evidence that they supported the Buddhist religion.[25] In fact, in the fifth and sixth century A.D. the Tamil threat to the Sinhalese Buddhist kingdoms had become very real because the above-mentioned three Hindu empires in South India were becoming more assertive.

In this context, it is also noteworthy that another king praised in the Mahavamsa is Dhatusena – another hero in the Sinhalese tradition – who in the fifth century A.D. (459-77) liberated Anuradhapura from a quarter century of Pandyan rule. The king was also honoured as a generous patron of

Buddhism.[26] Dhatusena was killed by his son, Kasyapa who is regarded as a great villain in Sri Lankan history. In fear of retribution from his exiled brother, the prince removed his capital from Anuradhapura to Sigiriya, a fortress and palace perched on a monolithic rock 180 meters high. Although the capital was transferred to Anuradhapura after Kasyapa was dethroned, Sigiriya is an architectural and engineering fete displayed in an inaccessible redoubt. The rock fortress eventually fell to Kasyapa's brother, who received help from an army of Indian mercenaries.[27]

Thus we see that in the seventh century A.D., Tamil influence became firmly embedded in the Island's history. By the 8th century A.D., there were Tamil villages collectively known as Damel-Kaballa (Tamil allotment), Demelat Valademin (Tamil villages), and Damel-gam-bim (Tamil villages and lands).[28] However, the next milestone in this chronology of the history of Tamils in Sri Lanka is the Chola period. In the 9th and 10th centuries A.D. Pandya and Chola incursions into Sri Lanka culminated in the Chola annexation of the Island, which lasted until the later half of the 11th century A.D.

The imperial Cholas established an empire which extended from Tamil Nadu over the waters as far as the Malayan peninsula and north as far as the Ganga. Actually in the middle of the 9th century, a Chola chieftain called Vijayalaya ruling small territory north of the river Kaveri established a Chola dynasty which was to expand into an empire.[29] The Chola, initially under Rajaraja the Great (985-1018 A.D.), were impatient to capture the royal insignia; they sacked Anuradhapura in 993 A.D. and annexed Rajarata – the heart of the Sinhalese kingdom – to the Chola empire. Rajaraja's son Rajendra in 1017 A.D. began the total annexation of the Island. The whole island was brought under Chola rule. For seventy five years, Sri Lanka was ruled directly as a Chola province. During this period, after the destruction of Anuradhapura, the Cholas set up their capital farther to the southeast, at Polonnaruwa, a strategically defensible location, which subsequently became the capital for the Sinhalese kings as well.[30]

The decline of Chola power in Sri Lanka was followed by the restoration of the Polonnaruwa monarchy in the 11th century A.D.[31] In 1215, following Pandya invasion, the Tamil dominant Arya Chakaravarthi dynasty established an independent Jaffna kingdom on the Jaffna peninsula and other parts of the North.[32] Jaffna under the Arya Chakaravarthis was much the most powerful kingdom in the island. The Arya Chakaravarthi expansion into the South was halted by Alagakkonara, a man descended from a family of merchants from Kanchipuram in Tamil Nadu.[33] He was the Chief Minister of the Sinhalese king Parakramdebahu V (1344-59 A.D.). Vira Alakeshwara, a descendant of Alagakkonara, later became king of the Sinhalese, but he was overthrown by the Ming admiral Cheng Ho in 1409 A.D.[34]

During the 14th century, thus, the fortunes of the Sinhalese were on decline. As Sinhala power declined, the Tamils moved southward to extract tribute from the Southwest and Central regions. By the middle of the 14th century the Jaffna kingdom had effective control over the northwest coast up to Puttalam.[35] A new era in Sri Lankan history began in 1505 when the Portuguese arrived, finding the Island divided into seven warring kingdoms and unable to fend off intruders. Here it needs mention that the Portuguese arrived to trade for cinnamom. During this extended period of domestic instability and frequent foreign invasions, Sinhalese culture experienced fundamental change. Rice cultivation continued as the mainstay of agriculture but was no longer dependent on an elaborate irrigation network.[36]

In the wet zone, large scale administrative cooperation was not as necessary as it had been before. Foreign trade was of increasing importance to the Sinhalese kings. In particular, cinnamom – in great demand by Europeans – became a prime export commodity. Because of the value of cinnamom, the city of Kotte on the west coast (near modern Colombo) became the nominal capital of the Sinhalese kingdom in the mid-fifteenth century. It was in this given scenario that the Portuguese ordered the king of Kotte to sell them his cinnamom at a price set by them.[37] The king refused and so the Portuguese used force. In 1518 the king of Kotte was forced to agree to give cinnamom to the Portuguese each year as a tribute. Increasing Portuguese demand led to a war in 1520-21, which the Portuguese won. In time the states of Kotte and Sitavaka began to quarrel. The rulers of Sitavaka were insulted by the increasing Portuguese influence in Kotte. So the Kotte and Sitavaka fought a number of wars. Each time Kotte was forced to look to the Portuguese for help. So unavoidably Portuguese influence in Kotte increased. Finally in 1597, the Portuguese acquired Kotte and Sitavaka. In 1619, they succeeded in taking over the kingdom of Jaffna in the North, although they never held control over Kandy. The coastal areas of the Island were conquered by the Dutch and then became part of the British Empire in 1796 A.D.

Sinhalese Nampota dated in its present form to the 14th or 15th century A.D. suggests that the whole of Tamil Kingdom, including parts of the modern Trincomalee district, was recognized as Tamil region by the name Demala – pattanama (Tamil City).[38] In this work a number of villages which are now situated in Jaffna, Mullaitivu and Trincomalee districts are mentioned as places in Demala – pattanama.[39] The English sailor Robert Knox described, walking into the Island's Tamil country, some aspects of their royal, rural and economic life and annonating some kingdoms within it on a map in 1681 A.D.[40] Previous to Robert Knox's publication, the only texts written before colonization of the British were the Mahavamsa, Dipavamsa and Kulavamsa whose goals were to glorify the significance of Buddhism in Sri Lanka, and the importance of Sri Lanka in the Buddhist world.

Most Sri Lankan Tamils live in the northern and eastern provinces and in the capital Colombo, and most Indian Tamils live in the central highlands.[41] Historically both groups have seen themselves as separate communities, although there has been a greater sense of unity. Sri Lankan Tamils are categorized into three sub groups based on regional distribution, dialects, and cultures.

Regional Manifestations

The first regional sub-group in which Sri Lankan Tamils are encapsuled is Puttalam Tamils, also known as Negombo Tamils. They are native Sri Lankan Tamils who live in the western Gampaha and Puttalam districts. The term does not apply to Tamil immigrants in those areas.[42] They are distinguished from other Tamils by their dialects, one of which is known as the Negombo Tamil dialect, and by aspects of their culture such as customary laws.[43] Most Negombo Tamils have assimilated into the Sinhalese ethnic group through a process known as Sinhalisation. Sinhalisation has been sped up by caste myths and legends.

Another sub-group of Sri Lankan Tamils based on regional distribution is eastern Tamils, who inhabit a region that spans the Trincomalee, Batticaloa, and Ampara districts.[44] Their history and traditions are inspired by local legends, native literature, and colonial documents.[45] In the 1500s, the area came under the neuronal control of the Kandyan kingdom, but there was considerable local autonomy under native Vannimai chiefs.[46] From that time on, Eastern Tamil social developments diverged from that of the Northern Tamils. Eastern Tamils are an agrarian based society. They follow a caste system similar to the South Indian or Dravidian kinship system. The Tamils of the Trincomalee district have different social customs from their southern neighbours due to the influence of the Jaffna kingdom to the North.[47] The indigenous Veddah people of the East coast also speak Tamil and have become assimilated into the eastern Tamil caste structure.[48] Most eastern Tamils follow customary laws called Mukkuva laws codified during the Dutch colonial period.[49]

Last but not the least, the Northern Tamils also known as Jaffna Tamils are also categorized into two groups: those who are from the Jaffna peninsula in the North, and those who are residents of the Vanni District to the immediate South. Jaffna's history of being an independent kingdom lends legitimacy to the political claims of the Sri Lankan Tamils, and has provided a focus for their constitutional demands.[50]

The kingdom of Jaffna is the direct predecessor to the concept of Tamil homeland. The kingdom was Tamil-Saivite and its demographical extensions were illustrated in the Jaffna – centric historiographical literature which arose in these times. The demography according to these literatures cover a territory from Kutiraimalai in the west coast (Puttalam district) to Verukal in the eastern coast (eastern province) encompassing more or less the present northern and eastern provinces.[51]

The kingdom was dominated by classes and feudal chiefs who had migrated from the various parts of South India, especially from Tamil Nadu. On many occasions, new settlements were created by them. The kingdom was partially agrarian and partially mercantile. A kingdom exclusively for the Tamil-homeland became thus possible only when there were no big powers in southern Sri Lanka and in the Tamil South India.[52] The political reality when the Portuguese came to Sri Lanka was that there were three kingdoms i.e. – the kingdoms of Kotte, Kandy and Jaffna.

As is mentioned earlier in this chapter, Sri Lanka faced its first colonial experience under the Cholas. The dry zone of Sri Lanka and its hyradulic pattern declined. The capital Anuradhapara was abandoned. Mass migration took place which considerably changed the demography of the North and the East of the Island. In Jaffna, Kantarotai was replaced by Nallur. As a sequence of these developments, the kingdom of Jaffna emerged in the latter half of the 13th century A.D. when both the Sinhalese and South Indian hegemony declined. In short, a Tamil state in Jaffna which was far anterior going back to Proto-historic times was given a fresh impetus by the Chola empire in carving out a homeland of specific dimensions for the Tamils in the North and the East.[53]

In fact, the Chola empire and the subsequent developments had a great impact on the demography of Vanni, East and Northwest. Especially the East was in the limelight under the Cholas, probably due to their activities in the Bay of Bengal. Tamil inscriptions of this and subsequent periods are found concentrated in the East up to Tirukkoyil in the down South.

Mass migrations of clan were a common phenomenon in the Vijayanagar South India, and their impact was felt in Sri Lanka too. Vanni, East and the Northwest have their own literary records narrating the settlements that arose in this period. The settlers ranged from agriculturalist to traders, artisans, mercenaries and fisher folk.[54] The indirect impact of the Vijaynagar empire prevented the political advent of Islam. But, since the early centuries of this millennium, muslim settlements came up in the coastal areas known for maritime trade contacts. In the Tamil homeland now there are a considerable population in Mannar, Mattakkalappee, Jaffna city and Puttalam in the Northwest (which was part of the Tamil homeland till recent decades).

The Portuguese and Dutch maintained the kingdom of Jaffna as a separate unit. Jaffna witnessed considerable economic growth under the Dutch due to certain specialized trade. This paved the way to the Jaffna centric social and cultural developments in subsequent times.[55] Towards the end of the Dutch rule, religious and linguistic revival took place which created a place for Jaffna not only to lead the Tamil homeland but also to be in a position ahead of the then Tamil South India in certain spheres of cultural achievements.

The late British period witnessed a gradual decline of economic independence of the Tamil homeland, especially Jaffna. Traditional subsistence, trading ports and trade routes declined. Missionary and native education brought in white collar jobs. The traditional trade which was cut off from its South Indian contact turned toward the Sinhalese areas in the South creating subsistence competitions.[56] The image of Tamils as exploiters and the resultant ethnic conflict arose in the early decades of the 20th century with the emergence of the powerful forces of Sinhala-Buddhist nationalism. The crisis is essentially one of devising socio-political means which will ensure a subsistence pattern for the Tamil people in their own land. A separate nation, autonomous state and affiliation with India are mere words in the absence of the incorporation of this fundamental factor.

Tamil Claims to Land: Fact and Fiction

When the Portuguese arrived in Sri Lanka in the early part of the 16th century, the seat of government of the island was at Kotte near Colombo. De Queyroz, a much quoted contemporary Portuguese historian, writes in his *"Conquest of Ceylon"* that 'after the City of Cota (Kotte) became the metropolis there were in the island 15 kinglets subject to the (Sinhalese) King of Cota who therefore was considered to be Emperor, and the same title is in these days (i.e. after the Portuguese occupation of Colombo) claimed by the (Sinhalese) King of Candea. These Kinglets were of Dinavaca, Uva, Valave, Putalao (Puttalam), Mantota (near Mannar), Tanagama, Muliauali, Triquilimale, Cutiar (Koddlyar, the Bay of Trincomalee and its hinterland), Batecalao (Batticaloa), Paneva (Panama), Vintena (Bintenna), Orupula, Mature, Candes and the point of the North, Jafnapatao (Jaffnapatam or Jaffna).' It is worth noting that foreign writers such as de Queyroz who wrote of the conditions of their times viewed local chieftains subordinate to the suzerainty of the sovereign as "Kinglets" or "Kings" subject to an "Emperor."[57] Right up to modern times it was the Indian tradition for even owners of large landholdings to call themselves "Rajas" though they had no temporal power at all. What is relevant for the present argument is that the "Emperor" at Kotte was suzerain of the entire country. Kandy (Candea) in the central hills became the seat of government in the late 16th century.[58]

Kings of Kandy Ruled Jaffna

The Dutch priest Baldaeus, who was with the Dutch forces which captured the Portuguese coastal settlements with the assistance of and on behalf of the Sinhalese King, wrote an authoritative work entitled *"A true and exact description of the Great Island of Ceylon"* in 1672.[59] He records that on 18 August 1613 King Senerat summoned his Councillors from the various parts of his kingdom to ensure the right of succession of his eldest son. The councillors who attended, included amongst many others, the Kings of Cotiarum, Batecaloa, Panua, Palugam (which together encompass, the present Eastern Province) and one Namacar, the envoy of the "King" of Jaffnapatam (part of the present northern Province). The succession of the Crown Prince to Senerat being agreed to by the Council, Senerat issued a proclamation when the Council reassembled on the second day, part of which read as follows:

'Cenuwiraed (Senarat) by the Grace of God, Emperor of Ceylon, King of Kandy, Setevaca (Sitawaka), Trinquenemle (Trincomalee), Jaffnapatam, Settecorles (Seven Korales), Manaer (Mannar), Chillaw, Chitaon Panua (Panama) Batecaloa (Batticaloa), Palugam (Palukamam) and Jaele (Yala), Prince of Ove (Uva), Denavaque (Denawaka), Pasdan Corle (Pasdum Korale), Velaren (Wellassa), Cotamale (Kotmale), Mewtre (Miwatura), and Ventane (Bintenna), Duke of Willagamme (Weligama on the Southern Coast), Gale (Gaile), Ody (Udunuwara) and Jattenore (Yatinuwara), Court of Quartercorle (Four Korales), Harkepatte (Harispattu), Odogodaskary (Udugoda Korale), Corwitty (Kuruwita) and Bategedre (Batugederal), Peace to all whom it may concern.

'Whereas we lay sick in bed and not knowing the time of dissolution we have therefore assembled together all our principal officers of state to consult with them as to secure the tranquillity of our country and to the well-being of our beloved son Comara Singa Astana (who did not eventually succeed Senerat on the latter's death in 1635 but was passed over in favour of youngest son Maha Astana who was crowned as Rajasinghe II).'

After appointing regents to rule the country till Kumarasinghe came of age, the Proclamation goes on thus 'and we do further command all kings and princes, all dukes, counts, ecclesiastics, nobles, governors, heads of all lands and provinces, captains and presidents of all councils, admirals, chancellors and all other persons ... of every province, town and village jointly and severally that they acknowledge the aforesaid princes, (i.e., the regents) as guardians and rulers of our Empire until such time as the hereditary prince shall come of age and for greater security we have jointly with the crown prince and all the assembled kings, princes, nobles and potentates affixed hereto our signature and confirmed it with our seal of office... Thus declared at the Imperial Palace at Digelege this 19th day of August 1613.' It will be noted that one of the Chieftains who bound himself was the King of Jaffnapatam through his representative Namacar.

Sometimes he pledged fealty to Portugal while acknowledging the Sinhalese king as his overlord. This precarious existence of the "Kingdom of Jaffna" ended in 1619 when a Portuguese general defeated the "Kinglet" Sangili (who was de jure a chieftain of Rajasinghe II of Kandy) at Atchuvely in 1619. Sangili himself was a usurper. Jaffnapatam was thereafter a Portuguese settlement for 40 years till it was captured by the Dutch in 1638. We are here concerned with the boundaries of this Kingdom of Jaffnapatam which alone might be claimed as the traditional homeland of the Tamils if such a concept were to be acknowledged at all.[60]

Jaffnapatam and the Eastern Province

Baidaeus, who accompanied the Dutch forces which took Jaffnapatam in 1658, lived and worked there as a missionary for eight years till 1665. We are fortunate to have his accurate and detailed description, complete with a map. Jaffnapatam, said Baldaeus, 'is divided into four provinces and is very thickly inhabited.' The four provinces were: Beligamme (Weligama at the time Sinhalese place names were still in use, now Valikamam), Tenmarache (Tenmaradchi), Waddemarache (Vadamaradchi) and Patchiarapalie (Pachchilaippali).[61]

In addition the adjacent isles as well as the island of Mannar (but no part of modern mainland Mannar District) belonged to the kingdom Jaffnapatam. The "Isles" are Ourature (modern Kayts), Caradiva (modern Tamil name Karaitivu), Pongardiva (new Pungidutivu), Analativa (Analaitivu), Nindundiva (Delft), Paletiva (Paletivu) and "some other isles" i.e., Manditivu, Kachchativu, and other islets which are now part of the territory of Sri Lanka. According to Baldaeus, the "Province" of Patchiarapalle (modern Pachchilaippali) bordered on the Kingdom of Kandy ruled by Rajasinghe II.

The Vanni (save a trip along the northern and north west coast) i.e., modern mainland Mannar District most of Kilinochchi District, Vavuniya District, as well as Mulativu District (all in the present Northern Province) and the whole of the present Eastern Province were part of the dominions of the Sinhala King. Jaffnapatam was little more than the Jaffna Peninsula ("Jaffnapatam" being derived from the Sinhalese "Yapa Patuna", Yapa – High ranking official, Patuna – entrepot) plus the adjacent islands and the island of Mannar. The area of this territory is only 430 square miles.[62]

The whole of the present Eastern Province was under the direct rule of the Sinhalese kings at Kandy, the "Kings" referred to by Baldaeus and de Queyroz having been only Vanniyas (Chieftains) and Disaves (provinces governors). Though the Portuguese and the Dutch built forts at Trincomalee, the huge bay called Koddiar Bay was under the control of the King (Emperor) at Kandy. Robert Knox and his party were captured at Koddiar Bay by King Rajasinghe's men. De Qyeyroz states that[63] Trincomalee, Koddiar, "Tambalagama" and "Gantale" were some of the territories of the Kingdom of Kandy.

Koddiar, Batticaloa and Puttalam were the main ports of the Sinhalese Kings who ruled in Kandy when the Portuguese, the Dutch and the British were successively in occupation of settlements on the northern, south western and southern coasts. The Dutch Governor Rycklof van Goens reported in December 1663 (at a time when the Dutch, having broken their treaty with Rajasinghe II entered into in 1638, were attempting to establish title even to Rajasinghe's dominions) that 'The country between the Waluwe (Walawe stretches east and north-east as far as Jale (Yala, now a wild life sanctuary) turns to the north and north west up to Trinquenemale. I have been able to visit this district as it is entirely inhabited by the King's (i.e. Rajasinghe's) people.'

Tamils, Muslims and Catholics in Sinhalese Territory

When the Portuguese persecuted the Arabs, Sinhalese Buddhist kings invited them to settle in their dominions. This was the origin of the large Muslim population in the Eastern Province at the present time. They also settled down on invitation in the Central Province and even in the North Central Vanni (Anuradhapura and Polonnaruwa districts) where traditional Sinhalese villages now have as their neighbours traditional Muslim villages, all dependent on agriculture under irrigation from village tanks. In 1762, Pybus, the British Ambassador from Madras to the Court at Kandy, was received by the King's officers at Mutur on the Southern beach of Koddiar (Trincomalee) Bay on 5th May, conducted in State through modern Trincomalee, Polonnaruwa and Matale Districts to Kandy and taken back to Mutur on 2nd July.[63]

'The district of Mutur had 64 villages under three Headmen who have the management for the General to whose Government it belongs, who (i.e., the General) resides at Candia (Kandy)' states Pybus in the diary of his journey.[64] The King's Disava (Provincial Administrator) is called "General" by Pybus. He is called "King" by de Queyroz and by Baladeus. In 1766 the Dutch Governor Falck, with an army behind him, forced King Kirti Sri Rajasinghe of Kandy to sign a treaty ceding to the Dutch a coastal strip four miles in breadth along the whole of the coastline of modern Eastern Province (as well as part of the western coast). Kirti Sri later refused to be bound by the treaty as it was signed under duress. But there could be no better proof that the whole of the present Eastern Province was acknowledgedly a Sinhalese domain till 1766, so that there is no question of this Province ever having been part of an independent Tamil Ealam or of "traditional homelands" of the Tamils. Tamils, Muslims, Mukkuvars (fisherfolk from the Malabar or Kerala coast in India) and Sinhalese lived under Sinhalese rule without discrimination. The private rights of each race were governed by customary laws. It is an outrage that the historical tolerance and hospitality of the Sinhalese are now exploited with the lie of Tamil "traditional home-lands" to deprive the Sinhalese of benefits of national investment on public land in a sparsely populated region which was, till the Sinhalese ceded the coastal strip to the Dutch in 1766 and the interior to the British in 1815, 16 parts of the Sinhalese dominions.

When the Portuguese persecuted the Muslims in the settlements occupied by the former, the Sinhalese Buddhist Kings settled the latter in the modern Eastern Province and the Central Province. When the Dutch persecuted the Catholics, the Sinhalese Buddhist Kings who had their seat at Kandy settled them too within their dominions. This is how there is a large Catholic settlement at Wahacotte, Matale District, in the heart of the country. In 1658 the Dutch issued a proclamation making the harbouring or giving of protection to a Roman Catholic priest a capital offence. Father Joseph Vaz, a hero of Roman Catholic history in this country, owned his life to the intercession and protection of a Sinhalese Buddhist King.

According to Professor Sinnappa Arasaratnam[65] the Dutch wished to conclude a new treaty with the Sinhalese King Wimaladharmasuriya II (1687-1707), as under their treaties with his predecessor Rajasinghe II (1635-1687) they held the settlements captured from Portuguese only as a form of security for repayment to them of the expenses incurred in fighting the Portuguese (which occupation of the former Portuguese territories until their expenses were paid, or, in the alternative, for the cession of the coastal strip between the Walawe Ganga and the Kalu Ganga, the small island of Pulliyantivu on which the Batticaloa Fort had been erected, and the inner bay of Trincomalee harbour. King Wimaladharmasuriya II rejected these proposals. The Sinhalese Kings throughout considered the Dutch as a security force employed for the protection of the coastal belts of the island.

Who are the Tamils?

The modern Northern Province (3352 square miles) is also sparsely populated with the exception of Jaffna Peninsula (approx. 430 square miles) even today. We have seen that only Jaffna Peninsula could for historical or demographic reasons be considered a traditional homeland of the modern Sri Lanka Tamils if such a concept were to be entertained. Even here the history of Tamil settlement is comparatively recent considering the antiquity of the history of Sri Lanka. 'The colonization of Jaffna by the Tamils cannot be of extreme antiquity,' writes H. W. Codrington in his work "*Ancient Land Tenure and Revenue in Ceylon*". 'Such Sinhalese place names as exist, and they are not a few, are not pre-medieval, and the Vaipavanmalai (Yalpana Vaipavanmalai composed in 1736 A.D., by Mailvagna Puravar, an inhabitant of Jaffna Peninsula on the instructions of the contemporary Dutch administration of Jaffna, and added to in British times) though unreliable as serious history, records the presence of the Sinhalese in the peninsula in the 15th Century.'[66] K. Balasingham, the eminent Tamil lawyer, politician and scholar writes that 'There is no proper history of Jaffna prior to the Arya Chakaravarthis' (i.e., before the latter part of the 13th century).[67] Even C. Rasanayagam in his heavilly Tamil-biased, "*Ancient Jaffna*" admits 'that Jaffna was occupied by the Sinhalese earlier than by the Tamils is seen not only in the place names of Jaffna but also in some of the habits and customs of the period.'[68] The evidence is that the people identified in modern times as Sri Lanka Tamils are mostly descendents of Malayalees from the Malabar or Kerala coast (Magha of Kalinga-modern Odisha and part of Andhra Pradesh–invaded the country in the 13th century with an army from Kerala), Tamils from the Coromandel coast who came with the advent of the Arya Chakaravarthi chieftains from the 13th century onward, Malaya from the armies of the Javaka invader Chandrabhanu (13th century), the Sinhalese who were original settlers as well as migrants from the Vanni when the Dry Zone irrigation systems collapsed, the comparatively few ancient Tamil invaders and non-military immigrants who would have been both original settlers in the Peninsula as well as immigrants from the Vanni after the collapse of the irrigation systems, Paravars (the Bharatha community) who came in Portuguese and Dutch times as pearl divers, soldiers and fishermen, Kalingas (from modern Odisha and Andhra Pradesh), Mukkuvars from the Malabar coast, Arabs, Moors from South India, and Portuguese who were given land grants and settled in Jaffna from 1619 to 1658. Most of the descendents of old Tamil invaders and traders who came from time to time from the 3rd century B.C. to the 11th century A.D., must have settled down in areas now predominantly Sinhalese and got absorbed into the modern Sinhalese population. They could not be among the Tamil population of today.[69]

To conclude, the ancestry of the Sri Lanka Tamils of the present time therefore is not clear. This had been an embarrassment to modern day historians. History is basically the capacity of a society in remembering its past. The mode of exerting this capacity varies from society to society. However, it should be noted that the study of history must be for history and knowledge's sake. History should never be didactic, nor should it be falsified and made into tools of politics. There is little consensus on the history of Tamils in Sri Lanka prior to the Chola period. Some Sinhala historians argue that there was no organized Tamil presence in Sri Lanka until the invasion from Southern India in the 10th century, whereas many Tamil historians contend that Tamils are the original inhabitants of the land and they were called Araipadi and Elapadi. However, the historical evidence is not conclusive either way.

According to anthropological evidence, Sri Lankan Tamils have lived on the island since 2nd century B.C. In fact, around 6th century A.D., the Buddhist monks in Sri Lanka imagined a mass Aryan migration during pre-historic times, which they thought was the basis for the formation of the Sinhala-Buddhist society. This myth created in response to the then prevailing situation is unfortunately still the foundation for the authoritative history of the Island, conditioning the minds of the people. In reality, there was no objective evidence for an Aryan migration. Early colonial and Sinhala historians began to look at the Middle historic Pali Chronicles, Dipavamsa and Mahavamsa, from a Sinhala community point of view, rather than a national point of view. The fact is that these chronicles were about the Theravada Mahavira sect and the ruling families of Anuradhapura. These did not cover other communities and were not about the whole of Sri Lanka.

In reality, by the time Prince Vijaya arrived in Sri Lanka to create the Sinhala race (500 B.C., according to the Mahavamsa), there was fairly advanced communities in North Central and Central Sri Lanka, which had migrated from Peninsular, and South India. It is a historical fact that the Tamil social formation in Sri Lanka over several centuries played a buffer between the Sinhalese and South Indian social formations. But the social formation of Sri Lankan Tamils territory has its own dimensions distinct from that of Tamil Nadu. But the prevailing political and economic conditions have made it an exerting question of Tamil nationalism, demanding a separate nation.

References

1. Rajesh Kadian, *India's Sri Lanka Fiasco,* Vision Books, New Delhi, 1990. p. 84.
2. Earth Trends, Environmental Information, Forests, Grasslands and Drylands-Sri Lanka (http//earthtrends, wri.org/pdf-library/country-problems/formcou-144PDF).
3. C. Christine Fair, "The Sri Lankan Tamil diaspora: Sustaining Conflict and pushing for peace" in Hazel Smith and Paul Stares (ed.), *Diaspora in Conflict: Peace-Makers or Peace Wreckers?,* United Nations University Press, New York, 2007. p. 177.
4. Ibid.
5. P. Sahadevan and Neil Devotta, *Politics of Peace and Conflict in Sri Lanka,* Manak, New Delhi, 2006. pp. 74-76.
6. James Brow, *Vedda Village of Anuradhapura: The historical anthropology of a community in Sri Lanka,* University of Washington Press, Seattle, 1978. The indigenous Veddas are physically related to Dravidian speaking tribal people in South India and early population of south-east Asia. They no longer speak their native language. See, Encyclopedia Britainca Online. London: Encyclopedia Britannia. 2009. http./ WWW.Britannica.com/ Ebchecked/ topic/624466/Vedda.
7. For a comprehensive discussion see, Satchi Ponnamabalam, *Sri Lanka, the National Question and the Tamil Liberation Struggle,* Zed Books, London, 1989.
8. V. Suryanarayan, "Prospects for Reconciliation" in B. Raman, N. S. Moorthy and Kalpana Chittaranjan (eds.) *Sri Lanka: Peace without Process,* Samskriti, Observer Research Foundation, New Delhi, 2006. p. 92.

9. Mohan K. Tikku, *Sri Lanka, A Land in Search of Itself,* National Book Trust, New Delhi, 2007. p. 15.
10. Eric Hobsbawm, *Nation and Nationalism Since 1780,* Cambridge University Press, Cambridge, 1993.
11. K. M. De Silva, *A History of Sri Lanka,* C. Hurst, London, 1981. p. 4.
12. See, Geiger's Preface to Mahavamsa, Geiger. W. translation of the Mahavamsa, Pali Text Society, London, 1912. p.23
13. See, Indo-European Flok-Tales and Greek Legend by W. R. Halliday, quoted in K. M. De Silva, *A History of Sri Lanka,* C. Hurst, London, 1981. p.130.
14. Iravatham Mahadevan, *Early Tamil Epigraphy: From the Earliest Times of the Sixth Century A.D.*, Harvard Oriental Series, Vol. 62, Cambridge, 2003. p. 48.
15. Karthigesu Indrapala, *The Evolution of an ethnic identity: The Tamils in Sri Lanka C.300 BC to C. 1200 CE,* Vijetha Yapa, Colombo, 2007. p. 157.
16. S.P.F. Senaratne, *Prehistoric Archaeology in Cyclon,* Colombo, 1969. pp. 13-21.
17. Iravatham Mahadevan, "Ancient Tamil Coins from Sri Lanka" *Journal of the Institute of Asian Studies,* XVI (2), March 2000. pp. 152-154.
18. Osmund Bopearachchi, "Ancient Sri Lanka and Tamil Nadu" in Chevillard, Jean-luc, Wilden, Eva, (eds.) *South-Indian Horizons: Felicitation volume for Francol's Gross on the occasion of his 70th birthday,* Publications du Department d'Indologie, Pondicherry, 2004. pp. 546-549.
19. K. M. de Silva, *A History of Sri Lanka* (1981). p. 129.
20. C. R. de Silva, *Sri Lanka: A History,* Vikas Publishing House, New Delhi, 1987, 2nd ed., 1997. pp. 30-32.
21. V. Nandrajan, *History of Ceylon Tamils,* Vasantham, Toronto, 1999. p. 40.
22. Sudharshan Seneviratne, "Peripheral Regions and Marginal Communities towards an alternative explanation of Early Iron Age: Material and social formation and Sri Lanka". Dissent and Ideology: Essays in honour of Romila Thapar (ed.) R. Champaka Lakshnni and S. Gopal, Oxford University Press, New Delhi, 1996. pp. 364-370.
23. Susantha Goonetillake, 'Sinhalisation: Migration or cultural colonialism' *Lanka Guardian,* Vol. 3, No. 1, May 1, 1980, pp. 22-29.

24. George W. Spencer (1990), "The Politics of Plunder: The Cholas in eleventh century Ceylon", *The Journal of Asian Studies*, 35 (3), p. 408.
25. S. Paranavitana (ed.), *History of Ceylon, Vol. I, Part I* (Colombo, 1959), pp. 293-294.
26. *Culvamsa*, Vols. I-II Translated and edited by W. Geiger (London, 1979), ch. XXXVIII, VV. 14-45.
27. Ibid., ch. XXXIX, V.V. 20-22.
28. K. Indrapala, *The Evolution of an ethnic identity: The Tamils of Sri Lanka*, South Asian Studies Centre, Sydney, (2007) pp. 214-215.
29. G. C. Mendis, *Ceylon Today and Yesterday*, Lake House, Colombo, 3rd ed. 1995. pp 30-31.
30. Ibid.
31. C. R. de Silva (1997), *Sri Lanka: A History*, Vikas, New Delhi. p. 76.
32. Ibid., pp. 100-102.
33. Ibid., pp. 102-104.
34. Ibid., p. 104.
35. S. K. Sitrampalam, "Tamils in Ancient Sri Lanka – A Multi-disciplinary Perspective", Prof. S. Vithiananthan Memoral Lecture delivered at the University of Jaffna, 2000.
36. K. M. de Silva, "Colonial History of Sri Lanka" course taught in connection with the intercollegiate Sri Lanka Education Program, Antumn, 1992.
37. Ibid.
38. K. Indrapala (2007), *The Evolution of an ethnic identity: The Tamils of Sri Lanka*, Vijitha Yapa, Colombo. p. 210.
39. Nampota; M. D. Gunasena and Company, Colombo, 1955. pp. 5-6.
40. Robert Knox, *An Historical Relation of the Island Ceylon*, Robert Chiswell, London, 1681. p. 166.
41. K. Indrapala (2007), pp. 269-275.
42. Steven Bonta, "Negombo Fishermen's Tamil: A Sinhala Influenced Dialect from a Billingual Sri Lankan Community". *International Journal of Dravidian Linguistics*, June 2008, p. 37.
43. James Glair, *Studies in South Asian Linguistics*, Oxford University Press, New York, 1998. p. 171.
44. Sivathamby Karthigesu, *Sri Lankan Tamil Society and Politics*, Century Book House, New Delhi, 1995. pp. 2-4.
45. Suganthy Subramanian (2006) (in Tamil) *Folk Tradition and Songs of Batticaloa District*, Kumaran Publishing, Colombo. pp. 1-13.

46. See Sivathamby Karthigesu (1995), *Sri Lankan Tamil Society and Politics*, New Century Book House, Delhi. pp. 7-9.
47. Ibid., pp. 5-6.
48. Gabriel C. Seligmann, *The Veddas* (http.//vedda.org/Selignann-coastal-veddas.htm), pp. 331-335.
49. H.W.Tambiah, *Laws and Customs of Tamils of Jaffna* (revised edition) Women's Education and Research Centre, Colombo, 2001. p. 2.
50. Karthigesu (1995), pp. 4-12.
51. K. Indrapala, "Chapter II-History" in K. Indrapala (ed.) Jaffna, Department of Information, Colombo, 1983, pp. 11-21.
52. Muruguar Gunasingam, *Sri Lankan Tamil Nationalism: A Study of its origins*, M.V. Publications, Sydney, 1999. pp. 66-82.
53. Putra Pujangga, *A Requiem for Jaffna*, Anantham Books, London, 1997. pp. 73-76.
54. S. Arasaratnam, "A Historical foundation of the Economy of the Tamils of North Ceylon", Chelvanayakam Memorial Lecture-1982, *Saturday Review*, Jaffna.
55. Ibid.
56. For a comprehensive account see P. Raghupathy, Early Settlement in Jaffna: An Archaeological Survey, Ph. D. Thesis, University of Jaffna, Sri Lanka, 1983.
57. Fernao de Queyroz, "The Temporal and Spiritual Conquest of Ceylon" translated by S. G. Perera, (Goa, 1667), p. 32.
58. De Queyroz, op. cit., p. 469.
59. Phillepus Baldaeus (1672), "A true and Exact Description of the Great Island of Ceylon", translated into English by Pieter Brohier published as Vol. VIII of the *Ceylon Historical Journal*. For the Portuguese Conquest of Jaffna, see p. 316.
60. Historians are confused and in turn confused others about the "Kingdom" of Jaffna.
61. Baldaeus, p. 316.
62. Ibid.
63. De Queyroz, p. 371.
64. See, "Diary of Mr. Pybus's Journey to and from the city of Candia, the capital of the Island of Ceylon and place of Residence of the Emperor". Edited by R. Raven – Hart and published under the title *The Pybus Embassy to Kandy, 1762*, Colombo 1958.
65. Sinnappa Arasaratnam (1987) "Wimaladharmasuriya II (1687-1707) and his relations with the Dutch" *Ceylon Journal of Historical and Social Studies*, Vol. 6, No. 1, pp 63-70.

66. H. W. Codrington (1938), *Ancient Land Tenure and Revenue in Ceylon*, Colombo, pp. 139.
67. K. Balasingham (1928), "The Laws of Ceylon", Vol. I , p. 165 quoted in K. Indrapala (2007), The Evolution of an ethnic identity: The Tamils of Sri Lanka, South Asian Studies Centre, Sydney, p. 238.
68. K. Indrapala (2007), The Evolution of an ethnic identity: The Tamils of Sri Lanka, South Asian Studies Centre, Sydney, pp. 265-66.
69. Ibid.

CHAPTER 2

Migration of Tamils in Pre-Independence Era

Sri Lanka – formerly Ceylon, in English, and Serendib in Arabic – is commonly referred to as the "Pearl of the Orient" due to its beauty and wealth of natural resources, flora and fauna. However, the irony is that in Sri Lanka live one of the most oppressed communities in the world. They are the Indian Tamils / Hill country Tamils living in the central highlands of central, Uva and Saberagamuwa provinces. As distinct from the Sri Lankan Tamils (also called Ceylon Tamils), the Indian Tamils migrated into Ceylon comparatively recently, that is, in the 19th and early 20th centuries from the Tamil speaking areas of South India. From day one of their arrival in Ceylon the Indian Tamils faced discrimination, hatred, humiliation and deprivation of the basic freedom and human rights.[1] Before we can understand the multi-dimensional facets of the syndrome "migration of Tamils", a careful analysis of its genesis seems urgent.

However, one cannot begin an academic discussion of the phenomenon known as "Migration of Tamils" in pre-independence era without a clear understanding of this fact that the movement of persons across land or over sea for reasons, social, economic and political, has greatly influenced the course of human civilisation, creating at the same time many a ticklish problem between the migrants and the government of the receiving countries.[2] Migration of Indians to other parts of the British empire in the nineteenth century and the early part of the twentieth century has created problems in many former British colonies. Most societies ranging from Guyana and Trinidad and Tobago in the Caribbean, to Myanmar in South East Asia, and Fiji in the South West Pacific and Uganda in East Africa have had great difficulties with demographic changes that followed the entry of large number of Indians that British planters and officials introduced.

So far as the question of Sri Lanka is concerned, its experience with Tamil migrants from India is the South Asian version of this.[3] This is so because the migrant Indian population in Sri Lanka did not transform the demography of the country as comprehensively as has happened in Fiji or Guyana and Trinidad and Tobago but the Indian Tamil population became a dominant presence in parts of Central highlands of Sri Lanka.

Migration Syndrome: Tracing the Genesis

In order to grasp the strands of the migration of Tamils, it seems pertinent to take a glimpse of the Tamil speaking communities in Sri Lanka. In Sri Lanka there are two groups of Tamils – the Sri Lankan Tamils also called the indigenous Tamils and the Indian Tamils / Hill country Tamils. The Sri Lankan Tamils are the descendants of those Tamils who reached Sri Lanka in the wake of the Chola invasions beginning with the rule of the Chola Prince, Elara.[4] This was more than a simple migration of people; it was an invasion that was responsible for pushing the Sinhalese southward and simultaneously establishing their own kingdoms.[5] These Indian migrants / newcomers not only introduced ethnic differences but also created a religious rift between the present Buddhists and the new Hindus.[6]

The Sri Lankan Tamils ultimately settled in northern and eastern provinces which constitute the dry zone of Sri Lanka as opposed to the wet zone, inhabited by the Sinhalese. The largest concentration of the Sri Lankan Tamils is to be found at Jaffna in the extreme north. The northern and eastern provinces are typically Tamil areas, the Sri Lankan Tamil population forming 94 per cent of the total population of the former province and about 53 per cent of that of the latter.[7] In a sense, the Sri Lankan Tamils are both Ceylonese and Tamils – Ceylonese because they enjoy Ceylonese citizenship, and Tamils because have cultural affinity to the Tamils of South India.[8]

Juxtaposed with the above mentioned group of Tamils, the second group of Tamils in Sri Lanka are the Indian Tamils who are descendants of bonded labourers sent from Tamil Nadu to Sri Lanka in the nineteenth century to work in tea plantation.[9] These Tamil speakers mostly live in central highlands, also known as the Malayakam or Hill country. It is important to note, after the British took control, Tamil migration greatly expanded and was encouraged. During the British Raj over half a million labourers from South India migrated to Ceylon. Successive batches followed till 1939 in which year the immigration of unskilled labourers came to be banned.[10]

Migration of Tamils: A Response to Market Forces

No doubt, it was the British colonial era project that speeded up the migration of Tamils. However in order to identify various phases and aspects of the migration of Tamils, it seems logical to create a historical content through summarizing related elements of Sri Lanka's history before the British occupation of Kandy in 1815. We need, at this point, to move through history from the sixteenth century onwards, in the years that led up to the European colonialism. The Portuguese first colonised the island in 1505. The Portuguese were more interested in controlling the island's commerce than in absorbing its territory. Apart from being able to establish control over some coastal parts of the island, the Portuguese never effectively controlled the entire island.[11] The result was that failed attempts at conquering the island, botched internal governing policies, and misguided Christian missionary activities together combined to close Portugal's chapter in Ceylon.[12]

It was approximately in the latter half of the 1600s that the Dutch supplanted the Portuguese in the coastal regions as colonial administrators, and ultimately controlled the bulk of the island, except for the kingdom of Kandy, in the centre of the island.[13] The Dutch, too, wanted control of the exportation processes and had very little interest in a political gain.[14] Thus the effects of Portuguese and Dutch colonial rule on the island's pre-capitalist economic formation are minimal. And what is more important, there is no visible sign of the migration of Tamils.

A New Agricultural Regime and Tamil Migration

The British, concerned that they may be defeated in conflicts with the French in South India, and requiring a safe part in the area, began to consider the eastern Sri Lankan harbour of Trincomalee. The British ejected the Dutch in 1796, and in 1802 Sri Lanka became a crown colony. With the British occupation of the Kandyan kingdom in 1815 Sri Lanka passed under the sovereignty of the British crown. It was during that time the British colonialists decided to introduce plantation economy in the island. The British, unable to persuade the Sinhalese to labour on the plantations, needed the Tamils to provide labour and to meet the demands of the growing market for Ceylon's products.[15] Thus thousands of Tamils began to make the annual journey to the coffee estates in the central and southern parts of the island. From the 1820s through the 1880s these Tamils worked as seasonal harvesters on the coffee plantations. After 1880 tea was subsequently introduced which required year round tending and could absorb family labour.

Under the British rule extensive plantations were developed and the island became a large-scale producer of tea, rubber, and coconut products. Hence, Sri Lanka's economic structure was impacted by a radical transformation as British capital was employed to replace the island's traditional subsistence agriculture by plantation farming. Coffee was the first plantation crop, the cultivation of which was encouraged in this way.[16] Consequent on the British occupation of the Kandyan territory in the central province of the island, the Kandyan Highlands offered a suitable soil and climate for the cultivation of coffee.

The expansion of the coffee plantations created a demand for waste lands. Up to 1832, waste lands at the disposal of the Crown were allowed to the planters, on a land grant system. The first plantations introduced on a commercial scale were coffee, and the land required for the plantation was sold for 25 pence per acre, in some instance, the price went up to #1 (one sterling pound) an acre.

The government replaced its outright land grant policy by a land sale policy in 1833, to accommodate the planters, who required more and more land for their export-oriented coffee and other cash crops. The government sold available lands at five shillings per acre. Despite the government's policy of the outright sale of available land, there was an acute shortage of land for the coffee plantations. Pressure from the planters for a solution led to the promulgation of the Crown Land Encroachment Ordinance No. 12 of 1840. By this ordinance, the Crown claimed all land that was not proved to have been rented previously. This led to an increase in activities in the coffee plantations, at the same time it also led to the creation of landless peasantry in the country.

Changeover from Coffee to Tea

It was during the stewardship of Sir Edward Barnes, who became Sri Lanka's governor in 1824, that coffee assumed pivotal significance in the Island's economy. The coffee plantation which covered the period from the 1830s to the 1880s reached its climax in 1878 when according to the report of Majoribanks and Marakkayar,[17] an area of 2,75,000 acres was brought under it. The ownership of coffee plantations, though mostly Europeans, was not wholly so, because a handful of Ceylonese planters were also known to have been the owners of coffee estates even as early as the 1830's and the 1840s.[18] However, the coffee plantation economy collapsed in the 1870s when a leaf disease ravaged the plantations and the planters switched over to the cultivation of tea and rubber. Tea, in particular was caught in that feverish search for an alternative exportable crop, which followed the blight and final disappearance of coffee.

Tea was introduced in the 1880s on a wide scale. The tea plantation economy expanded with the British entrepreneurial investment, export markets and consolidated companies transforming the structure of production and effectively changing the economic foundation of the old feudal society creating a basis for the development of the capitalist economic system[19]. The expansion of the coffee plantations created a demand for wastelands. Tea plantations began to replace coffee in the estates of the Central Highlands. Tea cultivation was promoted from 1860 onwards. The conversion from coffee to tea led to an important demographic development. Up to 1870, the demand for labour in the plantation sector had been seasonal. Labourers were required during the season to pick coffee beans. Therefore, the vast majority of the Indian migrant workers used to return to India.

When the tea and rubber plantations became dominant, the need for a permanent Indian labour force became a necessity. This led to the settlement of a large Indian Tamil community in the Central Highlands. Governor Sir Henry Ward (1855-1860) encouraged the recruitment of the Indian labourers. In 1873 the law to allow the immigration of Indian labourers was passed.

The Context, Pattern and Nature of Tamil Migration

The establishment and consolidation of the plantation economy in Sri Lanka required an adequate supply of labourers ready to be employed on estate work and willing to reside on estate areas. While the demand for labour in the coffee plantation sector was seasonal, the plantation of tea needed a continuous flow of labour throughout the year. But the labour whether for coffee or for tea plantation was not easily available locally. When opening up coffee plantations, the British had to take into account not only the ecological needs of the crop, but also the availability of vast tracts of uncultivated land and the labour for clearing and preparing that land. The Central Highlands of the island was selected due to its soil, climate and abundant forest and periodically cultivated Swidden land ideally suited for coffee. The irrigated low lands, being unsuited for coffee, did not interest the planters.[20]

The Sinhalese and the Kandyan labourers were prepared to undertake the work of clearing the bush but they declined to stay on the plantation areas permanently towards providing constant and dependable labour necessary for the cultivation of such crops as coffee and tea.[21] At the time plantations was opened up in the Central Highlands, labour, not land, was the scarce factor of production. A striking characteristic of the Kandyan Kingdom was its sparse population. According to the British Census Report of 1824, the population of the entire Kandyan Kingdom (which comprised roughly three-fourths of the whole island) was 256,835. The population of Kandy, the capital city in 1818 was only 3,000.[22] On the other hand, the profitability of plantation agriculture rests primarily on the availability of a large, regular, well disciplined and cheap labour forces.[23]

Unlike in neighbouring South India, there was no landless agricultural labouring castes in Kandy. The Sinhalese artisan castes themselves were primarily wet-rice cultivators possessing their own means of production. The elaborateness and complexity of the pre-colonial division of labour, especially its caste specificity, prevalence of serfdom, absence of agricultural labour castes, and primarily the availability of land, made it extremely difficult to find the large wage labour force needed by the coffee plantation.[24] However, in his famous despatch of 21 April 1847,[25] Emmerson Tennent, the officiating Lt. Governor of Sri Lanka, disclosed that despite their normal aversion to plantation work, a small number of the Sinhalese and Kandyan labourers could be prevailed upto to work on coffee estates. According to Dr. Silva,[26] the coffee planters were able to employ some local labourers from about the 1820's to the early 1840's.

However, it needs to be pointed out that the few Sinhalese who did work on coffee plantations provided mostly non-routine supplementary labour rather than routine field labour. The majority of the Sinhalese who ended up working on the European coffee estates were drawn largely from the coastal lowlands rather than the Kandyan regions and they worked in specialised occupations such as carpentry and masonry.[27] The Sinhalese labourers' decision not to become routine wage labour on the estates was quite rational given the availability of land at the time and the relative economic autonomy associated with small holder cash cropping. Their reluctance to become permanent wage labourers on the coffee estates does not imply indolence and disinterest in profit maximization as colonial officials and some social scientists would have us believe.[28] It is highly plausible that the rates of return from labour's cash cropping were higher than from wage labour on the estates although middlemen, traders and distributors did not pay fair price to the peasants for their coffee and other cash crops.

Obviously, therefore, the European planters were disappointed in the local labourers for coffee and subsequently, for tea plantations. Whatever supply of the lowland Sinhalese and highland Kandyan labourers for Coffee plantation was initially available soon petered out specially in face of the Kandyan resentment of any influx of the lowland workers.[29] Because the labour supplied by the Sinhalese semi-proletariat to the plantations was generally unreliable, rebellious and costly, the British planters sought a foreign labour force that was regular, cheap and easily controllable. This they found in landless agricultural labour castes of the South India (Tamils) which came to provide the large, regular and well disciplined labour force needed to the plantations in Sri Lanka.[30] Lt. Governor Emmerson Tennent also had drawn the attention of Grey to the desirability of obtaining South Indian labour in his despatch of 21 April 1847 thus: 'The great object of the colonial government should be to create a permanent and indigenous supply of labour within the island and, if this is not to be effected by stimulating the inert and contented Sinhalese, another expedient is still open by holding out such encouragement as may induce the Indian labourers to settle permanently in Ceylon. Such a settlement should be encouraged on the estates ....'[31]

Now the question that needs investigation is what factors prevailed upon the Tamils to submit to the inducement of the British planters and to migrate into Sri Lanka? The process of the migration of Tamils in the pre-independence era, as already pointed out in this chapter, was governed almost entirely by economic considerations. The push of poverty and the pull of opportunity resulted in a massive change, i.e., poverty at home and opportunity in the plantations overseas, converted what was intended to be no more than a temporary period of service into semi-permanent and, later on, permanent residence.[32]

What existed in pre-independence Indian society was the land-revenue policy initiated by the English East India Company that gradually contributed to rural pauperization in India. In the Permanent Settlement areas, the tillers of the soil were hit hard by the exploitation of landlords, while, in the Madras Presidency, the Ryots under the Ryotwari System were hit harder by the over-assessment of land-revenue and by the tyranny of the government officials entrusted with tax collections. As Nilmoni Mukherjee has pointed out, the assessment of revenue under the Ryotwari settlement was too high to make agriculture a really profitable occupation.[33] What is even more important, in many villages, one-third of the produce of the field was demanded as revenue from the petty Ryots with whom the settlement was made directly. This drove the peasants to resort to the money-lenders who were the survivors of the old trading classes with their occupation gone in the wider field due to the decline of national industries.[34]

In addition, as the money-lending business flourished in the Madras Presidency under the new land-revenue settlement, the Ryots came to be left more and more to the mercies of money-lenders for financial help. Some of the Ryots may have been better off but the majority of them lived in poverty and in debt. They had small patches of land which they cultivated with borrowed cattle but their chief means of subsistence was the wages they earned by working as labourers. Below them were the low-caste agricultural labourers who were thoroughly landless and a large segment of whom belonged to the depressed class and bore the stigma of slavery / serfdom. These labourers who thus occupied the lowest stratum of the Tamil society migrated in large numbers into Sri Lanka to work on estates[35]. Indignities issuing from their low-castes status plus slavery-ridden conditions in their own country as also their economic hardship goaded them to cross to Sri Lanka for a new life which would be free from any social stigma.

Another important factor that provided an additional momentum to the migration of Tamils into Sri Lanka was the existence of the institution of slavery in the 19th century Madras Presidency. The slaves employed as agricultural labourers / the agrestic slaves were exclusively Hindus of the lowest and most degraded classes such as Pullers and lived on the outskirts of villages in the Tamil-speaking parts[36] of the Madras Presidency, whereas the domestic slaves were principally Muslims, employed in Muhamedan families and to be found all over the Madras Presidency.[37] The agrestic slaves had a very miserable existence but the domestic slaves were, on the whole, better off.[38]

In this context, it is important to emphasise this fact that the plight of the agrestic slaves was perhaps nowhere more pitiable than in Malabar. The situation of the agrestic slaves is neatly summarised in an article by Campbell: 'The agrestic slaves in Malabar could be distinguished from the rest of the population there by their degraded, diminutive, squalid appearance, their dropsical pot-bellies contrasting horribly with their skeleton arms and legs.'[39] Campbell further adds, they were half starved, hardly clothed, and were in a condition, scarcely superior to that of the cattle employed in ploughing the land of their masters.[40] As other writers have pointed out, the agricultural labourers in Malabar were in some respects treated like a commodity of production.[41]

It is obvious from the above description that the agrestic servitude was, on the whole, deep seated in the South Indian society. It was, as noted by Dharam Kumar, less widespread and less rigorous in the Telugu districts than in Tamil Nadu and much less so than in Malabar and South Canara.[42] It was natural, therefore, for such a suffering section of the population of the Madras Presidency to have availed itself of the opportunity of migrating into Sri Lanka to escape the miseries of life.

In addition to the above-mentioned factors, a few historians subscribe to the view that the famine of 1876-78 which was perhaps the worst ever calamity to befall the Madras Presidency in the 19th century accelerated the process of Tamil migration into Sri Lanka.[43] The increase in the volume of Tamil migration in 1876-77 cannot be contested but the point which warrants clarification and consideration is whether or not this increase in the volume of migration could be ascribed to the outbreak of famine in the Madras Presidency. According to C. Bernard's (the then Additional Secretary to the Government of India) statement, based on Returns from sea-ports, the number of immigrants who reached Burma, Ceylon and other countries from the Madras Presidency by sea-passage during the 14 months of famine was 2,87,482 as against the average figure of 1,56,143 for the corresponding period in normal times.[44] Emigration by sea, according to Bernard's statement, therefore almost doubled during the period of famine. But as he further stated, 'there is nothing to show how many of these emigrants came from the famine districts.'[45]

It, therefore, stands to reason to conclude that famine did not lead to an abnormal increase of the migration of Tamils into Sri Lanka. It is possible that some might have migrated from the famine-stricken areas but their numerical strength was not such as to establish a cause-and-effect relationship between famine and migration. It was poverty and social fetters of the low caste Tamil agricultural labourers, on the one hand, and, on the other, the British capitalists' investment of private capital in the plantation economy of Sri Lanka, necessitating the influx of labour from abroad in the absence of an adequate and regular supply of local labour, which supplied the real cause of the migration of Indian Tamils into Sri Lanka. In this context, it seems difficult to digest the views expressed by a noted historian Rajaratnam that it (Tamil migration) was more a push from India than a pull by the planters that made Sri Lanka a heaven to the impoverished proletariat of South India.[46] The fact remains that behind the migration of Tamils into Sri Lanka, there was the interaction of both the push and pull factors – the push of poverty and the pull of opportunity.

The above-mentioned discussion of the genesis, context, pattern and nature of the migration of Tamils into Sri Lanka opens the way for a review of the commencement of migration and, thereafter, recruitment and treatment of Tamil migrant labourers. But before addressing these tasks, it may be worth considering the differences between the Sri Lankan Tamils and the Indian Tamils because it will provide the basic background on the implications of this analysis.

Sri Lankan Tamils and Indian Tamils

The Sri Lankan Tamils and the Indian Tamils are separate entities due to their historical origin, socio-economic conditions, political associations, territorial base, political demands and strategies as well as former's experience of living with the majority Sinhalese community. This is so despite their commonality in linguistic, cultural and religious terms. Both groups diverged and converged depending on their linkage with India which espoused their cause from time to time.[47] The two groups differed substantially in respect of social status and identity. The Indian Tamils had several names; Up-Country Tamils. Tamils of recent Indian origin, Plantation Tamils, Hill Country Tamils, Plantation people etc. Officially, they were called Indian Tamils. The term added to identify them more with India than with Sri Lanka. Thus the very official title alienates them from the mainstream Sri Lankan society.[48] Politically, they were disenfranchised and de-citizenized in 1948, which affected them psychologically, socially, politically and economically. On the contrary, the Sri Lankan Tamils considered themselves to be the original inhabitants of Sri Lanka, who once had a Tamil Kingdom in Jaffna and thereby claimed the north-east of Sri Lanka as their traditional homelands.

Moreover, the Indian Tamils were generally poor and marginalised compared to the social status of the Sri Lankan Tamils. There is a sense of inferior and superior complexes in the nature of the relationship between these two peoples as indigenous Tamils entertained a sense of imperviousness.[49] As mentioned earlier in this chapter, it was precisely because of their low social status that the Sinhalese looked upon the Indian Tamils as a slaving Tamil community, while the Sri Lankan Tamils regarded them with condescension.[50]

After this brief historical review of the differences between the Sri Lankan Tamils and the Indian Tamils, it remains important to identify the commencement of migration and other inter-related themes connected with this syndrome. The first batch of Tamil labourers is generally regarded as having reached the island in 1837.[51] While the first experiment of the British in recruiting Tamil labour began in the 1820s, as the Table mentioned below shows, it was with the rapid development of Coffee plantation in the 1840s that labour recruitment from South India became a systematic enterprise. As the statistics suggest, the transit labourers of the early decades rarely brought their wives or children. But later as the migrant Tamil community began slowly to evolve on the estates, more families came.

Migration of Tamil Estate Labourers 1839-856
(Annual Average Rounded to Nearest Hundred)

Period	*Arrival* *Men*	*Departure* *Woman and Children*	*Total*	*New Inflow* *Men*	*Women and Children*	*Total*
1839-42	4,800	400	5,200	6,400	500	6,900
1843-49	46,600	1,500	48,100	23,500	800	24,300
1850-59	48,600	7,500	56,100	36,300	2700	39,000
1860-72	52,400	17,300	69,700	54,700	12,400	67,100
1873-79	82,603	32,813	115,416	85,066	19,026	104,092
1880-86	36,659	9,423	46,082	43,233	12,310	55,543

Source: Donald Snodgrass, *Ceylon: An Export Economy in Transition* (Richard D. Irwin Inc, Homeword, 1966), p. 26.

Areas of Recruitment

There were, on the whole, two main regional centres of labour recruitment in India. One, and perhaps, the bigger of the two was the Madras Presidency, and the other was present day Bihar.[52] Most of the Indian Tamils were brought from southernmost Tamil districts of the Madras Presidency – Trichnopoly, Tinnevely, Madurai and Tanjore.[53] N. L. Juddington, Acting Controller of Indian Immigrant Labour, in his Administrative Report for 1831 also recorded that the majority of the labourers were recruited from the districts around Trichnopoly and that a circle, drawn with a radius of about fifty miles around Trichnopoly, embraced the most important recruiting districts.[54] The above Tamil speaking areas, around Trichnopoly, which are situated along the Coromandal coast, normally supplied the largest number of estate labourers.

The methods initially adopted by the planters to obtain the supply of Tamil labourers was not based upon the principle of indenture[55] as was the case with other plantation colonies such as Mauritius and the West Indies. The indenture system lasted several decades and operated in every colonial territory to which Indian workers were sent, with the exception of Sri Lanka where the distances to be traversed were short enough for more informal method of recruitment to be resorted to without the need for the indenture contract.[56] The colonial state in Sri Lanka, in fact, stopped short of state sponsorship of recruitment and supply of labour to the plantations. Throughout the nineteenth century, the planter lobby in Sri Lanka continued to agitate for state sponsorship of foreign labour migration.[57] But proximity to the source of labour supply in South India and the relative ease of labour recruiters and supervisors known as the Kanganies prevented the direct participation of the colonial state in this matter. Laissez-faire ideology was often invoked in justifying the non-interference of the state in the labour recruitment as well.[58]

The Tamil labour-force on an estate consisted of several gangs of varying size from 25 to 30 persons. Each such gang was placed under the supervision of a headman, himself a labourer, who went by the designation of Kangany. An estate labour was selected a Kangany by virtue of his efficiency in field work and aptitude for leadership. Armed with a licence to recruit labourers, a Kangany used to form his gang by recruiting labourers from the families which was related to him as also from such families as lived in the neighbouring villages. The Kangany system was thus built upon a patriarchal basis.[59] The recruitment of Tamil labourers from among the kinsmen and acquitances of a Kangany constituted one of the secrets of success of the Kangany system, at least, at its early phase. Such a system of recruitment not only prevented the break of the family life of the Tamil labourers but also nipped in the bud the possibility of their desertion and ensured their attachment to the estates and planters.

However, with the lapse of years the labourers came to be recruited by a Kangany not exclusively from his relatives and acquaintances but also from such persons of Tamil labouring class as could be induced by him to migrate either through his own endeavours or through the agency of a professional recruiters. The result was that the Kangany system lost its patriarchal character and subsequently its efficacy too. Under this system, the Tamil migrant labourers began their plantation life in debt to the planters via the Kanganies and remained subordinate debtors within a network made up of planters, Kanganies and Chetties, they were tied into an economic life of debt bondage.[60] Their readiness to accept this situation arose from the fact that the lower classes in South India were locked into similar systems of bonded agricultural labour from pre-British time.[61]

The evidence for the contention mentioned in the above paragraph does suggest that the Tamil migrant labourers had many financial obligations to meet before leaving for estates. And yet the advance money they got from the Kanganies could not cover all their needs.[62] To increase the cost advance meant putting more money into the Kangany's pocket, without the certainty of an increased return in the recruitment of Tamil migrant labourers. The solution was the introduction of Tin-

Ticket system in 1902, by which the Ceylonese Government undertook the responsibility of conveying the Tamil labourers, free of charge, from the Indian coast to the estates in Sri Lanka they were bound for, subsequently recovering the expenses from the superintendents of the estate concerned.[63] With the introduction of Tin-Ticket system of labour transportation/ recruitment, the colonial state began to play a more central role in the conveyance of South Indian Tamils to the plantations.

Thus, the history of the migration of Tamils into Sri Lanka in the 19th and 20th centuries was marked by the expansion of a plantation economy which transformed the rural environment. Further, and very significantly, these Tamil migrants needed to be kept socially and physically isolated from the Sinhalese living alongside their estates. This separation began in colonial time and largely sustained by post-independence politics, prevented the hill country Tamils and Kandyan Sinhalese from feeling part of the same community and nation. This made it easy for the elite to disenfranchise them without any significant protest from ordinary people.

Conclusion

In conclusion, it appears that the Sinhalese reluctance to become permanent wage labourers and take up the strenuous and regimented employment on the coffee estates marked the genesis of the Tamil migration into Sri Lanka in the first half of the 19th century. The reluctance of the Sinhalese to work in the plantations created a big labour problem for the British planters, who opened up the lucrative plantations of coffee, tea, rubber and coconut. The planters saw no reason to pay high wages when there was regular, cheap and easily controllable labour available in South India. Thus, thousands of South Indian Tamils began to make the annual journey to the coffee estates in the central and southern parts of the island. From the 1820s through the 1880s, these Tamils worked as seasonal harvesters on the coffee plantation. After 1860 onwards, when tea plantations began to replace coffee in the estates of the Central Highlands, the need for a permanent

South Indian labour force became a necessity. This led to the settlement of a large Indian Tamil community in the Central Highlands of Ceylon.

The migration of Tamils into Sri Lanka which had continued since then more or less at a regular flow, was finally banned by the Government of India in 1939. By the time the ban was imposed, plantation in Sri Lanka had appreciably thrived, changing the economic face of the Island. It is broadly true to say that migrant Tamils made a substantial contribution to the economic development of Sri Lanka. Thus who would deny that to this economic prosperity of this island the contribution of the Tamil migrants had been tremendous?

The Tamils, who arrived as migrants escaping from the life of serfdom in South India and with the hope of saving money, were not able to do so. The Tamil migrants soon came under a new form of serfdom arising out of their indebtedness to the planters and the Kanganies from which they and their descendants were rarely able to escape. Their sweat and blood sustained the worst form of exploitation economy that led the British planters with the surplus value and enriched the Sinhala land-owning classes. The Indian Tamils today carry with them the burden of the colonial legacy, although developments, both intentional and unintentional, are slowly breaking this down.

References

1. N. D. Wijesekera, *The People of Ceylon*, M. D. Gunasena, Colombo, 1949. p. 184.
2. H. P. Chattopadhyaya, *Indians in Sri Lanka,* O. P. S. Publishers, Calcutta, 1979. p. 1.
3. For a fuller analysis, see W. T. Jayasinghe, The Indo-Ceylon Problem: The Politics of Immigrants Labour (Colombo, 2002).
4. V. Nandarajan, *History of Ceylon Tamils,* Vasantham, Toronto, 1999. p. 40.
5. B. B. C. News, "Timeline: Sri Lanka", It can b e found here http://news.bbc.co.uk/zhi/Southasia/countryprofiles/1166237.stm.
6. Sri Lanka's Department of Census and Statistics, http://w.w.w., statistics;gov.ik/

7. Ibid.
8. H. P. Chattopadhyaya, (1979), p. 100.
9. C. R. de Silva, *Sri Lanka: A History,* Vikas Publishing House, New Delhi, 2nd ed. 1997. pp. 171, 181.
10. H. P. Chattopadhyaya (1979), pp. 35-36.
11. For further details see, Alan Strathern, "Theoretical Approaches to Sri Lankan History and the Early Portuguese Period" Modern Asian Studies, 2004, 38(1), pp. 191-226.
12. C. R. Boxer, "The American Historical Review", American Historical Association, 79, no. 3 (June 1974), pp. 828-829.
13. For more information on the Dutch expedition see http://www. iaf.nl/ sers/ anpoel/ nthonize/ utch title.html.
14. Nira Wickramasinghe, Gale Cengage Learning, "Ceylon" Encyclopedia of Western Colonialism since 1450. The complete article can be found here: http//www.gale cengage.com polf samples Sp 658434.pdf.
15. The entire account can be found here: http://w.w.w.info. lk?srilanka/Srilanka history/britishrule.htm.
16. H. P. Chattopadhyaya (1979), p. 13.
17. Report on Indian Labour emigrating to Ceylon and Malay' by N. E. Marjoribanks and Khan Bahadur A. K. G., Ahmad Tambi Marakkayar, 1917, Section II.
18. K. M. de Silva (ed.) *History of Ceylon,* Vol. III, University of Ceylon, Peradeniya, 1973. p. 97.
19. Sivasothy Sathesan, "British colonialism and the Tamil Eelam", http://w.w.w. sathesan.com/article 5/1.
20. Ashoka Bandarage, *Colonialism in Sri Lanka: The Political Economy of the Kandyan Highlands 1839-1886* (Lake House Publishers, Colombo, 1985), Chap. 2.
21. H. P. Chattopadhyaya, (1979), p. 16.
22. S. B. W. Wickramasekara, "The Social and Political Organization of the Kandyan Kingdom" M. A. Thesis, University of London, 1961, p. 2.
23. V. D. Wickizer, *Coffee, Tea and Cocoa,* Stanford University Press, Standford, 1951. p. 449.
24. For a discussion of the Pre-colonial division of labour, see Ashoka Bandarage, (1985), Chaps. 3 and 6.
25. Lot 5/34, N. A. of Sri Lanka – Despatch no. 6, Misc. of 21.4.1847 from Tennent to Grey (Corresponding to C. O. 54/235), p. 214.
26. K. M. de Silva (1973), pp. 97-98.
27. Governor Wards' despatch to the Secretary of State for the Colonies citied in *The Colombo Observer,* November 26, 1866; *see also* de Silva, ed. *The History of Ceylon* (1973), p. 213.

28. For example see Address by Governor Robinson quoted in Leopold Ludovice, Rice Cultivation: Its past History and Present Condition (Colombo, 1967); J. H. Boeke, Economics and Economic Policy of Dual Societies (Institute of Pacific Relations, New York, 1953), pp. 37-38.
29. Chattopadhyaya (1979), p. 18.
30. Ashoka Bandarage, op.cit., chap. 6.
31. Despatch No. 6, Misc., 21.4.1847, From Tennent to Grey, op. cit.
32. K. M. de Silva, "Colonial Expansion and Demographic Change: The British and Russian Experience" Ethnic Studies Report, Vol. XIX, No. 2, July 2001, p. 161.
33. Nilmoni Mukherjee, *The Ryotwari System in Madras* (Calcutta), p. 161.
34. N. C. Sinha, *Indo-British Economy 100 years Ago* (Calcutta, 1946), p. 54.
35. Chattopadhyaya, p. 23.
36. A. Sarado Raju, Economic Conditions in the Madras Presidency, 1800-1850 (University of Madras, 1941), pp. 273-276.
37. Ibid.
38. Ibid.
39. A. D. Campbell, "On the state of slavery in Southern India", *Journal of Literature and Science,* Vol. I, October 1833-December 1834, p. 249.
40. Ibid.
41. D. Kumar, *Land and Caste in South India* (Cambridge University Press, Cambridge, 1965), p. 34.
42. Ibid.
43. Dr. Lanka Sundaram, "Indian Labour in Ceylon", *International Labour Review,* Vol. XXIII, January-June 1931, p. 371.
44. Review of Madras Famine, 1876-78, Madras, 1881, Appendix B, Para. 5, p. 94 in H. P. Chattopadhyaya, *Indians in Sri Lanka,* O. P. S. Publishers, Calcutta, 1979. p. 13.
45. Ibid.
46. S. Rajaratnam, "Plantation Labour in Ceylon", *Young Socialist,* Colombo, No. 3, October-December 1961.
47. Urmila Phadnis, *Ethnicity and Nation-building in South Asia,* Sage, New Delhi, 1990. pp. 38-42.
48. S. I. Keethaponcalan (2003), "Politics and Violence in Sri Lanka: A Study of Indian Tamil Youth in the plantation sector" in *Comprehensive Security in South Asia: Ethnic Dimension,* Harman Publishing House, New Delhi. p. 309.
49. Ibid.

50. Statchi Ponnambalam, *Sri Lanka: The National Question and the Tamil Liberation Struggle*, Zed Book, London, 1983. p. 34.
51. Chattopadhyaya (1979), pp. 35-36.
52. C. Z. Guilmoto, "The Tamil Migration Cycle, 1830-1950 in India" *Economic and Political Weekly*, 16-23 January 1993), pp. 111-120.
53. V. Nandarajan, *History of Ceylon Tamils*, p. 124.
54. Quoted in Chattopadhyaya (1979), p. 37.
55. An indenture was generally a contract in which the cost of transport to the Colony requiring the service of the immigrant would be borne by a recruiting agent, in return for a specificed term of service, generally two or three years, after which migrants could go back home on a passage provided by the contractor.
56. K. M. de Silva, Ethnic Studies Report, op. cit., p. 161.
57. K. M. de Silva, *Social Polity and Missionary Organisation in Ceylon 1840-1855*, Longmans, London, 1965. pp. 238-267.
58. D. Wesumperuma, "The Migration and conditions of Immigrant Labour in Ceylon, 1880-1910", Ph. D. dissertation, University of London, 1974, p. 52. (Published by Vidyalankara Press, Kalaniya, 1988).
59. Chattopadhyaya, (1979), p. 42.
60. D. Wesumperuma, *Indian Immigrant Plantationi Workers in Sri Lanka: A Historical Perspective (1880-1910)*, Vidyalankara Press, Kelaniya, 1988. pp. 181, 298-90.
61. Ibid., pp. 181-182.
62. Michael Roberts, "The Master Servant Laws of 1844 in the 1860's and the Immigrant Labour in Ceylon", *The Ceylon Journal of Historical and Social Studies*, Vol.8, 1963, p. 25, Also see Ashoka Bandarage, *The Political Economy*, op. cit., chap. 6.
63. Wasumperuma, "The Migration and Conditions of Immigrant Labour in Ceylon, 1880-1990" Ph.D. dissertation, University of London, 1974, op. cit., p. 86.

CHAPTER 3

Problem of Citizenship and India's Role

Common borders, race, religion and history make India and Sri Lanka one of the closest neighbours in the region. But mere cultural similarities or even common religion or race do not necessarily lead to peaceful relations. To some observers outside India it must seem strange that India and Sri Lanka should ever quarrel on any issue. The close links – geographical propinquity, historical tradition and cultural affinity – between the two neighbouring countries of India and Sri Lanka should have normally operated against the development of any issue detrimental to normal relations between them.[1] However, the so-called Indo-Sri Lanka problem, which cropped up in course of time originated from the claim laid to Ceylonese citizenship by the Tamil-speaking Indian plantation workers in Ceylon. The status of these Indian Tamils led to the first major Indian intervention on the Island and thereby created a role for the Government of India in the affairs of Sri Lanka.

For 60 years or more, i.e. from 1928 to 1988, the status of Indian Tamil Community in Sri Lanka was one of the most controversial issues in the Island's politics; controversial within the island, and controversial outside it. Throughout this period of sixty years from 1928, the political arithmetic of how many Indians should be granted citizenship rights was one of the principal issues in the Island's political debates. Hence it seems pertinent to examine and analyse the intricacies of this vexed problem in order to grasp the considerations and reservations that guided each side (i.e. Sri Lanka and India) and the roadblocks that occurred in the course of the negotiations that took place over several decades.

Scenario during the Colonial Period

Some of the major political problems, which Sri Lanka has been facing and is still facing, such as the marginality of the Tamil estate labour force and the complexities of their citizenship issue, are commonly attributed to the plantation economy in particular. Before we can understand the neo-colonial manifestation of the problem of citizenship of Indian Tamil community in Sri Lanka, a careful analysis of its origin and evolution are necessary. During the early phase of coffee plantation development, that is until about the 1850s, almost all European officials of the state were also coffee planters. The Governor of the island, Edwards Barnes (1824-1831) and George Bird, a retired major in the colonial army, were among the first to open up coffee plantations in the Kandyan Highlands. These officials used the authority of their administrative positions to introduce legislation conducive to large-scale commercial agriculture. For example, Governor Barnes passed ordinances which enabled the colonial state to use pre-colonial free labour services (rajakariya) of the native peasantry towards the building of roads necessary for commercial expansion and the political integration of the island. In order to provide further incentives for export agriculture, he also exempted all land producing cash crops from export and import duties.[2]

In addition, the reforms introduced by the Coolebrooke-Cameron Commission of Inquiry in 1833 not only laid down the juridico-political framework for capitalist agricultural development in Sri Lanka, but also helped extend the participation of government officials in plantation agriculture. This was due to the fact that the Coolebrooke Commission allowed civil servants to make up for the loss in salaries and pensions created by its own fiscal recommendations through investments in commercial agriculture.[3]

The Crown Lands Encroachments Ordinance, No. 12 of 1840, the chief instrument used for securing land for plantations was designed and implemented by government officials, such as Geroge Turnour, who were also the pioneer coffee planters in the colony. The passage of this bill allowed the colonial state to lay claims to all uncultivated and unoccupied land unless the natives were able to prove ownership by the stringent criteria the state laid down. The land that the colonial state thus obtained as "Crown land" was at first made available to planters as free grants and in later years sold at the minimum nominal fee of five shilling an acre. The minimum fee was increased to one pound an acre in 1844.

Furthermore, the evidence of George Auckland, a prominent coffee planter in the colony, given before the British Parliamentary Committee enquiring into the peasant rebellion of 1848 in Sri Lanka, helps validate the thesis that the British in early and mid-nineteenth century Sri Lanka constituted a single "planter-officials" class.[4] Auckland's evidence reveals the complete identification of the colonial state with plantation development. Moreover, it highlights the absence of an independent judiciary in the colony.

The practice of appointing Britishers already resident in the island to official positions was common in the early years of colonial rule. This led to the effective control of many of the most coveted jobs in the higher bureaucracy by two British families in Sri Lanka – the Layards and the Templars – who came to be referred to as the "family compact."[5]

At least in the early years of British colonial rule in Sri Lanka, the colonial administration was far from the neutral bureaucratic type of authority that Max Weber has written about, but Weber himself acknowledged that the British Empire was basically an administration of notables. He pointed out that the Empire provided a vast system of public assistance to the British governing classes, especially for the younger sons of the gentry who did not inherit the ancestral estates and were therefore sent off to the colonies to make their fortunes.[6]

The early British colonial administration in Sri Lanka represented a personal form of rule by a few notables. The names of Turnour, Layard, Skinner, Buller, Woodhouse, crop up again and again in the colonial documents with regard to political, economic, judicial and other matters in the colony. George Auckland, quoted earlier, was himself a merchant, planter, a member of the Legislative Council and the proprietor of the Colombo Observer, the organ of the planter community and the semi-official newspaper of the colonial government.[7]

In the mid-1840's, the Colonial Office in London began to acknowledge that the neglect of official duties by the civil servants in Sri Lanka stemmed largely from their involvement in plantation agriculture. In 1844-1845, Lord Stanley, the British Secretary of State, ordered the civil servants to dispose of their properties and issued a strict prohibition against their participation in commercial activities.[8] The local governor at the time, Colin Campbell, modified this ruling by allowing civil servants to keep their estates, provided they did not manage them, thereby introducing the principle of separation of ownership and management. Campbell attempted to discourage from further commercial investments on the part of officials by claiming that promotions of those with planting interests within the administrative hierarchy would be delayed. In attempting to separate state officials from economic enterprise. Campbell also increased their salaries and pensions.[9]

In his evidence before the British Parliamentary Committee inquiring into the affairs of Sri Lanka in 1849, George Auckland noted that the process of extricating public servants entrenched in coffee planting was extremely difficult. In spite of Governor Campbell's orders, the formal separation of the bureaucracy and commercial enterprise was not yet effected.[10] Notwithstanding this formal separation, civil servants in Sri Lanka continued to retain ties of capitalist enterprise.[11]

Even after the state and economic enterprise were formally separated, the European planter community continued to enjoy a semi-official status in the colony. It was the most powerful pressure group in colonial Sri Lanka and was represented by the Chamber of Commerce and the Planters' Association, established in 1837 and 1854 respectively. As a nineteenth century critic of the colonial government, George Wall put it, the Planters' Association became "a power in the state".[12] While member of the British planter community found easy representation in the Legislative Council, it became an established practice for the Governor to consult the planters on all matters of importance in the colony.[13] For example, planter pressure was persuasive in the government's decision not to introduce a general land tax that would have been extended to the vast tracts of plantation lands in addition to the native paddy lands that were already under heavy taxation.[14]

Following the initial period of conquest and political consolidation, the plantation enterprise became the *raison d'etre* of British colonial rule in Sri Lanka. As historian Van Den Driesen has said, the colonial state came to regard the problems of the planters as synonymous with those of the country.[15] In fulfilling its commitment towards the plantation economy, the colonial state was compelled, advertently and inadvertently, to take actions that were detrimental to the village economy, particularly the interests of the Sinhalese peasantry. James Steuart, the Master Attendant of the colonial state (1825-1855) expressed this contradiction in the following manner.

> *We profess to govern for the exclusive good of the natives of the country and devote our attention almost exclusively to make the culture of the soil profitable to European adventures.*[16]

At the time plantations were opened up in the Central Highlands, labour, not land, was the scarce factor of production. A striking characteristic of the Kandyan Kingdom was its sparse population. According to the British Census Report of 1824, the population of the entire Kandyan Kingdom (which comprised roughly three-fourths of the whole island) was 256,835. The population of Kandy, the captial city in 1818 was only 3,000. On the other hand, the profitability of plantation agriculture rests primarily on the availability of a large, regular, well disciplined and cheap labour force.[17]

Unlike in neighbouring South India, there were no landless agricultural labouring castes in Kandy. The Sinhalese artisan castes themselves were primarily wet-rice cultivators possessing their own means of production. The elaborateness and complexity of the pre-colonial division of labour, especially its caste specificity, prevalence of serfdom, absence of agricultural labour castes, and primarily the availability of land, made it extremely difficult to find the large wage labour force needed by the coffee plantations.[18] Given the absence of social and economic pre-requisites for the emergence of wage labour in Sri Lanka, the colonial state attempted to create such a "free" (i.e. freed from the means of production) labour forces extremely by administrative fiat. The first step was taken by the Colebrooke-Cameron Commission when it abolished the pre-colonial forced labour services in 1833. The underlying motive in attempting to free forced labour (rajakariya) was the creation of a wage labour force needed for capitalist economic development in the island. The few Sinhalese who did work on the coffee plantations provided mostly non-routine supplementary labour rather than routine field labour.

The British brought the plantation workers of the Indian origin to Ceylon when the island was under their colonial overlordship. They were British subjects. 'But owing to the survival in the law of traditions derived from feudal system, citizenship was a matter not of relationship towards a country but to relationship towards the king. Those who elsewhere would be described as "citizens" or "national" of the respective countries were in the commonwealth referred to as "subjects" of the king, or "British subjects". Since there was one king throughout the commonwealth, even after some of the colonies obtained dominion status or independence, there was a common citizenship implied in the phrase "British subjects".'[19] According to Sir Ivor Jennings, 'the relationship between the subject and the king was described as allegiance, so that all persons who were born in the king's dominions were said to be born within the king's allegiance. Accordingly, the Indian plantation workers, who were in Ceylon during the period when Ceylon received its dominion status, were all British subjects and even after that period of time their successors, such as children, are also British subjects.'[20] However, the fact was that the Indian Tamils were gradually given the franchise to participate in the political activities of the Island.

In the 1920s, franchise rights were based on a residence of six months and certain property qualifications. It was under these circumstances that the Imperial Conference held in London in 1921, accepted the resolution, proposed by India, that the Indians, who were lawfully domiciled in the dominions, should not be discriminated against politically or otherwise on the ground of their Indian origin or descent. But the property qualifications which the government of the country prescribed for the exercise of franchise were fixed too high for the estate labourers to satisfy.[21] The electors, for instance, were required to possess such property qualifications as (a) a clear annual income of Rs. 600 or (b) the ownership of immovable property, either in their own rights or in the rights of their wives, to the values of Rs. 1,500 after allowing for any mortgage debts thereon or (c) the occupation, as owner or tenant, for six months prior to the preparation of the electoral register, of a house, warehouse, shop etc. of the annual value of Rs. 400, if situated within the limits of a municipality, local border, sanitary board or urban district council, or of Rs. 200, if situated elsewhere.

The prescription of such high property qualifications for the experience of franchise had the inevitable effect of leaving the bulk of the Indian Tamil population disqualified from exercising political rights.[22] The previously imposed literacy test and property qualifications proved prejudicial to the interests of Indian Tamils in as much as the lack of their opportunities for reading and writing and their indigent condition conspired against their acquiring the eligibility for franchise.

Donoughmore Commission: Indian Tamils Enfranchised

Actually, the Indian problem in Sri Lanka first emerged in the wake of the landmark recommendations of the Donoughmore Commission in 1928 on the introduction of universal suffrage to the Island. The Donoughmore Commission sought to provide the people of Sri Lanka with a constitution so as "to transfer to the elected representatives complete control over the internal affairs of the island".[23] The Commission further recommended that in the first place, we consider it very desirable that a qualification of five years residence in the island (allowing the temporary absence not exceeding eight months in all during the five years period) should be introduced in order that the privilege of voting should be confined to those who have an abiding interest in the country, or who may be regarded permanently settled in the island . . . this condition will be of particular importance in its application to the Indian emigrant population. Secondly, we consider that the registration of voters should not be compulsory or automatic, but should be restricted to those who apply for it . . . ."[24]

When the Donoughmore Commission report was being debated upon in the Ceylon Legislative Council in 1929, its recommendations for five years continuous residence and the dropping of the literacy and property qualifications in respect of the Indian immigrant population were subjected to severe criticism on the ground that such recommendations, if implemented would virtually enfranchise the entire Indian estate population on the island and the Indian voters would then inevitably swamp the Sinhalese ones in the Kandyan areas.[25] The result was that an unexpected storm of protest from the Sinhalese politicians followed. The Sinhalese leadership was against the large number of plantation workers of the Indian origin being given voting rights, as recommended by the Donoughmore Commission. Moves were made to restrict the number of Indian Tamil voters. While introducing such a resolution, a prominent Sinhalese politician declared, "It is said that this resolution of mine is brought with the object of keeping out a large number of Indian voters. There is no use of any camouflage in this matter. I will boldly state that is so."[26]

From the above description it is obvious that the vast majority of Sri Lankan politicians refused to accept the position that all migrant Indians in the island were entitled to vote on the same terms set out in the Donoughmore report for the indigenous population. From their point of view it would have meant: '(a) a dilution of the electoral strength of the Kandyan Sinhalese in most of the constituencies in the Kandyan areas; (b) the possibility of the Indian Tamils being returned as representatives of Kandyan Sihalese Constituency in the event of the splitting of Kandyan Sinhalese vote between rival candidates; (c) the likehood,. . . of British planters, and/or Indian estate Kanganies (overseers) herding the Indian vote in favour of the candidate of their choice'.[27] They accordingly demanded that besides the test of past residence, as recommended by the Donoughmore Commission, the immigrants should be required to give an indication of their future intention to remain in Sri Lanka and to become a permanent part of the island's population. The Sinhalese demand, was, in other words, heading toward an insistence on domicile as a condition of franchise.

These misgivings were conveyed to Governor Sir Herbert Stanley, and modifications were accordingly made to the Donoughmore Commission recommendations by the Colonial Secretary. Sir Herbert Stanley approved of the Sinhalese stand, with the result that instead of mere residence, domicile (either of origin or of choice) was now made the standard test for franchise. For the undomiciled persons to enjoy franchise rights Sir Herbert proposed two alternative requirements – either literacy and property qualifications or a certificate of permanent settlement to be granted to the applicant by a duly appointed officer.[28] The franchise status quo of the Tamils of the Indian origin which was devised by Sir Herbert Stanley, was referred to Lord Passfield, the Secretary of States for colonies. Governor Stanley incorporated change in the order in council 1931, after his proposal was accepted by Lord Passfield, the Secretary of States for colonies. This arrangement, though a deviation from the Donoughmore Commission proposals, enabled Indians to participate in the run up to the general elections to the state councils, and to the parliamentary elections.

Citizenship Rights Circumscribed

The above-mentioned conditions for citizenship rights circumscribed, in effect, the franchise of the Indian residents and were resented both by the Indian community in Sri Lanka and by the Government of India. The Indian community grumbled against the administrative efforts to reduce the strength of Indian voters. Meanwhile economic pressure brought on by the Depression of the 1930s exacerbated the issues relating to the presence of the Indian Tamils in Sri Lanka. Due to the gravity of the circumstances, the leadership in Sri Lanka wanted emigration restricted, to the extent of even replacing Indian labour with local labour. It was under these circumstances that the Sinhalese politicians in the Ceylon State Council (the legislature) moved to restrict Indian entry into the island by ordering the Ceylonisation of the Public Services including manual workers.[29]

Attempts to Resolve the Issue

The above-mentioned circumstances resulted in two conferences between Sri Lanka and India. To explore the possibilities of finding out a satisfactory basis for formal negotiations on all issues of common interest requiring adjustment the leaders of the two governments met together at a conference at New Delhi, the Indo-Ceylon Relations Exploratory Conference, as it was called, which commenced on 4 November 1940 and ended on 12th.[30] The most prominent Sri Lanka politicians of the day including D. S. Senanayake and S.W.R.D. Bandaranaike were participants at these discussions. The Indian delegation was composed of G. S. Bajpai and Ramaswami Mudaliar. The Exploratory Conference of 1940 at Delhi was inconclusive.[31] It could offer no solution to the problems of citizenship status of the Indian immigrants in Sri Lanka. This discussion/negotiation which terminated unsuccessfully in 1940 was resumed in 1941 at a conference in Colombo where an agreement was reached on all points, including, inter alia, the Immigration Bill and the Question of Franchise.[32] A Joint Report was signed on 21 September 1941.

The India/Ceylon Joint Report in regard to franchise states: "It was agreed that those Indians who could not claim domicile of origin or of choice or a literacy and property qualification could vote only if they possessed certificates of permanent settlement which would be granted on the following conditions."[33] In respect of residence the recommendation was "7 years for married and 10 years for unmarried persons. . . provided that continuous absence of an immigrant for more than one year prior to application constitute break in any qualifying period of residence".[34]

Opportunity Missed

However, although it was a Joint Report, the Central Legislative Assembly of India did not ratify the Report, and in January 1943, repudiated it altogether. According to H. P. Chattopadhyaya, the Indian delegates were not plenipotentiaries. They were merely charged with exploring the possibilities of an agreement on the franchise and citizenship questions. Their "agreed conclusions" could not, therefore, be approved by the Central Legislative Assembly in India.[35] The result was that the opportunity to reach a settlement was missed. The Sri Lankan attitude to the issue was greatly influenced by two factors. Firstly, the economic depression of the 1930s caused severe unemployment, and Indian labour was seen as competitors who deprived the indigenous labour of gainful employment. Secondly, the transient nature of the Indian labour between India and Sri Lanka on the question of domicile became a critical issue in order to assure an "abiding interest" in the country and a desire to settle "permanently".[36]

Soulbury Commission: Stalemate Continued

The Soulbury Commission, appointed in 1944, which paved the way for the independence of Ceylon, recognized the "anxieties arising out of the likelihood of large-scale enfranchisement of the Indian emigrants, and despite strong representation from the Ceylon Tamil and Indian Tamil organizations, decided that the Indian question was an internal matter to be disposed of by the future legislature. The Commission, therefore, left the existing basis of franchise in Sri Lanka undisturbed".[37] The Soulbury Commission Report also stated that ... "if the qualifications of these Indian immigrants for franchise had depended solely on the condition of five years residence in the Island, as recommended by the Donnoughmore Commission, the Constitution of 1931 would not have been accepted by the Legislative Council."[38]

Naturally, therefore, the Soulbury Commission could not concede that the Indian Community in Sri Lanka be enfranchised. The Soulbury Commission could not grant the Indian request for "balanced representation" on the ground that such a request purported to impose communal representation which was viewed by it as undesirable. The further Indian demand for the statutory provision that not more than half the members of the proposed cabinet be chosen from any community was also rejected by the Sinhalese political elites,[39] and was not conceded by the Commission either.

Infructuous Negotiations Continues: Delhi Talks

Intermittent infructuous negotiations between the colonial governments, and the nationalist politicians of both countries, continued right up to independence. Just prior to Sri Lanka's independence, in December 1947, Prime Minister Nehru of the newly independent India and D. S. Senanayake, the Prime Minister-designate of a soon-to-be independent Sri Lanka, met in New Delhi to thrash out the old problem of citizenship status of the Indian Tamils.[40] The discussion between the two Prime Ministers centred mainly on two questions: (a) who among the Indians resident in Sri Lanka should be considered eligible for the Ceylonese citizenship; and (b) how they should be admitted to such citizenship. At the end of the discussion, Nehru requested Senanayake to set down in writing the qualifications which he would consider adequate for citizenship. Senanayake agreed and committed to paper his proposals regarding the qualifications for citizenship.[41]

On Senanayake's written proposals Nehru offered his comments. However, the Government of Sri Lanka could not finally endorse Nehru's suggestions. In fact, the Delhi talks of December 1947 on the acquisition of citizenship status by the person of Indian origin were set at naught, when the Government of Sri Lanka sought to redefine the condition of

Ceylone citizenship by the citizenship legislations of 1948-49.[42] W.T. Jayasinghe points out that these talks (Delhi talks of December 1947), brokered by the colonial office on the eve of Sri Lanka's independence, collapsed even though the terms offered by D. S. Senanayake were more generous to the Indians that those he had agreed to in 1941.[43] However, the crucially important fact that deserves attention is that the collapse of these talks forms the essential background to the controversial citizenship legislation of 1948-49.

Ceylon Citizenship Act (1948): Real Motive Unearthed

The Ceylon Citizenship Act, which came into operation on 15 November 1948, though providing the qualification to be a citizen, was designed to disqualify persons of Indian origin. The provision said that "only a person born in Ceylon prior to the date of the Act coming into force of a father born in Ceylon could be recognized as a citizen.[44] This decitizenized all persons of Indian origins since proof of birth of two generations was necessary. The scheme of citizenship either by descent or by registration, as embodied in the Act of 1948 was obviously very much restrictive. The Act made no provision for the grant of citizenship only by virtue of a person's birth in Sri Lanka. Citizenship was, in effect, restricted to the persons having family connections with the country for at least two generations. Most of the Indian immigrants found it very difficult to prove to the satisfaction of the authorities that their father was born in Sri Lanka, as required under Section 4(1)(a) of the Act. Compliance with section 4(1)(b) requiring proof of birth in Sri Lanka of the applicant's paternal grandfather and paternal great grandfather was even more difficult, as the Registration of Births Ordinance came into force only after 1895. It took sometime more to complete arrangements for registration.[45] The citizenship provisions under the Act of 1948 were, in fact, unacceptable to the Indians in Sri Lanka. The provisions were restrictive, rigid and stringent.[46]

From the above discussion, it would thus appear that the Act of 1948 offered very narrow space to the person of Indian origin in Sri Lanka for obtaining Ceylonese citizenship. This was followed by discussions that led to the India and Pakistan (Residents) Citizenship Bill of 1949. It laid down qualifications for citizenship as registered citizens (SIC).[47] The procedures too were a hinderance. Nevertheless 2,37,000 applications covering 8,24,000 persons were made under the Citizenship Act. This means that nearly all plantation workers applied for citizenship. Devaraj observes: "Applications were rejected on the most flimsy grounds. The rejections were so arbitrary that some felt that the entire exercise was a meaningless one. To crown it all, there came to light an administration circular in which deputy commissioners who were semi-judicial officers were asked to reject applications on the basis of a percentage."[48]

Attempts to Resolve the Matter: Nehru-Senanayake Talks

The Ceylon Citizenship Act of 1948-49 was not a permanent solution to the problem and attempts to resolve the matter came up for discussion again in 1953 after D. S. Senanayake's death. The talks between the two Prime Ministers, Jawaharlal Nehru and Dudley Senanayeke in London, were more important for the formula that the latter introduced on that occasion than for any success achieved in reaching an agreement on it.[49] The formula recognized three categories of Indian residents in Sri Lanka: firstly; those who qualified for Sri Lanka citizenship under the prevailing citizenship laws; secondly, those who did not qualify for citizenship but subject to future review would be granted permanent residence on work permits; and the third, Indian citizens who would be gradually compulsory repatriated to India.[50] While D. S. Senanayake was intent on giving citizenship to only 50,000 persons, the proper implementation of the Act was entailing a far greater number. The problem created by the scale of rejection impelled Dudley Senanayake who succeeded D. S. Senanayake as Prime Minister in 1952 to take the matter up with Nehru which he did at the above mentioned meeting in London. While Dudley proposed a more liberal implementation of the Citizenship Act by granting citizenship to 4,00,000 persons, he also envisaged a compulsory repatriation to India of 3,00,000 persons.[51]

Nehru rightly disagreed with any form of compulsory repatriation of the Indian residents in Sri Lanka. The two Prime Ministers, thereupon, left the matters where they were for the time being. A change of government took place in Sri Lanka in October 1953. Senanayake came to be succeeded by Sir John Kotelawala. Nehru invited Sir John Kotelawala to New Delhi to discuss with him outstanding issues relating to the Indian question. The invitation was accepted, and the two leaders met in New Delhi in January and October 1954. Kotelawala put forward a set of proposals essentially replacing compulsory repatriation by "inducement which were to be offered to those not registered as Ceylon citizens to apply for Indian citizenship.[52] The matter remained unresolved.

Srimavo-Shastri Pact of 1964: A Breakthrough to Solve the Citizenship Problem

Nothing further happened on settling the citizenship problem until the Srimavo-Shastri Pact of 1964. In the general election of July 1960, Mrs. Srimavo Bandarnaike led her Sri Lanka Freedom Party to victory and formed the government in the same year. It was then estimated that as many as 9,75,000 persons of Indian origin were still without registration either as Ceylonese or as Indian citizens and were, therefore, stateless. It was left to Mrs. Bandarnaike to confer with the then Indian Prime Minister, Lal Bahadur Shastri, on the fate of that huge body of stateless persons during her visit to New Delhi in 1964. In October that year, the Sri Lankan Prime Minister Mrs. Srimavo visited New Delhi to speed up the deportation of the plantation Tamils rendered stateless by the legislation of 1948.[53] The official Conference ended inconclusively. As Mrs. Bandarnaike was preparing to go home, she received an unexpected invitation for one final meeting with her Indian counterpart Lal Bahadur Shastri. At this eleventh hour meeting an agreement was casually drawn up; India agreed to accept 5,25,000 out of an estimated 9,75,000 stateless Tamils whereas the Sri Lankans would provide citizenship to 3,00,000 others.[54] It was also agreed that the repatriation would take place over fifteen years. The fate of 1,50,000 other plantation Tamils was to be settled later.

This important agreement was signed without consulting either the plantation Tamils or the people of Tamil Nadu – where these expatriates had extended families and where they were expected to settle on return to India. The broad mechanism of resettlement was not even discussed. Even the chosen time span of fifteen years was not examined. The Indian politicians looked upon the Agreement with a critical eye. While Sri Ranga, M.P. called it 'a shameful agreement',[55] M.R. Masani, M.P. described it as 'unsound in principle' and as a 'violation of basic human rights'.[56] Another M.P., Manoharan, referred to the Agreement as a criminal document.[57] Also, that the Government of India, despite its vaunted bureaucratic skills, took decisions without fully understanding the implications of their actions.

On her return to Colombo after accepting the agreement, Mrs. Bandarnaike made an official statement that those stateless persons, who would be granted the citizenship of Sri Lanka, would be placed on a separated electoral roll and not on the general electoral roll of the country,[58] meaning thereby that such citizens would be treated as second class citizens. This was, however, not in keeping with the spirit of the Agreement.

This whole episode was like a barter trade agreement, throwing people from one country to another without consideration of their feelings. On the implementation of the Shastri-Srimavo pact of 1964, now hinged the settlement of the question of citizenship status of 8,25,000 stateless persons of Indian origin – 3,00,000 of whom to be granted Ceylonese citizenship and the remaining 5,25,000 to be recognized as Indian citizens and to be repatriated to India. It was on 24 April 1968[59] that the Government of Sri Lanka and the Indian High Commission at Colombo issued public notices calling for applications for admission to the citizenship of the respective countries from among the persons of Indian origin covered by the agreement of 1964. A time limit of two years ending on 30 April 1970 was fixed within which applications were to be entertained. The call for applications was responded too profusely. According to the estimate of the Ceylon Workers Congress, about 4,00,000 persons applied for Indian citizenship and about 7,00,000 persons for the citizenship of Sri Lanka.[60]

Commenting on the above figures, S. Thondaman wrote to the then President of India V.V. Giri, on 18 March 1972 that, whereas the terms of the agreement of 1964 provided for the coverage of 8,25,000 people and a residue of 1,50,000, its implementation showed that the actual number of persons involved was approximately 11,00,000.[61] According to the estimate of Vincent Coelho, a former High Commissioner for India in Sri Lanka, on 30 April 1970 – the closing date for submitting application for Indian citizenship – the Indian Mission in Colombo received application for Indian citizenship from 4,58,422 persons while the Government of Sri Lanka received applications from over 6,30,000 persons for Ceylonese citizenship. According to Coelho, therefore, the total number of stateless person as in 1970, worked up to 10,88,422 (4,58,422 plus 6,30,000).[62] *The Statesman* flashed the following comments giving out information that 4,00,000 persons asked for Indian citizenship as against an expected under of 5,25,000 persons, while 6,25,000 persons claimed the citizenship of Sri Lanka, though the agreement of 1964 provided for the absorption of 3,00,000 Indians only.[63]

From the above description/analysis, it might appear that the Srimavo-Shastri Pact was a dangerous document. Those who applied for the Ceylonese citizenship were more numerous than those who sought admission to the citizenship of India, a larger number of persons of Indian origin, in other words, having expressed their desire to stay on in Sri Lanka's as Ceylonese nationals. The increase in the number of stateless persons was obviously due to natural increase from 1964 to 1970. The absorption of this natural increase would be the responsibility of the governments of the two countries concerned in accordance with the terms of the agreement.

Indira – Srimavo Supplementary Agreement (1974)

When Mrs. Bandarnaike began a second set of negotiations in 1974 with Mrs. Gandhi, the breakthrough made in 1964 was consolidated. It was decided that the 1,50,000 stateless persons whose fate was left undecided in 1964, with their natural increase, should be split equally between the two countries.[64] It was also agreed that until such time as the remaining 75,000 were repatriated to India, they would continue to enjoy all the existing facilities in Sri Lanka, except the facilities for remittances. Though Colombo and New Delhi finally agreed on the modus operandi of ending the statelessness of the persons of the Indian origin, the iniquitous distinction created by the Ceylon Citizenship Act of 1948, between citizenship by descent and citizenship by registration continued to exist, relegating the citizens by registration to the status of second class citizens.

Final Rectification

In fact, the process of granting citizenship under above-mentioned agreement/pacts was slow due to the link with the repatriation of those who applied for Indian citizenship. These repatriation agreements were the harbingers of the destruction of these communities, which had evolved into a composite group with a distinct culture of its own. In 1984-85 to stop India intervening in Sri Lankan affairs, the UNP government eventually granted citizenship right to all stateless persons.[65] The 15 years pact (already mentioned earlier in this chapter) was to have expired in October 1979. After giving it a two years extension upto October 1981, the Indian government held that it was no longer operative. On 30 January 1986, "The Grant of Citizenship to Stateless Person Bill" was debated in Parliament in which the government proposed granting Sri Lankan Citizenship to the shortfall of 94,000 persons who had not applied for Indian citizenship when the pact expired in 1981.[66] Prime Minister Premadasa told Parliament that 4,21,207 of the 5,06,000 who had applied for Indian citizenship had been granted it (together with their natural increase of 1,70,582).

Of them 3,37,066 (plus natural increase of 1,23,835) had been repatriated to India.[67]

Since the registration process was still very slow, another bill – Grant of Citizenship to Stateless Person (Special Provisions) Act No. 39 of 1988 was passed in November 1988 to try to expedite the processs.[68] This was opposed by Sri Lankan Freedom Party (SLFP) who voted against it.[69] The people of Indian origin who were until then deprived of the rights flowing from citizenship were overwhelmed by their achieving their long dreamed goal.[70]

In nutshell, India had shown concern about "stateless" Indians in Sri Lanka, a legacy of British colonialism, and these Indians were mostly working in the island's tea plantations. While such concern was legitimate, later, particularly in the 1970s, the early 1980s and more so after 1983, Indian concern began to cover all Tamils. For Sri Lanka, its foremost objective was to break India's intransigent position on the stateless issue of Indian Tamils. And it was also thought out to be a requirement for nation-building in the multi-ethnic island along the lines desired by the Sinhalese Buddhist nationalists. It needs to be emphasized that with the grant of citizenship the struggle of the people of Indian origin did not end. They had to struggle further to obtain the rights of citizenship envisaged and this struggle goes on.

References

1. Sir John Kotelawala, *An Asian Prime Minister's Story*, George Harrap and Co. Ltd., London, 1956. p . 98.
2. I. H. Van Den Driesen, "Coffee Cultivation in Ceylon, (1), *The Ceylon Historical Journal*, July 1953, p. 38.
3. K. M. de Silva, "The Development of the Administrative System, 1833 to c. 1919," in K.M. de Silva ed., *History of Ceylon* vol. 3, Colombo, Ceylon University Press Board, 1973. p. 213.
4. The team "planter-officials" is generally attributed to historian Van Den Driesen.
5. K. M. de Sliva, "The Development ..." , op.cit., p. 214.
6. Han, H. Gerth and C. Wright Mills eds., From Max Weber: Essays in Sociology (New York: Oxford University Press,

1958), p. 210. See also Ralph Pieris, "Some Neglected Aspects of the British Colonial Administration in the Early Nineteenth Century,"*Ceylon Historical Journal*, vol. 12, Nos. 1-2 July and Oct. 1952,p. 73.

7. Parliamentary Papers; Great Britain, (BPP), 1850, Vol. 12, p. 2.
8. K. M. de Silva, "The Development ....", op. cit., p. 214.
9. Jean Grossholtz, "Forging Capitalist Partiarchy: The Effect of British Colonial Ruler on Sri Lanka," (unpublished manuscript), p. 116. See also K. M. de Silva, "The Development," pp. 214-215.
10. BBP, vol. 12, p. 20.
11. Grossholtz, "Forging Capitalist Patriarchy", p. 117.
12. George Wall, *Ceylon: Her Peasant Condition, Revenues, Taxes and Expenditure*, Colomby Colombo Observer Press, 1868. p. 122.
13. K. M. de Silva, "The Development....." p. 236.
14. Bandarage, *The Political Economy*, chap. 2.
15. I. H. Van Den Driesen, "Some Trends in the Economic History of Ceylon in the Modern Period", *CJHSS*, vol. 3, 1960, p. 2.
16. Quoted in G. C. Mendis, (ed.),1956 The Colebrooke-Cameron Papers (Oxford: Oxford University Press), vol. 1, p. 57.
17. V. D. Wickizer, *Coffee, Tea and Cocoa*, (Standford: Stanford University Press, 1951), p. 449.
18. For a discussion of pre-colonial division of labour, see Bandarage, *The Political Economy*, chaps. 3 and 6.
19. Ivor Jennings, *The Constitution of Ceylon* (Bombay, 1953, third edition) Oxford University Press, London, p. 27.
20. Ibid.
21. Vide Report of the Controller of Indian Immigrant Labour for 1924, p. 11, para 78.
22. H. P. Chattopadhyaya (1979), p. 206.
23. Rajesh Kadian, *India's Sri Lanka Fiasco*, Vision Books, New Delhi, 1990. p. 86.
24. Donoughmore Commission Report, 1928, p. 82.
25. H. P. Chattopadhyaya (1979), p. 207.
26. Hugh Tinker, Separate and Unequal (C. Hurst, London, 1976), pp. 117-18.
27. Lalit Kumar, India and Sri Lanka (1977), p. 14.
28. H. P. Chattopadhyaya, (1979), p. 208.
29. Rajesh Kadian, (1990), p. 87.
30. H. P. Chattopadhyaya, (1979), p. 214.
31. Ibid., p. 215.
32. J. S. Bains, India's International Disputes (1962), p. 89.
33. Lalit Kumar (1977), p. 28.

34. Ibid.
35. H. P. Chattopadhyaya, (1979), p. 217.
36. Neville Ladduwahetty, "The need for building bridges: Another view", *The Island*, June, 1999.
37. H. P. Chattopadhyaya, (1979), p. 217.
38. Ibid.
39. A Jeyaratnam Wilson, *Politics in Sri Lanka*, 1947-1973, Macmillan Press Ltd., London, 1974. pp. 29-30.
40. Rajesh Kadian (1990), p. 88.
41. H. P. Chattopadhyaya, (1979), p. 219.
42. Clive Parry, *Nationality and Citizenship Laws of the Commonwealth and the Republic of Ireland*, Oxford University Press, London, 1957. p. 798.
43. Professor Hugh Tinker, a British expert on the subject of the Indians living in the Empire, and a person whose sympathies were clearly with the Indian Communities, had little hesitation in blaming Nehru for the breakdown of the negotiation with D. S. Senanayake in 1947. Hugh Tinker, *Separate and unequal* (1976), also see W. T. Jayasinghe, *The Indo-Ceylon Problems* (2002).
44. H. P. Chattopadhyaya, (1979), pp. 225-227.
45. Ibid.
46. S. U. Kodikara "Persons of Indian origin in Ceylon" Foreign Affairs Report, Vol. XIII, No. 1, January 1964, pp 13-14
47. Clive Parry (1957), p. 820.
48. C. Devaraj, "Indian Tamils of Sri Lanka" in Ethnicity and Social Change, Social Scientists Association, Sri Lanka, 1985.
49. W. T. Jayansinghe (2002), pp. 113-119.
50. Ibid.
51. H. P. Chattopadhyaya, (1979), p. 233.
52. Ibid., p. 235.
53. Rajesh Kadian (1990), p. 88.
54. Ibid., p. pp. 88-89.
55. Lok Sabha Debates, Vol. XXXV, 1964, 3rd Series, 10th Session, Col. 1216, 23.11.1964.
56. Ibid., Col. 1238, 23.11.1964.
57. Ibid., Col. 1527.
58. Lok Sabha Debates, Vol. LVII, 1966, Cols. 1482-1492.
59. Ibid., Vol. XVII, 1968, Cols. 999-1001, 24.7.1968.
60. H. P. Chattopadhyaya, (1979), p. 261.
61. Ibid.
62. Vincent Coelho, *Across the Palk-Strait: India-Sri Lanka Relations*, New Delhi, 1976. p. 133.

63. "Not Under Duress" Editorial, *The Statesman*, Calcutta, 17, February, 1973.
64. Rajesh Kadian (1990), p. 90.
65. For a Comprehensive analysis of the stateless issue, See P. Sahadevan, *India and Overseas Indians: The Case of Sri Lanka,* Kalinga, New Delhi, 1995. pp. 112-36.
66. Ibid.
67. For details see W.T. Jayasinghe (2002).
68. Ibid.
69. *The Hindu*, December 6, 1988.
70. "Stateless Tamils' long struggle bears fruit" Tamil NET, October 7, 2003.

CHAPTER 4

Tamil Organisations – Moderate and Extremists

Compared to other British colonies in the region, Sri Lanka achieved independence relatively easily on 4 February 1948, with a brief political movement. The Sri Lankan elite did not have to fight for independence either through non-violent mass movement or by armed struggle against British imperialism.[1] Sri Lanka's progress from semi-responsible government to dominion status has been rather peaceful. There were hardly any pressures on social and political structures. English language, western ethos and secularism were dominant features of the elite of all categories at that time.[2] The first government led by D. S. Senanayake tried for a stable equilibrium of ethnic forces within Sri Lanka's multi-ethnic polity.[3]

However, the cracks surfaced with the Sinhala-Buddhist cultural awakening which had an inevitable populist twist and moreover, when the power slipped into the hands of a broad based middle class after 1956. It is not surprising, therefore, that this attitude led to considerable reservation in the minds of Tamil political activists.[4] The resignation of S.J.V. Chelvanayakam, member of All Ceylon Tamil Congress (ACTC), from D. S. Senanayake government and the founding of a new party (The Federal Party) by him in 1949 is a manifestation of this political climate.

Evolution of Tamil Moderate Outfits

After it gained independence in 1948, Sri Lanka, till the present era of ethnic conflict, has been in the dual process of the ethnicisation of politics and the politicization of ethnicity. An overview of Sri Lankan Tamil politics since independence clearly shows that the Tamils had been mainly "reactive" to Sinhala politics. Since their hopes and aspirations were never fulfilled by the Sinhala-dominated governments, frustration became intense, demands became more radical, culminating in the slogan of a "separate State of Tamil Eelam". From a consensual associational politics from 1948-56, when the Tamil leaders were a part of the Government, it became competitive politics, to conflictual politics to conflagrational politics.[5]

In Sri Lanka, the preparation for ethnic war was a lengthy process; the most crucial part of it was mobilisation of the people for war. Political mobilisation took almost 25 years before the militant/extremist leadership was born to conduct a decade long process of military mobilisation of Tamil youth in the early 1970s. The trend toward Tamil exclusivity, despite periods of accommodation with the Sinhalese political parties, had begun before independence. The first political moderate organisation formed specifically to protect the interests of Tamil ethnic minority was the All Ceylon Tamil Congress (ACTC). It was founded under the leadership of G. G. Ponnambalam in 1944. The Party played a remarkable role in injecting political consciousness of the Tamils in terms of their possession of a separate identity. Before independence, the All Ceylon Tamil Congress demanded "balanced representation" or the "50-50 formula". It signified that fifty per cent of the seats should be awarded to the Sinhalese majority and fifty per cent to the ethnic minorities, as well as a mandatory representation of the minorities in the cabinet. It clearly manifested Tamil anxieties about the domination of Sinhalese majority after independence.

The ACTC won 7 out of 95 seats in the 1947 General elections. Under the policy of "responsive cooperation",

ACTC, under the leadership of Ponnambalam entered into a coalition with the ruling UNP Senanayake government while Ponnambalam became a minister. Chelvanayakam opposed Ponnambalam's decision to join the UNP government which created a rift in the party. Finally Chelvanayakam broke away from the ACTC on the issue of Indian citizenship which he felt would greatly hurt the collective Tamil interests in the island.

Focus of Tamil Political Strategy

The resignation of S.J.V. Chelvanayakam and the founding of a new party Tamil Federal Freedom Party in December 1949 was a crucial turning point in Tamil nationalist politics in post-colonial Sri Lanka. The Federal Party (F.P.) put forward the demand for federal system of government, provincial autonomy to Tamils and citizenship to stateless Tamils.[6] Thereby the focus of Tamil political strategy shifted from sharing power at the centre through representation in its capacity as "minority" to the right to regional autonomy entitled to a "nation". In his speeches months before launching the FP, Chelvanayakam propagated the idea of Tamils constituting a separate nation.[7] Vanniasingham, Chelvanayakam's deputy, provided the broad outlines of the form of federal structures which Tamils would enjoy:

> *What we Tamil want is a federal constitution made up of two linguistic provinces with a federal centre at Colombo dealing with only defence, foreign affairs and inter-provincial communications. Each linguistic province will be its master in all internal matters...*[8]

Thus, in 1949, the FP enunciated the principles for resolving the problem on the basis of two nations, Sinhalese and Tamils. The FP advocated: (a) an autonomous region for the indigenous Tamil speaking peoples comprising the northern and eastern provinces linked to the rest of the island under a federal set up; (b) parity of status for the Tamil language with the Sinhalese language; (c) citizenship rights for all Indian Tamils who wished to make the Island their permanent home.[9] The FP soon became the leading political instrument of the Tamils and played a catalytic role in Tamil nationalism in Sri Lanka. FP strategy advocated a Constituent Assembly and opposed the imposition of a Constituent Assembly on the Tamil-speaking people. It strongly opposed attempts to settle Sinhalese in state-aided agricultural settlements in the East which the Tamil considered a part of their "traditional Tamil homeland" areas.

Ponnambalam equated the idea of federalism with secessionism and in a statement on 11 April 1949 described it "mid-summer madness" for the Tamils to ask for the partition of the country and segregation of the different communities.[10]

Moderate Outfits and Developmental Rhetoric

The Federal Party (FP) convention in 1951 declared that Tamils were a separate nation:

> *[The] Tamil-speaking people in Ceylon constitute a nation distinct from that of the Sinhalese by every fundamental test of nationhood, firstly, that of a separate historical past in this island at least as ancient and as glorious as that of the Sinhalese, secondly by the fact of their being a linguistic entity entirely different from that of the Sinhalese .... And finally, by reason of their territorial habitation areas which constitutes over one-third of this land....*[11]

The FP, under Chelvanayakam, tried to rally Tamils around the cause of Tamil nationalism. It tried to invoke Tamil nationalism among the Tamils in the East, played in the cause of Indian Tamils and wooed Tamil-speaking Muslims in the East. In 1956 elections, FP emerged as the dominant Tamil political force by defeating the conservative Tamil Congress.

In the 1950s and the 1960s, Tamil politics was characterised by a sense of grievance and political operation. The rhetoric and language of Tamil politics was developmental – for example, it carried grievances with regard to education, employment and land. In addition, it was democratic, i.e., it was against laws that appeared to discriminate against the Tamil language and for political structures which would allow for autonomy in predominantly Tamil areas. Consciousness was centred around language and economic rights.[12] During this period, the Party launched several economic non-violent movements. Satayagraha and civil-disobedience which mobilised around the Question of Tamils' separate identity. The FP twice entered into agreements with successive Sri Lankan governments – Bandaranaike – Chelvanayakam Pact 1957 and Senanayake – Chelvanayakam Pact 1965, which could not be implemented due to opposition from Buddhist clergy and political competition between the UNP and SLFP. In 1968, FP withdrew from the UNP government because its leaders felt that Party's association with the UNP could not secure rights for the Tamils.[13]

The cumulative effects of the ethnic riots of 1956, 1958 and 1961 added to the university admission policy of 1970s wherein a quota system was introduced for admission in the universities in proportion to the ethnic composition of population and adoption of the first Republican Constitution in 1972, which eliminated the guarantees given to the Minorities, further agitated minds of the Tamils.[14] The FP, in 1970, made representation to the Ministry of Constitutional Affairs which was drafting the 1972 Constitution. The FP suggestions included:

- A federal form of government with an autonomous Tamil State, an autonomous Muslim State and three autonomous Sinhala states;
- Tamil language Regulation 1966 to be incorporated into the Constitution;
- Mother Tongue to be the compulsory medium of instruction for all Tamil children.[15]

The Birth of the Eelam Dream

Unlike in the 1960s, the 1970s saw the Tamil political parties completely shut out of power in Colombo. The Federal Party continued to be moderate in its demands. Its manifesto for the 1970 elections rejected separatism. The Federal Party requested only the following:

- Equal standing for Tamil and Sinhala as official languages of the state;

- Sri Lankan citizenship for stateless Plantation Tamils;
- A secular state, with no religion being promoted above the others;
- The protection of the fundamental rights of all citizens;
- The abolition of caste and untouchability;
- A decentralized government.

In comparison to the calls for a separate state, this was hardly extremist. Yet it was anathema both to Sinhala-Buddhist nationalists as well as to the increasingly authoritarian politicians of the 1970s. When every single one of their demands was comprehensively repudiated in the 1972 constitution, the Federal Party withdrew from the constitution-writing process.

For the first time, mainstream Tamil politicians were openly separatist in their speeches. Two of them, Chelvanayakam and A. Amirthalingam, met with politicians from Tamil Nadu to request their support for a prospective Tamil State.[16] The prevailing radicalization also served to unify previously splintered Tamil political groups. United in their opposition to the constitution, they formed the Tamil United Front (TUF) in 1972. Outside the TUF, there were an estimated 40 small Tamil revolutionary groups already in existence by the time of the introduction of the new constitution.[17]

While the TUF were not yet explicitly separatist, and were primarily motivated by their opposition to the constitution, the Tamil revolutionary groups began to react violently to a set of incendiary policies introduced by Srimavo Bandaranaike in 1970 and 1971. Tamils were banned from using foreign currency to attend universities in India (in effect cutting off their access to Tamil-language university study) and the import of books, films and magazines from Tamil Nadu was banned. The constitution was regarded as excessively pro-Sinhala; the measures, however, were seen as repressive and anti-Tamil. In August 1971, an SLFP minister visiting Jaffna avoided assassination as he was not in his car when a bomb exploded in it. This was the first militant act by the revolutionary Tamil youths who would later fight a 25-year civil war.[18] Nine months later, the Tamil youth movement had its first casualty:

a group of young separatists shot and seriously injured an SLFP member and killed his driver. Violent separatism was not yet fully in the mainstream of Tamil political discourse, being at this stage restricted to the youth, but by the early 1970 it had emerged as a serious social and political threat.

Discrimination and the Failure of the Federal Party

Here it seems pertinent to pause and reflect on the failure of the Federal Party. Bandaranaike's death was an immense blow to the chances of parliamentary compromise. His successor as head of the SLFP, and a year later as Prime Minister, was his wife Srimavo, the world's first female Prime Minister. Srimavo Bandaranaike quickly moved to regain control of the left-wing pro-Sinhala political space. She passed a bill on December 31, 1960, declaring Sinhala the sole official language.[19] The bill was not only the fulfilment of the key Sinhala-Buddhist demand but also became a source of discrimination and a means to redress the colonial preference for the Tamils. The new bill meant that every government employee was required to know Sinhala. The civil service had been the career of choice for educated Tamils for a century. In 1956, before the passage of the original Sinhala Only Act, 30% of civil servants were Tamils. By 1975, the number had fallen to 5% (Tamils were 25% of the population and 15% of the citizenship).[20] Civil disobedience proved ineffective as the government once again declared a state of emergency, banned the Federal Party and outlawed strikes.

In response, the Tamil political parties allied with Dudley Senanayake, the son of D.S. Senanayake and the new head of the UNP. Senanayake came to power in 1965 in a "rainbow coalition" that included parties of all ethnic agendas. The Senanayake-Chelvanayakam pact of March 24, 1965 was remarkably similar to the Bandaranaike-Chelvanayakam (BC) pact eight years earlier. The UNP government agreed to enact the provisions of Bandaranaike's Tamil language bill, making Tamil the language of law courts and administration in the Northern and Eastern Provinces. Tamils considered the pact only a partial solution, as Sinhala was still the sole language in all other parts of the country, once again disadvantaging the Tamils in terms of employment. To placate angry Sinhala-Buddhist nationalists, Senanayake enacted several pro-Buddhist decrees, which served to further upset the Tamil minority.

The failure of the Federal Party to achieve a negotiated solution that was acceptable to most Tamils, and their alleged betrayal in joining the pro-Sinhala UNP government, led to the alienation of more militant or extreme Tamil groups and, by 1970, to the end of Chelvanayakam's tenure as the most respected and powerful Tamil politician. "Thantai Chelva", as he was known, had always resisted both calls for violence as well as the notion of a separate state.[21] "The SLFP victory in the election of 1970 meant that there was no Tamil presence in the government and that the Federal Party had lost its political clout. The end of the Federal Party era marked the rise of soft and later militant separatism as the dominant ideology of the Tamil movement in Sri Lanka.[22]

The 1970s: Militancy and the Road to Civil War

At a societal level, the decade following Bandaranaike's shooting had brought little progress on the front of ethnic reconciliation. By 1970, young Sri Lankans were becoming frustrated with the nation's weak economic growth and social unrest, two factors that were clearly linked. In March 1971, Sinhalese youth groups, led by the Marxist Janatha Vimukthi Perumana (literally People's Liberation Front; better known as the JVP)[23] launched a month-long insurgency to protest against the politicians' failure to help Sri Lanka progress.

In this backdrop of social protest and violence, politicians of both main parties, the SLFP and UNP, tired to appeal to Sinhala-Buddhist nationalism. Srimavo Bandaranaike, SWRD's widow, and her ideological opponent J. R. Jayewardene of the UNP, both used anti-Tamil nationalist rhetoric to divert discourse away from their economic and social policy failures.[24]

During this period, constitutional reform was attempted as a means of changing society. New constitutions were introduced in 1972 and 1978, each with the aim of somewhat advancing Sinhala-Buddhist nationalism.[25] Yet despite a complete hold on political power, the nationalists were impatient at their inability to fully dismantle the Tamil elite, whose privileged status they continued to see as an unfair colonial anachronism.

The constitution of 1972 is a tremendously important document in the history of Sri Lanka as a whole and in the context of the ethnic conflict in particular. The process of drafting began in July 1970, when Srimavo Bandarnaike convened Parliament as a Constituent Assembly and it became the law of the land on May 22, 1972. It reflected the long-held Sinhala desire for an indigenous constitution to replace the colonially imposed Soulbury Constitution. The constitution declared Sri Lanka a socialist state and had a number of other economic policy provisions, which shall be omitted here. But with regard to Tamils and the ethnic conflict, the key features of the 1972 constitution are as follows:

- Sinhala was made the sole official language of the state, and the use of Tamil was not granted as a constitutional right.
- Chapter II of the constitution stated the following: "The Republic of Sri Lanka shall give to Buddhism the foremost place and accordingly, it shall be the duty of the state to protect and foster Buddhism."
- The Soulbury Constitution's protection of civil and human rights was severally weakened.
- Parliamentary legislation was no longer subject to judicial review: this greatly increased the power of ministers and legislators.

With this constitution, the ruling SLFP not only took the country in a left-wing direction but also fulfilled promises that it had made to Sinhala-Buddhist nationalists since at least 1956. Yet the nationalist provision of the constitutions angered not only Tamils but also secular Sri Lankans of all ethnicities. Several Tamil Members of Parliament had resigned in mid-1971, during the drafting process, in protest against the perceived anti-Tamil nature of the document. In retrospect, the 1972 constitution encouraged many Tamils to support radical demands for an independent Eelam.

A seemingly innocuous but in fact controversial aspect of the constitution was the naming of the nation-state as "The Republic of Sri Lanka (Ceylon)". The name "Lanka" had been associated with the island, in both Sinhala and Tamil, for millennia, but the unambiguously Sinhala "Sri" upset Tamils, who had previously protested its use on vehicular license plates.[26] Thus we see that the feeling of alienation and anger with the government were intensified and trickled down and reached the common people. Tamil representatives took no part in discussions and debates and did not accept the final outcome.[27]

Moderate Tamil Political Groups: Agenda of Separatism

Consequently, the demand for a separate state gained momentum in the 1970s. Separatism as an objective was proclaimed by the major Moderate Tamil political groups viz., the FP, the TC, the Ceylon Workers Congress and the Tamil Progressive Front.[28] In 1975, sections of the two dominant Moderate Tamil Parties, the Federal Party (FP) and the Tamil Congress (TC) united to form the Tamil United Liberation Front (TULF). The first meeting of the TULF was held in 1976 at Vaddukoddai. It adopted a resolution calling for a separate state the "Tamil Eelam". The resolution declared that the Tamils in Sri Lanka:

> *[by] Virtue of their great language, their religion, their separate culture and heritage, their history of independent existence as a separate state over a distinct territory for several centuries till they were conquered by the armed might of the European invaders, and above all by their will to exist as a separate entity ruling themselves in their own territory, are a nation distinct and apart from the Sinhalese.*[29]

The FP, the major constituent unit of the TULF – the newly formed front – had declared even earlier that the Tamils are in every way fully equipped to be regarded as a separate nation and to live as a separate nation and that the only path for them to follow is the establishment of their right to self-rule in their traditional homeland based on the internationally recognised principles of the right of self-determination of every nation.[30]

New Dimension to Tamil Politics

The demand for Eelam by moderate Tamil organisations was first step towards the threatened disintegration of the Island on ethnic lines. It challenged the unitary character of the Sri Lankan Constitution. The Tamil feeling of alienation had moved to the extreme when the General Elections were held in 1977. The TULF returned with an overwhelming majority from the Tamil dominated areas and won 17 out of 24 seats that it contested in the North and East and hence became the official Opposition Party in the House.[31] After securing a massive mandate, the TULF began to campaign for a separate Eelam very enthusiastically. Sivasithamparam, the President of the TULF stated in Parliament:

> *[The] mandate that we obtained, was based on our demand for a separate Tamil Eelam... the Tamil people have given their mandate in no uncertain terms. Fifty seven per cent of the population of the Northern and Eastern Provinces, sixty-three per cent of the population of the Northern Province alone, have given the green light to the mandate that we asked for.*[32]

The Return of the UNP and the Path to Civil War

The conservative UNP, under the 70-years old J.R. Jayewardene, won a massive victory in the elections of 1977. Despite his opposition to the BC pact of 1957, Jayewardene was no longer seen as pro-Sinhala to the same extent as, for instance, the populist UNP minister Ranasinghe Premadasa, and with Tamil voters overwhelmingly opting for the TULF over militant parties, the prospect of a compromise suddenly seemed conceivable again. Such expectations were to prove hopelessly optimistic in the years to come, however, and by the middle of his twelve-year administration Jayewardene and the militants had plunged the nation into civil war.

The UNP's first major act was to redraft the 1972 constitution. The westminister system that the country had inherited with was scrapped, with Parliament being elected by proportional representation and a new head of state: a Gaullist-type executive President. Jayewardene intended to counter the weight of Parliament, and he was elected President a few months later. There remained a Prime Minister as head of government, but the President was the real source of power; indeed, the 1978 system, which continues to this day has left Sri Lanka with a government remarkably similar to the French Fifth Republic.

Proportional representation severely damaged minority candidates and parties. The threshold for a presence in parliament was set at 12.5%, high enough to marginalize every minority party other than the TULF.[33] On the issue of language and religion, the 1978 constitution hedged its bets. Sinhala was the "official" language, Tamil a "national" one; Buddhism was given "the foremost place", yet "freedom of thought, conscience and religion" were guaranteed. The constitution even enfranchised some Plantation Tamils. After the Sinhala-Buddhist fervour of the 1972 document, this was an encouraging attempt at compromise.[34]

Moderate Tamil Outfits Sidetracked

However, at this juncture, the moderate Tamils were sidetracked by the extremist/militant Eelamists. Naturally therefore, the TULF could hardly perform the role of strong opposition party in an era of emerging militancy and extremism, in which the state initiated and sponsored violence increasingly had got deadlocked with the violence of Tamil militants.[35] Every outbreak of communal violence hardened the Tamil feelings and attitudes and to that extent marginalized the role and influence of moderate and democratic Tamil political organisations.[36] Thus the Federal Party (FP), the Tamil Congress (TC) and CWC gradually got sidelined.

Democratic Channels Closed: The Tamil Youth Restive

By 1970s an incipient armed struggle by the Tamil youth started cropping up on Sri Lanka's political scene. Militant Tamil youth felt that peaceful political agitation by the moderate Tamil political organisations had got nothing for the Tamils, and, it was the "boys" turned to secure rights for the Tamils. Even before the 1970s, some elements within Tamil political parties and also outside it tried to raise the demand of a separate state and take a more militant course of action. The failure of the 1961 Satayagraha led to a feeling in a segment of the Federal Party (FP) that Gandhism had failed to secure their rights. As a consequence, they decided to form an underground group to fight for a separate state. Most of them were civil servants and have been influenced by Leon Uris 'Exodus'. At a meeting in Colombo they christened their group Pulip Padai (Army of Tigers). The group was to remain secret even from Federal Party stalwarts, and was to choose its members carefully. On 12 August 1961, the Pulip Padai members converged at the historic Koneswaran temple in Trincomalee and, standing in its holy precincts facing the sea, took a solemn oath to fight for a Tamil homeland.[37]

In 1969, Nadoraja Thangavelu alias Thangadurai and Selvaraja Yogachandran alias Kuttimani formed an informal group named Tamil Liberation Organisation (TLO).[38] It included Prabhakaran as well. Its members decided to plunge headlong into a violent struggle.[39] In early 1970s, Ponnudurai Satyaseelan founded the Tamil Manavar Perravai (Tamil Students League), which was joined by Sivakumaran who had for some time remained with TLO.[40] Sivakumaran attempted to assassinate Sri Lankan Deputy Minister for Cultural Affairs Somaweera Chandrasiri in September 1970 and Alfred Duriappah, the Jaffna Mayor, in February 1971. It ceased to operate in the middle of 1972.

The formation of the Tamil United Liberation Front (TULF) in 1972 led to creation of the Tamil Elaingyar Peravai (TYL-Tamil Youth League) in January 1973. Although strictly not a TULF affiliate, it functioned as one and brought numerous young Tamils under one banner. Forty youth, many of whom became leading activists of the militant movement, established TYL. The TYL organised processions and hunger strikes and whatever else the TUF exhorted it to do. According to Aunamalai Varadaraja Perumal, 'Amirthalingam gave support to our activities.'[41] Although TYL was critical of TULF, TYL did not oppose TULF until 1979. The TYL was split in 1975. While one group backed the TUF leadership, the other formed Eelam Liberation Organisation (ELO) and advocated an armed struggle.

The mid-1970s marked the emergence of separatism as a destabilising factor in Sri Lankan politics. Both the JVP uprising in 1971 and creation of Bangladesh deeply influenced the Tamil Youth and acted as models for carrying on armed insurgencies.[42] First, the JVP uprisings in 1971,[43] which was crushed with the international military assistance. The uprising showed that a 'relatively weak state could be fought and with luck and grit, [could be] overcome.'[44] The bloody struggle also provided a good insight to the Tamil radicals into the mechanism of warfare and state power. Second, the creation of Bangladesh through the armed struggle of Mukti Bahini with the aid of India in 1971 proved that a 'sovereign Tamil nation could never become a reality without a similar struggle and the kind of sanctuary the Mukti Bahini had.'[45] The Tamil militants tried to emulate the second model. Sivarajah rightly points out another three objective conditions that acted as a catalyst in the Tamil insurgency. These were: (a) Promulgation of a new constitution in 1972; (b) the excesses committed by the Police on the last day of the Sixth International Tamil Research Conference which was held in Jaffna in 1974; and (c) the anti-Tamil riots of 1977.[46]

Mushrooming of Tamil Extremist Outfits

Against this backdrop, there was an intensification of separatist agitation and mushrooming of Tamil extremist outfits in the second half of 1970s. It saw the emergence of Tamil Eelam Liberation Organisation (TELO), Peoples Liberation Organisation of Tamil Eelam (PLOTE), Eelam People's

Revolutionary Liberation Front (EPRLF), Eelam Revolutionary Organisation of Students (EROS) and Liberation Tigers of Tamil Eelam (LTTE). In September 1977, Thangadurai set up a militant group called the Tamil Eelam Liberation Army (TELA) and a political affiliate known as Eelam Liberation Army (ELA) and a political officiate known the Tamil Eelam Liberation Organisation (TELO). They intended to function on the lines of the Irish Republican Army and its political wing, the Sinn Fein.[47] After the arrest of Thangadurai and another top leader of TELO Kuttimani on April 3, 1981, Sri Sabaratnam took over the leadership of the group.

In 1979, Uma Maheshwaran who was chairman of the LTTE's Executive Council developed personal as well as ideological differences with Prabhakaran. Uma Maheshwaran broke away from the LTTE and set up PLOTE in 1980. The main objective of the PLOTE was the creation of a sovereign state – the People's Democratic Republic of Tamil Eelam. It put great emphasis on "mass mobilisation"... as it saw 'the liberation struggle as a protracted struggle in which the revolutionary armed struggle was an essential component.'[48] It favoured a "hit and run strategy" to sustain the liberation struggle and organised its branches all over the Tamil areas.

The EROS was formed in London, on 23 November 1975 by E. Ratnnaasakathy with an agenda to set up a separate state which would extend from Point Pedro to Badulla and Mannar to Batticaloa, including Pottuvil. Its slogan was: 'we are eelavar; our language is Tamil; our nation is Eelam,'[49] EROS was the only group that gave importance to the Tamil-speaking people living in the hill-country and considered them as the "classical proletariats" to be included as its vanguard in the struggle against the aggressive Sinhalese state.[50] It followed a Marxist – Leninist ideology to resolve Tamils problem in the North, East and the plantation areas. EROS military strategy and tactics differed from those of other extremist groups. It included attacks on economic targets and the army, so that the Sinhala state was weakened and demoralised.

As a result of a split in the Eelam Revolutionary Organisation of Students (EROS), the Eelam People's Revolutionary

Liberation Front (EPRLF) was set up on 4 October 1981. The founding President of the EPRLF was Gunasekeran, while its Secretary General was Padmanabha and Commander-in-Chief was Devananda. The main objective of the EPRLF was to establish a People's National Democratic State of Eelam. The group viewed the Eelam liberation struggle as part of the fight against imperialism. It also adopted Marxism – Leninism as its ideology. The outfit considered the 'armed struggle as the only viable and effective means to achieve the liberation of Eelam.'[51] The group set up following bodies: The General Union of Eelam Students (GUES), the Rural Workers and Peasants Front (FRPF), the Eelam Youth Front (EYF), the Plantation Proletariat Front (EPF) and the Fishing Workers Union (FWU).[52] It had its own military wing, called the People's Liberation Army. The Tamil insurgent groups carried out sporadic attacks against Sri Lankan police outposts in the North and East, in addition to targeting moderate Tamil politicians, suspected informants and Sinhalese civilians.[53]

The Liberation Tigers of Tamil Eelam actually originated in 1972 when LTTE's Commander Velupilai Prabhakaran founded the Tamil New Tigers in mid-1970s, which later became LTTE.[54] Prabhakaran who was politically motivated from his younger days, developed the military organisation of the Tamil New Tigers (TNT) and then the LTTE.[55] According to Dissanayaka, Prabhakaran killed Tanabalassingham to assume the Leadership of the TNT and later on 5 May 1976[56] renamed the group as Liberation Tigers of Tamil Eelam.[57]

Growth of the LTTE

The international community assumed that the violence of 1983 would press both sides to negotiate rather than escalate. India offered to mediate, but Indira Gandhi's credibility as a mediator was severely undermined by the efforts of the Research and Analysis Wing (RAW), India's external intelligence agency, which armed the LTTE and other militant groups and helped them set up training camps in Tamil Nadu.[58] Unsurprisingly, the UNP government thus rejected India's advances.

The training camps in India proved crucial to developing and enhancing the LTTE's military capabilities. The Sri Lanka military was powerless to carry out strikes against India, the dominant power in the region. The hawkish Lalith Athulathmudali was appointed as Minister of National Security, and he created a 5,000 person commando force, known as the Special Task Force (STF) which, while unable to shut down the camps, intercepted the movement of supplies and militants from Tamil Nadu to Jaffna, seizing several Indian fishing vessels in the process, which further damaged Indo-Lankan relations. By March 1984 there were 2,000 militants in the Tamil Nadu camps. Their numbers had been strengthened by many of the 35,000 refugees of the 1983 riots who had received asylum in Tamil Nadu.[59]

What enabled the LTTE to achieve primacy over all the other Eelam militants? At least four major reasons can be identified:

- The LTTE's cadres were the best organized and most disciplined;
- The LTTE's capacity for executing ruthless violence against both the Sinhala government as well as rival Tamil groups;
- The charisma of its leader, Prabhakaran, who at the time faced little opposition to his leadership from within the LTTE;
- Its single-minded focus on only one goal: establishing an authoritarian state of Tamil Eelam in the Northern and Eastern Provinces of Sri Lanka.

Of these, the last is perhaps the most significant. Other Tamil militant groups, such as the Eelam Revolutionary Organisation of Students (EROS) and the Eelam People's Revolutionary Liberation Front (EPRLF) were often hindered by confused agendas, such as desiring the creation of a Marxist state in all of Sri Lanka as opposed to just Eelam. The LTTE successfully associated itself with the aspirations of the Tamil people for independence, and thus did a better job than any other group of achieving mass popularity. The leaders of the six biggest Tamil groups met in Madras in October 1983 to attempt to resolve their differences without success.[60] Instead, the LTTE won a series of violent encounters against these groups in Jaffna, Madras and London in 1983 and achieved leadership of the movement essentially by conquest.

The LTTE is renowned worldwide for its funding model, for efficiently levying Tamil politicians in India, and more importantly, refugees in Switzerland, Canada and other countries for financial support for their cause. They did not merely collect remittances, however, they also had a large international smuggling operation. Their financial strength enabled them to have state-of-the-art technology and in later years to launch their own navy and air force (in 2007). This was an astonishing achievement. A British military expert wrote in 1999 that for an insurgent group to possess a navy was 'probably unique in the history of insurgency warfare'.[61] It allowed the LTTE to grow from a typical militant group to a guerrilla army, albeit one that engaged in many of the activities of terrorist groups. Young recruits were indoctrinated into the ideology of dying for the cause, and the LTTE were pioneers of suicide terrorism.[62]

In Jaffna, the LTTE showed no mercy to Tamils who refused to join or assist their cause. They killed antimilitant academics, social workers, activists and local politicians. They took control of schools, hospitals and other public institutions: this was the first step in establishing a *de facto* LTTE-run state in Jaffna. Above all, they not only defeated but also decimated rival militant groups. In April-May 1986, they killed 200 members of the Tamil Eelam Liberation Front. Later that year, they organized a series of attacks on the EPRLF in Jaffna. Unlike the LTTE, the other militant organizations had only one source of funding, India. When the Indian government cut off its assistance after 1985, they were financially crippled.

According to government figures, between 1976 and July 1983, 73 persons were slain by the Tigers underground militants,[63] and from 1978-83, the Tigers were responsible for more than 265 bombings, robberies, assaults, and other criminal acts.[64] There were shooting incidents, more significant of which was the killing of Alfred Duraiappah, the Major of

Jaffna in 1975 by V. Prabhakaran, who later emerged as LTTE's chief supreme. The LTTE was very quick in establishing its international linkages. Since the early 1980s, the LTTE has established a global network of offices and cells that spans at least 40 countries and is unrivalled by any other extremist organisation worldwide. Funds come from the countries where there are the large Tamil diasporan communities.[65]

According to Rohan Gunaratna, LTTE's secretive linkages with three Tamil political-militant organisation helped LTTE to develop its international component. They were tactical and not enduring relationships. These included support from TULF, EROS and Tamil Liberation Front.[66] LTTE's link with the TULF was established even before it obtained a formal mandate from the Tamil people for a separate Tamil state in 1977. Rohan further observes that TULF leader Amithalingam clandestinely supported the LTTE to emerge as a powerful force.[67]

Another TULF MP V. N. Naratnam who was an executive committee member of the Inter-Parliamentary Union introduced many influential and wealthy Tamils who were living abroad to the LTTE. EROS which had links with Fatah, the military wing of Palestine Liberation Organisation (PLO). It offered training opportunity to EROS which, in turn, EROS shared with the LTTE. The third organisation, the TLF, the precursor of the Tamil Liberation Organisation (TLO) based in London, organised many demonstrations and rallies against Sri Lanka's government. During the second half of the 1970s, TLO was gradually absorbed by the LTTE and began to function as the international arm of the LTTE. Powerful international linkages of LTTE proved to be a major morale booster for the Tamil insurgents.

To conclude, Sri Lanka's discriminatory policies towards Tamils directly led to the emergence of moderate and extremist Tamil organisations to protect the interests of Tamil ethnic minority. Beginning in the 1950s Sri Lanka's Sinhalese politicians began advocating ethnocentric policies to win the majority community's vote. Indeed, ethnic outbidding and ethno-centrism were so blatantly promoted and so enthusiastically embraced in Sri Lanka that ethnocentric associations triumphed over the Island's civil associations. The first political organisation formed specifically to protect the interests of the Tamil ethnic minority was the All Ceylon Tamil Congress, founded under the leadership of G.G. Ponnambalam in 1944. A number of incidents in the following years, each worse in its impact than the preceding one, resulted in the formation of other moderate Tamil political groups viz. the TC, the Ceylon Workers Congress and the Tamil Progressive Front. After 1956, Tamil moderate political outfits began demanding autonomy for the northern and eastern regions of the country – albeit within a federal framework. Subsequently the above-mentioned major moderate Tamil political organisations joined hands and formed the Tamil United Front in 1972.

However, during the late 1970s and early 1980s the militants' aspects began to materialise. The result was that the moderate Tamil political organisations were sidetracked by some forceful and dynamic extremist political groups. These groups included the Tamil Eelam Liberation Organisation (TELO), People's Liberation Organisation for Tamil Eelam (PLOTE), the Eelam People's Revolutionary Liberation Front (EPRLF) and the Liberation Tigers of Tamil Eelam (LTTE) founded in 1972 by V. Prabhakaran. The most effective among them has been the last one, the LTTE, which sidelined all others and has emerged as the principal and most lethal voice of militant Tamil aspirations. The LTTE has built up its strength on highly motivated, committed and trained cadres and a wide array of small arms and sophisticated weapons procured from international markets and a sympathetic external patron, India.

Since 1987 only the LTTE has fought the war and all other groups have surrendered their arms under the India-Sri Lanka Peace accord of 1987 and joined the political mainstream. The LTTE has ensured a constant supply of manpower to sustain its armed campaigns through its tactics of strategic targeting of certain social groups and harnessing the Tamil national sentiment of the youth to its goal of national liberation.

Such confrontationist politics between the Sri Lankan government and the moderate political outfits and war between LTTE and the Sri Lankan forces has resulted in multi-dimensional crises in the Island and seriously affected Sri Lankan nation and state. Its fabric of unity has been badly torn.

References

1. Rober Oberst, "Democracy and the Persistence of Westernized Elite Dominance in Sri Lanka" *Asian Survey,* (California), Vol. 25, No. 7, July 1985, p. 760.
2. Marshal R. Singer, The Emerging Elite: A Study of Political Leadership in Ceylon, MIT Massachusetts, 1967, p.37.
3. Zeylanicus, *Ceylon Between Orient and Occident,* Elek Book Ltd., London, 1970. p. 224.
4. Michael Roberts (ed.), "Problem of Collective Identity in a Multi-Ethnic Society: Sectional Nationalism vs. Ceylonese Nationalism 1900-1940" Collective Identities, Nationalism and Protest in Modern Sri Lanka, Marga Institute, Colombo, 1979. p. 352.
5. V. Suryanarayan, "Prospects for Reconciliation" in B. Raman, N. S. Moorthy and K. Chittaranjan (ed.) Sri Lanka: Peace Without Process (Samskriti, in Association with Observer Research Foundation, New Delhi, 2006), p. 99.
6. E.F.C. Ludowyk, *The Story of Ceylon,* Navrang, New Delhi, 1985. p. 286.
7. A. Jeyaratnam Wilson, *SJV Chelvanaykam and the Crisis of Sri Lankan Tamil Nationalism 1947-1977: A Political Biography,* Hurst and Company, London, 1994. pp. 29-30.
8. A. Jeyaratnam Wilson (1994), p. 30.
9. Ibid., p. 41.
10. Ibid.,p. 30.
11. Cited in Sivarajah Ambalvanar, *Politics of Tamil Nationalism in Sri Lanka,* South Asia Publishers, New Delhi, 1996. pp. 106-107.
12. Radhika Commaraswamy, "Myths without consciences: Tamil and Sinhalese Nationalist Writings of the 1980s" in Charles Abeysekera and Newton Gunasinghe, (ed.), Facts of Ethnicity in Sri Lanka, Social Scientists Association (SSA), Karunaratne and Sons Ltd., Colombo, 1987. p. 74.
13. Krishna Gopal, "Ethnicity and Conflictual Nationalism in Sri Lanka: Ramifications and Emergent Scenario" in Gopal Singh (Ed.) *South Asia: Democracy, Discontent and Societal Conflicts,* Anamika Publishers, New Delhi, 1998. pp. 84-85.

14. Jehan Perara, "Sri Lanka: The Federal Alternative" *Lanka Guardian* Vol. 8, No. 4, June 15, 1985, p. 11.
15. Nadesan Satyendra, "A Record of Broken Pacts and Evasive Proposals" http:/www.tamilnation.org/conflictresolution/tamil_eelam/
16. Patrick Peebles, *The History of Sri Lanka,* Greenwood Press, Westport, 2006, pp. 112-119.
17. Ibid.
18. Ibid.
19. Ibid., p. 110.
20. Ibid., p. 111.
21. Chellamuthu Kuppuswamy, *Prabhakaran: His Life and Struggle For Eelam,* Oxygen Books, Chennai, 2009. pp 45-47.
22. Peebles, p.124.
23. K.M. de Silva, *History of Sri Lanka* (1981), p. 541.
24. Nira Wickramasinghe, *Sri Lanka in the Modern Age: A History of Contested Identities,* C.Hurst, London, 2006. p. 129.
25. Ibid., p. 238.
26. Alfred Seyarastnam Wilson, *Sri Lankan Tamil Nationalism,* C. Hurst, London, 2000. pp. 157-158.
27. Sinnappah Arasaratnam, "Sinhala-Tamil Relations in Modern Sri Lanka" in *Ethnic Conflict: International Perspective* (Eds.) Jerry Boucher, Dan Landis and Karan Arnold Clark, Sage, London, 1987, p. 48.
28. Krishna Gopal, in Gopal Singh (Ed.), *South Asia: Democracy Discontent and Societal Conflicts* (1998), p. 86.
29. Ketheshwaran Loganathan. Sri Lanka: Lost Opportunities-Past Attempts at Resolving Ethnic Conflict (Centre for Policy Research and Analysis, Faculty of Law, University of Colombo, 1986), p. 58.
30. The Mirror (Colombo), 10 September 1973.
31. Ambalvanar Sivarajah, "The Rise of Militancy in Tamil Policies" in Mahindra Werake and P.V.J., Jayasekera (ed.), *Security Dilemma of a Small State, Part II, Internal crises and External Intervention in Sri Lanka,* South Asia Publishers, New Delhi, 1995, pp. 124-125.
32. Ibid.
33. Nira Wickramasinghe (2006), pp.252-255.
34. Peebles (2006), pp.135-136.
35. Urmila Phadnis, "Role of State in Ethnic Conflict in Sri Lanka" *Lanka Guardian,* Vol. 13, No. 15, December 1, 1990, p. 20.
36. *The Hindu* (Madras), 19 March 1986, p. 1.

37. M. R. Narayan Swamy, *Tigers of Lanka: From Boys to Guerrillas*, Konark Publishers, Delhi, 1994, p. 24.
38. Kuttimani was a smuggler in Velvettiturai, a coastal village and also hometown of Prabhakaran. Ibid., p. 25.
39. Ibid.
40. Ibid., p. 25.
41. Ibid., p. 26.
42. Rohan Gunaratna, Sri Lanka's Ethnic crisis and National Security, South Asian Network on Conflict Research (Unie Arts Ltd., Colombo, 1998), p. 106.
43. See, A. C. Alles, The JVP: 1969-1989 (Lake Home Investment Ltd., Colombo, 1990), pp. 275-276.
44. M. R. Narayan Swamy, Tigers of Sri Lanka: From Boys to Guerrillas, op.cit., p. 27.
45. Ibid., p. 28.
46. Ambalvanar Sivarajah, *Politics of Tamil Nationalism in Sri Lanka*, South Asia Publishers, New Delhi, 1996. p. 129.
47. M. R. Narayan Swamy (1994), p. 36.
48. Ambalvanar Sivarajah (1996), p. 133.
49. Ibid., p. 134.
50. Ibid., p. 136.
51. Ibid., p. 138.
52. Ibid.
53. Peter Chalk, "The Liberation Tigers of Tamil Eelam Isurgency in Sri Lanka" in Rajat Ganguly, Ian Macduff (ed.), *Ethnic Conflict and Secessionism in South and South East Asia: Causes, Dynamics Solutions*, Sage Publications, New Delhi, 2003. p. 130.
54. Manoj Joshi, "On the Razor's Edge: The Liberation Tigers of Tamil Eelam" Studies in Conflict and Terrorism, January – March 1996, pp. 19-42.
55. Rohan Gunaratna, *International and Regional Security: Implication of the Sri Lankan Tamil Insurgency*, Unie Arts Ltd., U.K., 1997. pp. 8-10.
56. Dissanayaka, T.D.S.A., The Dilemma of Sri Lanka (Swastika Pvt. Ltd., Colombo, 1993), p. 77.
57. M. R. Narayan Swamy, op.cit., p. 31.
58. Ramchandra Guha, *India After Gandhi: The History of the World's Largest Democracy*, Macmillan, London, 2007, p. 610.
59. Kuppuswamy, p. 85.
60. Ibid.
61. Ramchandra Guha (2007), pp. 593-597
62. Ibid.

63. Government of Sri Lanka, The Facts and the International Commission of Jurists Report on Ethnic violence in Sri Lanka (Pamphlet) (Ministry of State, Colombo, 1983).
64. Ibid.
65. Rohan Gunaratna, International and Regional Implication of the Sri Lankan Tamil Insurgency, 1997, U.K.: International Foundation of Sri Lanka, Unie Arts Ltd., p. 8.
66. Ibid., In countries where LTTE is proscribed, it operates through organisations such as the United Tamil Organisation, the World Tamil Movement and the Tamil Rehabilitation Organisation USA.
67. Rohan Gunaratna, International and Regional Security: Implication of the Sri Lankan Tamil Insurgency, p. 8.

CHAPTER 5

Complexities of Tamil Problem in Sri Lanka

Sri Lanka is an exquisite little island rich in colour, excitement and new experience. However, it is an irony that Sri Lanka offers a striking example of political, economic and religious problems left by colonisation.[1] The conflict between the Tamils and the Sinhalese which had grown/evolved during the past couple of decades on the island of Sri Lanka, took a significant turn since mid-January 2009. And in May 2009, the government of Mahinda Rajapaksa launched its final campaign against the Tamil strongholds and killed many of its leaders including the Liberation Tigers of Tamil Eelam founder, Velupillai Prabhakaran. The crushing defeat of the Liberation Tigers of Tamil Eelam has set an uncommon precedent in the annals of insurgent warfare, in that it debunks the popular notion that intractable and established insurgencies are unwinnable.

Even though the defeat of the Liberation Tigers of Tamil Eelam (LTTE) in Sri Lanka means that the achievement of a separate Tamil State is no longer plausible, LTTE supporters within the Tamil diaspora will not easily relinquish the struggle, inculcated of decades of LTTE ideology. Hence in such a type of fluid situation what comes up for consideration is the complexities of Tamil Problem in Sri Lanka. In order to understand how to address the problem, it is necessary to be familiar with the past.

Grappling with the Past

The early history of Sri Lanka is shrouded in myth. In this mythic history, the Buddha visits Sri Lanka and establishes the Island as the repository of his teaching, thus fusing Sinhalese Buddhism, nationalism and ethnic identity. A fundamentalist Buddhist acceptance of this mythic version of history is prevalent in contemporary Sri Lanka.[2] Though many tribes and clans from predominantly southern India gradually populated the Island, the most powerful and dominating of settlers were the Sinhalese who originated from northern India.[3] Upon their arrival, which historians have calculated to be in the fifth century B.C., the Sinhalese were probably able to share the Island and have great influence because of their intermarriage and relations with the aboriginal peoples. By 200 B.C., the Sinhalese occupied most of Sri Lanka, and Sinhalese kingship and royal families governed various regions of the island.[4] The Sinhalese people, though they were the majority, lived peacefully with the non-Aryan population of the Island. As historian K. M. de Silva points out:

> *Sri Lanka, in the first few centuries after the Aryan settlement, was a multi-ethnic society (a conception which emphasises harmony and a spirit of live and let live) rather than a plural society (in which tension between ethnic or other distinctive groups is a main feature.)*[5]

So far as the question of the arrival of the Tamils is concerned, the Tamils tend to have darker skin than the Sinhalese and originate from the southern part of India. They speak Tamil which is a Dravidian language commonly spoken in South India; Tamil is a language totally different from the language of the Sinhalese and is derived from Sanskrit in North India.[6] While it is hard to tell when the Tamils came to Sri Lanka, historian S. A. Pakeman states; "There is ample historical evidence that well before the beginning of the Christian era, invasion from South India had begun, and these continued sporadically all through the history of Ceylon (Sri Lanka) up to the coming of the Portuguese early in the sixteenth century."[7]

Various tribes from South India invaded and settled in northern parts of the Island, spreading down to the northeast and northwest coasts. The northern peninsula of Sri Lanka, Jaffna peninsula, became a principal settlement of the Tamils. During the 19th century, they designated the peninsula as the Tamils' independent kingdom. Due to the differences in religion and language and tensions over land rights, the Tamil kingdom of Jaffna was often at war with the Sinhalese kings until the coming of the Portuguese.

European Colonialism and Tamil Problem

Though Sri Lanka is positively identified for having its own unique and distinct characteristics, 443 years of European domination cannot be overlooked as it laid the foundation for political, economic, social and religious infrastructure that now defines post-colonial Sri Lanka. In 1505, the Portuguese landed on Sri Lanka and successfully negotiated a trade agreement with the Sinhalese kingdom of Kotte.[8] The Portuguese continued to rule Sri Lanka until the Dutch forced them out in 1658. The Sinhalese kingdom of Kandy continued to exist with autonomy[9] under the Dutch, but the Tamil kingdom and the remnants of the Kotte and Sitawake Kingdoms remained under colonial rule. The colony remained firmly in Dutch hands until the middle of the 18th century, when British imperial ambitions in India brought Britain to Sri Lanka in attempt to drive the Dutch from the Indian sub-continent.[10]

The British took the major east coast port of Trincomalee in 1796, and effectively took the Island from the Dutch in 1797. Once again, the dominant Sinhalese kingdom, Kandy, pursued a trade agreement and autonomy treaty with Great Britain which was doomed to fail from the beginning. The British did not intend to keep Ceylon (as they called it), but assumed that with the cessation of hostilities with the Dutch, it would be returned.[11] However, it was not, and Ceylon become the first crown colony (literally a colony of the crown), meaning that it was under direct British rule. Peace lasted no more than a year. The ensuing war lasted from 1803-1815, but resulted in absolute British domination of Sri Lanka.[12]

The British built the Island's society around plantation agriculture and initially began with the main crop being cinnamon. However, as a result of various agricultural disasters throughout the 19th century, the keystone crop changed many times from cinnamon to coffee, cocoa, tea, and rubber. Some of these required more labour than the Island could initially provide, so the British brought in the ethnically similar Indian Tamils to work on plantations. These Tamils were considered to be different by Tamils who had lived in Sri Lanka for 900 years. The British effectively created a new ethnic rivalry on the island.[13]

Generally, the Sinhalese and the Tamils had lived in peace (with occasional territorial disputes), but now with the introduction of this third but ethnically similar group, a critical imbalance in representation on the political level severed 900 years of Sinhalese and Tamil co-existence.[14] The British undertook the education of the Sinhalese, limiting their attempts to educate the Tamils. American missionaries educated the Tamils, and actually gave them a better education, resulting in Tamils receiving more role in the civil service of the empire, and in turn gaining a tremendous amount of influence.[15]

World War I was a critical point in Ceylonian history. In 1919, all the major Sinhalese and Tamil political organisations banded together to form the Ceylon National Congress and this new Congress immediately submitted a proposal for a new constitution that would increase local control over Executive Council and the budget.[16] Amendments in 1924 led to greater Ceylonian representation on the Executive Council. This momentous amendment/reforms gave Ceylon tremendous autonomy under the empire, and yet strengthened its ties with Britain in the upper classes, and lessened the overall nationalistic movement. However, to ascertain why a representative government as chartered by the 1924 Constitution had not succeeded and to suggest Constitutional changes necessary for the island's eventual self-rule,[17] a royal commission visited Ceylon in 1927 under the Earl of Donoughmore. This resulted in a new Constitution, known as the Donoughmore Constitution, which was designed to address the grievances and failures of the previous 1924 constitution. This failed to produce anything more than a splintering of more nationalist groups and movements.

In 1945 Great Britain agreed to grant Ceylon independence. Before independence was granted, Lord Soulbury was sent with a commission to examine a new constitutional draft that the Sri Lankan Minister had proposed. The Commission made recommendations that led to a new constitution. The new constitution was known as the Soulbury Constitution. In 1948 Ceylon was granted independence with a Parliamentary system implementing a bicameral legislature. All seemed well, and a bright future seemed to guarantee a prosperous nation. But history has a way of making itself fail to adhere to our assumptions.

The Dynamics of Tamil Problem

Unlike the Indian experience, Sri Lanka's attainment of independence was notably untraumatic. In effect, Sri Lanka independence followed on the coattails of the Indian struggle for independence. The British left Sri Lanka amicably and were perceived as a trustworthy ally by both the Sinhalese and Tamil elites (as evidenced in the 1948 Ceylon – UK Defence Pact).[18] In the initial period following independence, the bonds between the elites of the two groups engendered a sense of "Ceyloness" which took precedence over the ethnic divisions, especially since the English language remained a common medium of communication and the medium of instruction in the secondary schools and university. Gradually, however, post-independence cohesion eroded. According to Kenneth Bush, various suggestions have been put forward to explain the apparent advantaged position of the Sri Lankan Tamils at independence: British "divide and rule" policy; access to superior English medium education; economic necessity; Tamil industriousness.[19]

No doubt, each suggestion contributes to the explanation. However, the consequence of this phenomenon was that, at independence, the Tamils came to be viewed by the Sinhalese as being "over represented" in higher education, the professions, and the civil service.[20] This became a source of discontent and a political target for Sinhalese nationalists. The ethnic differences proved to be a temptation too strong not to be exploited and manipulated by politicians who quickly learned that an ethnic majority could be transformed into an electoral majority.

Tamils of Indian Origin: Target of Discrimination

When Sri Lanka became independent in 1948, Sinhalese leaders used their majority in the newly elected Parliament to improve their community's economic and political positions. From the first year of independence, the Senanayake government immediately passed legislation to disenfranchise and even deny citizenship to many estate Tamils who were brought to Ceylon from India by the British.[21] This can be shown in the Ceylon Citizenship Act of 1948, and the Indian and Pakistani Residents Act No. 3 of 1948 and the Ceylon Parliamentary Elections Amendment Act No. 48 of 1949.[22] Senanayake carried out these actions to ensure that he, claiming to be a descendant of the original Buddhist monarchs, preserved the Sinhalese hegemony. This angered the Tamil people because they wanted representation in the new government also. In 1949, the Tamil people formed the Tamil Federal Party and wished to create a Tamil state on Ceylon. Tension continued between the Sinhalese sponsored Sri Lankan Freedom Party and the Tamil Federal Party for many years.

As the Sinhalese nationalists assumed control of the government through the electoral process, they enacted legislation which limited Tamil employment and educational opportunities. As a result the Tamils' share of government jobs dropped from 50 per cent to 11 per cent between 1956 and 1980.[23] Sinhalese control of university education was instituted in 1971 through a government initiated admission scheme. Tamil youths were required to score higher on entrance tests, and were subjected to district quotas, which drastically restricted Tamils' admission to university programmes (especially engineering and medicine).[24]

Sinhala-only Legislation Marginalized Tamils

Until 1956 English was the official language of Sri Lanka. The medium of instruction in all secondary and tertiary level educational institution was English while all official correspondence had been in English until then. With the enactment of the Official Language Act No. 33 of 1956, a sudden change was brought about in the country. Sinhala was made the official language and all official correspondence had to be in Sinhala. All those employed in the State services had to learn Sinhala.[25] The language by itself was not the only matter at issue. It is an important aspect of one's ethnic identity. Relegating Tamil to a lower status offended the Tamils and inflamed their feelings. Tamils were suddenly called upon to obtain proficiency in a language that was as alien to them in order to secure employment in the public sector, hold on to their jobs in government services, and to receive promotions. Generations of parents in the Tamil areas had communicated with their children in the Tamil language and Tamil was the only language of instruction in schools for centuries until the Island came under the British rule.[26]

There was, therefore, very little social interaction between the Tamil and the Sinhalese peoples, except at the level of the English educated elite. The enactment of the legislation making Sinhalese the only official language of the nation was a blow to the aspirations of Tamils, who, like the Sinhalese, were liberated from English rule. Tamils had hoped that independence from foreign rule would liberate them from the needs to educate their children in an alien language, to seek public service jobs, and to communicate directly with the government officials in their own language. This right was denied to them when provisions were not incorporated in the 1956 Sinhala only language bill for the reasonable use of Tamil.[27] This became a great concern to the Tamil people, especially the Tamil youth who were directly affected by the Sinhala only legislation.

History of Broken Promises

The strident positions taken by leaders of Sinhalese parties on the language issue prior to the enactment of Sinhala only legislation also infuriated Tamil leaders. The third Prime Minister of independent Sri Lanka, Sir John Kotelawala of the United National Party, had assured the Tamil people in 1955, during his visit to Jaffna that both Sinhalese and Tamil would be made the official languages of the country, if his party were returned to power in the general elections of 1956.[28] This statement was deliberately twisted by Sinhalese activists to suggest that, if both languages were given equal status, Sinhalese people would be forced to study Tamil. This provided the opportunity for S.W.R.D. Bandaranaike of the Sri Lankan Freedom Party, who was championing the Sinhalese – Buddhist cause, to declare that Sinhala would be made the only language of Sri Lanka with a provision for the reasonable use of Tamil.[29]

This stand of the Sri Lankan Freedom Party was challenged by Prime Minister Kotelawala of the United National Party when he also announced, contrary to what he had promised the Tamils earlier, that Sinhalese will be made the only official language of the nation.[30] No sooner was this proclamation made by the United National Party, Mr. Bandaranaike declared that Sinhala will be made the official language in twenty – four hours if his coalition party won the elections.[31] Prime Minister Bandaranaike proceeded to make Sinhala the only official language in 1956, without making any provisions for even the reasonable use of Tamil. It became obvious to Tamil leaders that Sinhalese officials were willing to make any promises to the Sinhalese electorate that would return them to power and were unconcerned about the adverse impact that any of these decisions might have on the Tamils and long-term Sinhalese-Tamil relations.

In 1956, Ceylon elected a new Prime Minister S.W.R.D. Bandaranaike, partly under the pretence that he claimed to be the "protector of Buddhism".[32] In 1957, the new Prime Minister and the leader of the Tamil Federal Party, S.J.V. Chelvanayakam, created the Bandaranaike – Chelvanayakam Pact, a document drafted to repeal the disenfranchisement legislation of estate Tamils and allow Tamil to be the official language of the Northern and Eastern Provinces of Ceylon. However, the Buddhist reaction rallied by the Sangha and J. R. Jayawardene – then a leading UNP Member of the opposition – was so strong that the pact was dropped. As early as 1956 "language riots" began to flare up, resulting in the deaths of hundreds. Thousands of Tamil refugees fled from the Sinhalese South to Tamil areas in the North.[33]

Successive governments, such as the Srimavo Bandaranaike's government of early 1970s, not only rejected Tamil demands, but went to the extent of reaffirming Sinhala as the official language, without making any provision for the use of Tamil language even in Tamil areas.[34] Discrimination against the Tamil people continued as Srimavo continued to promote Sinhalese hegemony. At this point, the Tamil people took action and started a series of non-violent protests in response to the discrimination. During the 1970s, two new constitutions would allow the consolidation of power in the hands of the Sinhalese elite.

In 1972, a new constitution for Ceylon was drafted that changed everything. It started by renaming Ceylon as Sri Lanka and even contained a bill of rights that ensured religious freedom. This is quite significant since there was no bill of rights in the original constitution of Ceylon. However, the Tamil people still were not given the right to speak their language.[35] In the 1977 elections, the people of Sri Lanka elected UNP representative, J.R. Jayawardene, as head of state. He helped draft the 1978 constitution which is still used today. The constitution included the use of Tamil and English as official languages, allowed to the Tamils to have representatives in proportion to their population, and ensured easier access to education. Although this may seem to be a step towards resolving the discrimination against the Tamil people, the basic freedoms outlined in this constitution have never been enforced for a variety of reasons. The best explanation of this lack of enforcement is stated by David Little: '[T] he possibility of improved ethnic relations was ... undermined by the government's failure to implement its policies wholeheartedly.'[36] In addition to this, legislative groups had less authority than assumed and were limited by budget cuts and corruption to enforce such legislation.[37]

Tamil Problem Gets Complicated: Warnings Ignored

The 1977 landslide victory of J. R. Jayawardene's UNP over the Sri Lankan Freedom Party was followed by an outbreak of violence. Although it began as a confrontation between UNP and SLFP supporters, it was quickly redirected towards both the Sri Lankan Tamils resident in the Sinhalese South, and the plantation Tamils in the Central Province. Perhaps because the defeated SLFP had earlier extended its rule under unpopular Emergency legislation, Jayawardene was hesitant to declare a state of emergency. The widespread killings, assaults, rapes, looting and destruction were allowed to continue over a period of two weeks. Thousands of Tamil refugees were pushed northwards in search of security. The violence reinforced Tamil distrust of government promises to improve Tamil-Sinhalese relations.[38]

In August 1981, the next wave of communal violence swept the Island. Increased Tamil militancy in the North, the detention of Tamil youths incommunicado, and the retributive police looting and arson in Jaffna escalated tensions; but now the violence was organised and systematic. Tamil sources claimed that attacks had been organised by "people close to the government" and that the police and armed forces did not intervene until a state of emergency was declared days after the violence had begun.[39] President Jayawardene stated: "I regret that some members of my party have spoken in Parliament and outside words that encourage violence, and the murders, rapes and arsons that have been committed."[40]

Despite Jayawardene's expression of regret, the government was unable to avoid the anti-Tamil violence that erupted in July 1983, when thirteen Sinhalese soldiers were killed in an ambush by Tamil militants in Jaffna. This incident is usually identified as the cause of this round of violence, but it is more accurate to identify the ambush as the match that lit the fuse to the powder-keg of ethnic tension. Eyewitness reports stated that, where the armed forces were present during acts of violence, they would either stand by and ignore, or actually participate in, the attacks on Tamils and their property.[41]

From the above paragraph it is obvious that the security forces were directing the hysteria-driven mob and no efforts were made by the government to stop the carnage by imposing a curfew or by showing any compassion to the Tamils. These responses from the government once again outraged the Tamil community, and convinced its members including moderates, that it was no longer possible for them to live peacefully under Sinhalese domination.[42] The stage was set for the violent confrontation between Tamil militants and government forces, which has continued into the late 1990s.

From Carnage to Civil War

From the carnage of 1983, the ethnic violence escalated into a civil war in 1986-87. Civilian Tamil communities were subjected to the terror of both the Sinhalese military and Tamil guerrilla groups. By comparison, very few Sinhalese civilians were attacked by the Tamil militants, despite repeated and frequent atrocities carried out by the security forces upon unarmed Tamils.[43] Indeed, conditions deteriorated to the point where, in January 1987, the Jayawardene government imposed a fuel and economic blockade on all the Tamil areas of Northern Sri Lanka – essentially putting the entire area under siege – and simultaneously initiated a full-scale military offensive, which included regular artillery shelling and air raids on residential areas containing hospitals, schools and temples, as well as Tamil homes.[44]

The justification for these actions were offered by an official government spokesperson: 'The government reserves the right to attack such targets till such time as the killing of civilians is stopped, and the peace process is allowed to continue.'[45] The rhetoric of Sinhalese political leaders became increasingly antagonistic, as illustrated in the speech in Parliament by Prime Minister Premadasa on 24 April 1987: 'When the lives of our people are in danger, we are not prepared to go in for a political solution .... Any friend who tells us to find a political solution will be considered as the biggest enemy.'[46]

Plight of Tamil Civilians: India Shares the Agony

The Indian government's interest in Sri Lankan affairs increased from 1983 through 1987. As Jayawardene government became set on the final military solution, the Indian government found itself unable to influence events within Sri Lanka. As a result, India's credibility as a mediator rapidly evaporated.[47] The Indian Parliament and media responded by stepping up their calls for direct intervention by Indian troops. The impetus for such intervention was most likely the pressure from the many citizens of Tamil Nadu who were related to the Tamils in Sri Lanka. The Indian government decided that military intervention was necessary. However, a practical reason was needed to avoid international scorn.[48]

The Indo-Sri Lankan Peace Accord of 1987 was the Indian government's way of satisfying its own Tamil citizens and the Sinhalese government in Colombo. The accord stated that the Indian government never would allow a separate Tamil state; however, it did recognise the northern and eastern areas as "areas of historical habitation"[49] by Tamil-speaking Sri Lankans and that 'Sinhalese shall be the official language of Sri Lanka. Tamil and English will also be official languages.'[50] Sinhalese was first, but Tamil and English were equal to Sinhala satisfying the Tamils. The Indian Army moved in to help restore order to the North and East. The Indian army, not knowing how to distinguish guerrillas from citizens, killed 2,000 Tamil civilians and caused significant property damage.[51]

The Indian Peace Keeping force (IPKF) was an unqualified disaster – the force was unable to defeat or even substantially damage the LTTE.[52] Simultaneously, nationalist sentiment opposed the presence of Indian army in Sri Lanka. By the end of March 1989, IPKF was called back to India. Later in 1991, when a member of LTTE assassinated the Prime Minister of

India, Rajiv Gandhi, India dismantled its aid network, and support for the LTTE among the Tamil politicians evaporated.

The Road to Defeat

The 1990s started with the assassination of Defence Minister Ranjan Wijeratna in 1991. This was followed by the assassination of Rajiv Gandhi (as already mentioned in the above paragraph), inter alia, because India's Peace Keeping Force had been used to fight against the Tamil rebels. In 1993, President Premadasa, elected in 1988 after the creation of the Indo-Sri Lankan Accord, was assassinated.[53] The people elected Chandrika Kumaratunga to the Presidency in 1994. She immediately began peace talks with the LTTE. In October 1994, the LTTE made four demands: lifting the embargo on non-military goods to Jaffna, ending the ban on sea-fishing, dismantling of the army base at Pooneryn, and allowing armed LTTE cadres to move freely in the Eastern Province.[54] The government conceded the first two and said that the other two could only occur after the cessation of hostilities. The LTTE accepted a ceasefire in January 1995, but at this point, neither side was willing to risk peace for fear of losing power to their internal rivals.[55]

However, in April 1995, the LTTE backed out of the agreement and continued to commit various terrorist acts throughout the 1990s. The government would then retaliate against Tamil citizens, and the cycle would go on. The millennium saw failed attempts at ceasefires and negotiations. Finally in 2002, a formal ceasefire was declared between the LTTE and the Sri Lankan government, moderated by the Norwegian government. However, in 2006 the situation became even worse; the violence between the Tamil groups and the government re-escalated to the levels before the 2002 cease-fire agreements. In May 2009, the government launched its final campaign against the Tamil strongholds. With the death of Velupillai Prabhakaran and the top leadership of the Liberation Tigers of Tamil Eelam, Sri Lanka can look forward to a future of peace and development.

The military defeat of the LTTE on 18 May 2009 has brought the twenty six year old Sri Lankan conflict to an end. The immediate legacy is a huge humanitarian problem in parts of the North involving the care and resettlement of displaced people, their reintegration into local communities, and the provision of resources for them to begin to reconstruct their lives.[56] Beyond that, the victory over the LTTE poses a long-term political challenge to Sri Lanka's government. If it is to win the hard-won peace and rebuild the country, an essential requirement will be its willingness and ability to rebuild bridges with the Tamil community.

The Road to Rebuild

There are, however, roadblocks on the road to peace and tranquillity. To enjoy the fruits of military victory, it is important that Colombo consider Sri Lankan Tamils as partners in progress and not merely throw some crumbs at them. There are political constraints that make this process difficult, if not impossible in the short term. At the moment, the ability of President Mahinda Rajapaksa to deliver a creditable political package to the Tamils is severely limited. That is if he wants to do so in the first place. He has his armed forces and a chauvinist Buddhist and Sinhalese establishment to contend with.[57]

Any viable solution to the Tamil problem will require substantial devolution of powers to Tamil majority areas in the north-east of the country. That might not be easy. Politically, federalism finds little favour in Sri Lanka. Having examined federal experiments in nations experiencing ethnic conflict throughout history. Sri Lankan historian K. M. de Silva would rather advocate innovative local government institutions because they are likely to be a more appropriate means of recognising ethnic and religious diversity in areas like the Eastern Province with its mixed population.[58]

The Tamils in North and East of Sri Lanka have been living in oppression and appalling conditions for over three decades and this continued even after the military victory. However, this situation started changing during the run up to the January 2010 Presidential elections. The incumbent President issued order for lifting all restrictions at checkpoints at the entrance of the Northern Province. While it was expected that people would be allowed to move around without much restrictions, reports say that permanent presence of army in North would soon add to roadblocks, checkpoints, patrols, systematic surveillance, harassment and intimidation, of locals.[59]

In sum, the complexities of Tamil problem in Sri Lanka demands a complex and unique answer, mixing different political theories together to suit Sri Lankan society. The multi-ethnic and multi-religious nature of the nation creates a unique mix of political desires, motives and voices. After it gained independence in 1948, Sri Lanka, till the military defeat of the LTTE in May 2009, has been in the dual process of ethnicisation of politics and the politicisation of ethnicity. The state effectively came into being managing and serving not only the common affairs of the elite but also the common affairs of the majority community. In the manner that the state turned into an instrument of legitimising the tyranny of the majority, it also turned into a coercive agency. The state in its desire to satisfy the demands and aspirations of the majority community used both coercion – repressive state apparatus such as the military, and the police and the consent of the people – through the voting system. Hegemonic groups gave their consent.

The result was that misguided nationalists, both Sinhalese and Tamils, came close to destroying the country. If the government gives way to ultra-Sinhala nationalists, who advocate treating the Tamils as second-class citizens, there will never be a united Sri Lanka. A government that has defeated the armed Tamil formations must now contain ultra-Sinhala nationalism and build a truly united and equal Sri Lanka. Indeed, given the period of Tamil grievances built over the last seven decades or so, the problem requires serious attention on the part of the Sri Lankan government. Unless that is done, the Tamil problem has the potential to resurface in the years to come.

References

1. K. M. De Silva, "Grappling with the past, Coping with the present, Thinking of the future: Culture, Tradition and Modernity in Sri Lanka," *South Asian Survey*, 2001.
2. Kenneth Bush, "Ethnic Conflict in Sri Lanka" *Conflict Quarterly*, Spring 1990, p. 43.
3. Zeylanicus, *Ceylon between Orient and Occident*, Elek Book Ltd., Great Britain, 1970, p. 23.
4. C. W. Nicholas, *A Concise History of Ceylon*, Ceylon University Press, Colombo, 1961, p. 21.
5. K.M. de Silva, *A History of Sri Lanka*, C. Hurst and Company, London, 1981, p. 21.
6. Zeylanicus (1970), p. 24.
7. S. A. Pakeman, Ceylon (Frederick A. Praeger, New York, 1964), p. 20.
8. Steven Kemper, 1991, *The Presence of the Past: Chronicles, Politics and culture in Sinhala Life*, Cornell University Press, Ithaea. p. 104.
9. Richard Nyrop, Area Handbook for Sri Lanka (U.S. Library of Congress, Washington D.C.), http:/icweb2.10cgov/frd/cs/sri_lanka/lk_bibl.html.
10. K. M. de Silva (1981), p. 146.
11. Ibid., p. 148.
12. Lennox A. Mills, *Ceylon under British Rule: 1795-1932*, Charles Birchall and Sons, London, 1933, p. 177.
13. Jonathon Spencer, Sri Lanka: History and the Roots of Conflict (Routledge, New York, 1990), p. 166.
14. K.M. De Silva (1981), p. 231.
15. Lennox A. Mills (1933), p. 195.
16. Ibid., p. 221.
17. Jonathan Spencer (1990), p. 235.
18. Kenneth Bush (1990), p. 49.
19. Ibid.
20. The Sinhalese even accused the Tamils of conspiring with the British to monopolise most of the public service jobs, and to obtain political leverage through communal representation in the Legislative Council. See, W. Howard Wriggins, *Ceylon: Dilemma of a Nation*, Princeton University Press, Princeton, 1960, p. 79.
21. David Little, *Sri Lanka: The Invention of Enmity*, United State Institute of Peace Press, Washington D.C. 1994, p. 56.

22. See Russell R. Ross (ed) Sri Lanka: A Country Study (Federal Research Division, Library of Congress, Washington D.C., 1990), pp. 38-52.
23. Marry Anne Weaver, "The Gods and the Stars" *The New Yorker*, 21 March 1988, p. 40.
24. For details refer to: Chandra Gunawardene, "Ethnic Representation, Regional Imbalance and University Admission in Sri Lanka" Comparative Education, No. 1, 1975, p. 11. Judith Kapferer." The Demand for Education Sri: Antecedents and Consequences." In Kenneth Orr ed., Appetite for Education in Contemporary Asia (Australian National University, Canberra, 1984) Robert Kearney, "Educational Expansion and Political Vitality in Sri Lanka: The 1971 Insurgency" Asian Survey, No. 9, 1975, p. 15.
25. Chelvadurai Manogaran, "Colonisation as politics: Political use of space in Sri Lanka's National Conflict in C. Manogaram and B. Pfaffenberger (eds.) *The Sri Lankas: Ethnicity and Identity,* West view Press, Boulder, Colorado 1994. pp. 84-125.
26. Robert Kearney, "Language and the Tamil Separatist Movement in Sri Lanka," *South Asian Survey* 18 (6 June 1978), pp. 521-534.
27. Ibid.
28. Chelvadurai Manogaran "Origin of Conflict in Sri Lanka and Sinhala Ethnic Nationalism," Proceedings of International Conference on Tamil Nationhood, Ottawa, Canada, (1999).
29. Chelvadurai. Manogaran (1990).
30. Ibid.
31. Kenneth Bush (1990), pp. 46-49.
32. David Little, Sri Lanka: The Invention of Enmity (1994), United States Institute of Peace, Washington D.C., p. 66.
33. Tarzie Vittachi, *Emergency 58: The Story of Ceylon Race Riots*, A. Dentch, London, 1958, pp. 153-174.
34. C. Manogaran (eds.) *The Sri Lankan Tamils* (1994), p. 120.
35. The Tamil talked of secession and quickly realised that their non-violent tactics were not working to create any sort of change. See, C. R. De Silva, "The Sinhalese-Tamil Rift in Sri Lanka" in Wilson A. Jeyaratnam and Dalton, Dennis (ed.) *The States of South Asia*, University of Hawaii Press, Honolulu, 1982. pp. 155-174.
36. David Little (1994), pp. 86-87.
37. Ibid.
38. Kenneth Bush (1990), p. 50.
39. Virginia Leary, "Ethnic Conflict and violence in Sri Lanka," A Report of a Mission to Sri Lanka in July-August 1981 on behalf of the International Commission of Jurists, ICJ, Geneva, 1981.

40. Quoted in *New York Times*, 11 September 1981, A2.
41. Patricia Hyndman, Sri Lanka: Serendipity under Siege (Spokesman, Nottingham, 1988). See also Gananath Obeyesekere, "The origins and Institutionalization of the violence" in James Manor (ed.) *Sri Lanka in Change and Crisis,* Vroomttelm, London, 1984. pp. 153-174.
42. Manogaran (1999), Until 1983, Tamils were the Victims of Sinhalese mob violence in Sinhalese areas. This situation changed dramatically as Tamils began to arm themselves and to retaliate.
43. Patricia Hyndaman, *Sri Lanka: Serendipity under Siege* (1988), p. 53.
44. See, "Jaffna Bombed for Third Day", *The Hindu*, 25 April 1987, p. 1.
45. *The Hindu*, 22 April, 1987, p. 1.
46. "Talks Only After Peace", *The Hindu*, 25 April 1987, p. 1.
47. Kenneth Bush (1990), p. 51.
48. Santha K. Hennayake, "The Peace Accord and the Tamils in Sri Lanka," *South Asian Survey*, 29, No. 4 (1989), p. 402.
49. Ibid., p. 408.
50. Ibid., p. 409.
51. Ibid., pp. 410-412.
52. Ramchandra Guha, *India After Gandhi: The History of the World's Largest Democracy,* Macmillan, London, 2007, p. 613.
53. Molly Moore, "Suicide Bomber kills leader of Sri Lanka: President Slain During May Day Celebration in Island Nation", *Washington Post,* May 02, 1993, See. A.
54. See Patrik Peebles, *The History of Sri Lanka,* Greenwood Press, Westport, 2006, pp. 36-53.
55. Ibid.
56. R. Hariharan, "Sri Lanka: Need to restore trust" *The Hindu,* May 18, 2010.
57. Apratim Mukherji, "Sri Lanka: History Revisiting?" *Mainstream* (New Delhi), Vol. XLVI, No. 49, Nov. 22, 2008, pp. 3-4.
58. K. M. de Silva, "The Federal option and its Alternatives" in de Silva and G. H. Peiris eds., Pursuit of Peace in Sri Lanka, 1995, Pinter, London, pp. 203-29.
59. Ashik Bonofer and David Morgan "The Tamils in Sri Lanka and the Sri Lankan State" in Ketheshwaran Loganathan, Sri Lanka: Lost opportunity, 1996, Centre for Policy Research and Analysis, Faculty of Law, University of Colombo, p. 58.

CHAPTER 6

Extremism and the LTTE

South Asia has been home to numerous ethno-nationalist extremism since the region was de-colonized with the departure of the British in 1947. Many of these extremist movements benefited tremendously from the activities of co-ethnics and co-religionists organized in transnational diasporas throughout the world. Among these conflicts, the civil war in Sri Lanka has been perhaps the most enduring and seemingly intractable – with the notable exception of the Kashmir conflict.[1] Although no exact date is ascribed to the start of the conflict, most writers note that it began to militarize in the 1970s. During this period, numerous Tamil extremist groups were formed. By the early 1980s, one group had emerged as pre-eminent – the Jaffna based Liberation Tigers of Tamil Eelam (LTTE) under the leadership of Velupillai Prabhakaran.

When one examines the political opportunity-set available to the Tamil extremists, there is little to suggest that the extremism should have been as enduring as it has been. First, the Tamils were virtually excluded from political processes from the inception of the independent Sri Lankan State. Second, the rival Sinhalese ethnic groups comprised nearly three-quarters of the population and were firmly in grasp of all state powers; Sinhalese elites were and remain unified in their support for a unified state. Third, for most of the conflict there has been no influential state support for the Tamils in Sri Lanka.[2] The Sri Lankan state perpetrated frequent and large-scale acts of repression to put down extremist activities. Thus the important question arises: how have the Tamil militants been able to sustain extremist activities/insurgency for this long with such efficacy and lethality in such unfavourable circumstances?

To answer this question, it seems logical to appropriate the argument put forward by Wayland and expand upon it.[3] Wayland notes that scholarship on contentious politics generally concurs that, to be successful, social movements – and their extremist forms – require changes in the broader political context in addition to their own organization and internal resources. These changes are referred to as the "political opportunity structure" and are needed both to activate latent grievances and to provide incentives for collective action – principally by conditioning participants' expectations for success or failure. These are 'factors external to a movement that influenced the movement's emergence and chance of success'.[4]

In her analysis of the Tamil extremism, Wayland widens the notion of the political opportunity-set to include transnational factors and argues that this expanded notion of political opportunity structures explains the success of the LTTE in Sri Lanka despite numerous structural impediments. The Liberation Tigers of Tamil Eelam, also known as the Tamil Tigers evolved into a widely known extremist group since its formation in 1976. Although the group made strides towards recognition as a political faction, the LTTE till the middle of 2009 resorted to extremist tactics.[5]

The Tamil Extremism

Tamil nationalism is a reactive phenomenon. The Tigers too were made, not born. Both Tamil nationalism and the subsequent phenomenon of LTTE were products of ethnocentric policies embraced by successive Sri Lankan governments.[6] As Nigel Harris has aptly observed,

> *Successive (Sinhalese) governments were more pre-occupied with securing their own base among the Sinhalese . . . at virtually any cost – or rather, in the political auction, preventing themselves being pushed out by their rivals. If the Tamils had not existed, Colombo would have had to invent them. And, in an important sense, it did. It was Colombo that forced the inhabitants of the North to become different, to cease to be Sri Lankan and become exclusively Tamil.*[7]

In the decades following independence, Colombo continued to pursue policies that were aimed at bolstering the relative position and strength of the Sinhalese majority. As Gunaratna notes; 'the majoritarian rule and exclusivist ethnic policies of the successive Sinhaha majority governments in the aftermath of independence crystallized the development of an extremist ideology among Tamil leaders.'[8]

Actually, an overview of Sri Lankan Tamil politics since independence clearly shows that the Tamils had been mainly reactive to Sinhala politics. The decentralized federalist British Colonial government had given rise to a growing sense of Tamil national consciousness in the North, and the Tamil politician G.G. Ponnambalam founded the All Ceylon Tamil Congress. Ponnambalam had requested a 50-50 arrangement whereby half the seats in Parliament would be reserved for minorities; this was perhaps an excessive request when minorities were only 30% of the population; and was rejected.[9] Nevertheless, the first Sinhala government, led by D.S. Senanayake of the United National Party (UNP), reached out to Jaffna Tamils and Muslims, whom he included in his administration. The one minority that was consciously excluded were the Plantation Tamils, who were denied Sri Lankan citizenship, making them into a stateless people. Ponnambalam and S.J.V. Chelvanayakam of the Federal Party, the other prominent leaders of the time, did not immediately argue for the cause of the Plantation Tamils.[10] Their failure to do so has been seen by some Jaffna Tamils as a historic error that prevented the formation of a unified Tamil movement.[11]

Senanayake's inclusive approach was seen as insufficiently pro-Sinhala by Sinhala-Buddhist nationalists, who had seen independence as the chance to achieve their long-held dream of unitary state. Their first champion was Solomon West Ridgeway Dias (S.W.R.D.) Bandaranaike who founded the Sri Lanka Freedom Party (SLFP) to take power away from the moderate Colombo elite. Senanayake and his successor, Sir John Kotewala, were deeply westernized, and the language of administration was English. Senanayake believed that using English would avoid the inevitable offence to Tamils that adopting Sinhala would cause – a solution that was adopted in India as well, where the decision in 1965 not to make Hindi the official language may well have prevented a Sri Lanka – type civil war.[12]

In 1956, the SLFP began the "Sinhala only" campaign, which claimed Sinhala as the only official language of Sri Lanka. The bill was quickly enacted after the party's electoral victory. In its original form, this bill contained some clauses listing the appropriate uses of Tamil and English, but these were deleted under pressure from Sinhala-Buddhist extremists. The Federal Party, now the dominant Tamil political force, protested the planned bill and demanded parity for Tamil and Sinhala, citizenship for Plantation Tamils and a fresh, federalist constitution. Parliament passed the Sinhala only act but the newly elected Prime Minister Bandaranaike did not enforce it immediately, and instead met with Tamil Federal Party leader S.J.V. Chelvanayakam.[13]

The Bandaranaike – Chelvanayakam (BC) Pact did not meet the demands of the Tamils, but made some concessions. Tamil was official in the North and East as the language of education, and Tamil speakers would face no opposition to its use. However, Sinhala would be the official language of the Central government. There would be no true federalism, but regional councils with considerable powers.[14]

The BC Pact received criticism from extremists on both sides, but most of all from certain UNP members who tried to wrest control of the Sinhala – Buddhist movement from Bandaranaike. Under immense pressure, with monks campaigning outside his house, Bandaranaike revoked the pact; in protest, the Federal Party launched mass civil disobedience.

The government declared a state of emergency, as ethnic riots broke out throughout the country. After the riots had ceased, Bandaranaike passed an Act allowing the use of Tamil in administration and law courts in Tamil-speaking areas. The Act would prove to be his undoing, as he was assassinated by a Buddhist monk in September 1959.[15]

Realm of Politics to Realm of Extremism

Bandaranaike's death was an immense jolt to the prospects of parliamentary compromise. His successor as head of SLFP, and a year later as Prime Minister, was his wife Srimavo. Srimavo Bandaranaike quickly moved to regain control of the left-wing pro-Sinhala political space. She passed a bill on December 31, 1960, declaring Sinhala as the sole official language.[16] The bill was not only the fulfillment of the key Sinhala-Buddhist demand but also became a source of discrimination and a means to redress the colonial preference for the Tamils. The new bill meant that every government employee was required to know Sinhala. The civil service had been the career of choice for educated Tamils for a century. Civil disobedience proved ineffective as the government once again declared a state of emergency, banned the Federal Party and outlawed strikes.[17]

In response, the Tamil political parties allied with Dudley Senanayake, the son of D.S. Senanayake and the new head of the UNP. Senanayake came to power in 1965 in a rainbow coalition that included parties of all ethnic agendas. The Senanayake – Chelvanayakam Pact of March 24, 1965 was remarkably similar to the BC Pact eight years earlier. The UNP government agreed to enact the provisions of Bandaranaike's Tamil language bill, making Tamil the language of law courts and administration in the Northern and Eastern provinces. Tamils considered the pact only a partial solution, as Sinhala was still the sole language in all other parts of the country, once again disadvantaging the Tamils in terms of employment. To placate angry Sinhala-Buddhist nationalists, Senanayake enacted several pro-Buddhist decrees, which marginalized the Tamils.[18]

The failure of the Federal Party to obtain a negotiated solution that was acceptable to most Tamils, and their alleged betrayal in joining in the pro-Sinhala UNP government, led to the alienation of extreme Tamil groups. Moreover, the victory of SLFP in the election of 1970 meant that there was no Tamil presence in the government and that the Federal Party had lost its political clout. The end of Federal Party era marked the rise of soft and later extremist ideology colouring the Tamil movement in Sri Lanka.[19]

At this point, in the early 1970s' Ceylon experienced strife on both ends of the political spectrum. The government needed to strengthen its position, and did so by reviving the inter-community tensions of the past. At societal level, there was little progress on the front of ethnic reconciliation. And what is worth noting, young Sri Lankans were becoming frustrated with the nation's weak economic growth and social unrest, two factors that were clearly linked. Following the victory of the Sinhala Nationalist Party in 1970, a group of Marxist ideologues known as Janatha Vimukthi Peramuna (JVP) led a 1971 insurrection against the Sinhalese nationalist government.

In this backdrop of social protest and violence, politicians of both main parties, the SLFP and UNP, tried to appeal to Sinhala-Buddhist nationalism. During this period, constitutional reform was attempted as a means of changing society. New constitutions were introduced in 1972 and 1978, each with the aim of somewhat advancing Sinhala-Buddhist nationalism.[20] In retrospect, the 1972 constitution encouraged many Tamils to support radical demands for an independent Eelam. In fact, a seemingly innocuous and controversial aspect of the constitution was renaming Ceylon as Sri Lanka. On this controversial aspect of the constitution we have the comments of Wilson: 'The name "Lanka" had been associated with the island, in both Sinhala and Tamil, for millennia, but the unambiguously Sinhala "Sri" upset Tamils, who had previously protested its use on vehicular license plates.'[21] Yet despite a complete hold on political power, the nationalists were impatient at their inability to fully dismantle the Tamil elite, whose privileged status they continued to see as an unfair colonial anachronism.

Extremism: Period of Formation and Identity

The mid-1970s marked the emergence of extremism as a factor in Sri Lankan politics. The prevailing radicalization also served to unify previously splintered Tamil political groups. United in their opposition to the constitution, they formed the Tamil United Liberation Front (TULF) in 1972. Outside the TULF, there were an estimated 40 small Tamil extremist groups already in existence by the time of the introduction of the new constitution.[22] These Tamil extremist groups began to react violently to a set of incendiary policies introduced by Srimavo Bhandarnaike in 1970 and 1971. Violent separatism was not yet fully in the mainstream of Tamil political discourse, being at this stage restricted to the youth, but by the early 1970s it had emerged as a serious social and political threat.

The Emergence of Prabhakaran

Prabhakaran was born on 26 November 1954 in Valvetthithurai, a small town in northern Sri Lanka that was a known smugglers' heaven.[23] His father was an ardent supporter of the moderate Tamil politician S.J.V. Chelvanayakam – a man known as "Gandhi of Eelam" due to his espousal of non-violent methods – but from an early age Prabhakaran had no taste for moderate politics.[24] At the age of 16, he dropped out of school to co-found the Tamil Students Federation. He launched his first terror attack on September 17, 1972; he intended to kill Alfred Duraiappah, the Tamil SLFP Mayor of Jaffna, with bombs.[25] He failed then but killed Duraiappah in 1975. Not without a sense of irony, Prabhakaran named his group the Tamil New Tigers (TNT).

On March 5, 1976 the TNT led a bank robbery, using amateur, homemade weapons. By the end of the decade Prabhakaran himself had murdered 11 opposition politicians, but his organization was still considered politically weak, a fringe element with little respect or attention from moderate

Tamils. The most powerful pro-separatist group of the time was the Tamil Liberation Organisation, founded in 1969. Aware of the potency of the word "Liberation", Prabhakaran renamed his organization on May 5, 1976, and the Liberation Tigers of Tamil Eelam was officially born.[26]

Between the years 1978 and 1983, the extremist group known as the LTTE, the strongest of the extremist Tamil separatist groups materializing from the former Tamil Student's Movement, was responsible for approximately 265 bombings, robberies, assaults, and other various crimes. Coincidentally, the Tamil United Liberation Front (TULF) was gaining political control of the Northern and Eastern parts of the country. The TULF had long been pursuing the creation of a separate Tamil state, to the great aversion of the government. The country's first popular election of a President was in 1982. The TULF encouraged its followers to boycott the elections because its candidates were not allowed to run. The United National Party (UNP) incumbent, Junius Jayawardene, won the election.[27]

Jayawardene's first substantive action was to hurry the Sixth Amendment to the constitution through Parliament, banning Sri Lankan citizens or parties from advocating separatism. This effectively barred the TULF from Parliament, since its very raison d'etre was separatism, and it had been elected on the platform of pursuing separatism through the political process. Thus the TULF lost representation in Parliament.[28] This move closed the possibility of a formal political solution to the ethnic conflict. Instead, the LTTE now ran the movement for Eelam.

Growth of the LTTE

In 1983, the LTTE conducted its first military operation – an ambush on a police patrol in Jaffna.[29] The LTTE's ambush had three consequences. First, it solidified Sinhalese resentment against the Tamil extremists; second, it strengthened the Tamil resolve and resulted in the launching of the first Eelam war; third; it further eroded the international community's support for Tamil statehood. The international community assumed that the violence of 1983 would press both sides to negotiate rather than escalate. India offered to mediate but Indira Gandhi's ability as a mediator was severely undermined by the efforts of the Research and Analysis Wing (RAW), India's external intelligence agency which armed the LTTE and other extremist groups and helped them set up training camp in Tamil Nadu.[30]

The training camps in India proved crucial to developing and enhancing the LTTE's military capabilities. The Sri Lankan military was powerless to carry out strikes against India, the dominant power in the region. What enabled the LTTE to achieve primacy over all other Eelam extremist outfits? At least four major reasons can be identified:

- The LTTE's cadres were the best organised and most disciplined;
- The LTTE's capacity for executing ruthless violence against both Sinhalese government as well as rival Tamil groups;
- The charisma of its leader, Prabhakaran, who at the time faced little opposition to his leadership within the LTTE;
- Its single-minded focus on only one goal: establishing an authoritarian state of Tamil Eelam in the Northern and Eastern Provinces of Sri Lanka.

Of course, the last is perhaps the most significant. Other Tamil militant groups, such as the Eelam Revolutionary Organisation of Students (EROS) and the Eelam People's Revolutionary Liberation Front (EPRLF) were often hindred by confused agendas. The LTTE successfully associated itself with the aspirations of the Tamil people for independence, and thus did a better job than any other group of achieving mass popularity. The leaders of six biggest Tamil groups met in Madras in October 1983 in an attempt to resolve their differences, without success.[31] Instead, the LTTE won a series of violent encounters against these groups in Jaffna, Madras and London in 1983 and achieved leadership of the movement essentially by conquest.

Funding

The LTTE received funding and military support from many sources, mainly by Tamils in other nations. According to Rohan Gunaratna, a professor specializing in LTTE research at St. Andrew's University in Edinburgh, 'the Tigers are on the cutting edge of arms trafficking'[32] and Indian Tamils once contributed a majority of the LTTE's external funds. As the death toll and human rights violence rose within the conflict, however, most Indians ceased to back the extremist group. The loss of Indian support did not hurt the Tigers.[33] The LTTE soon began to rely on a large population of expatriates in countries such as Canada, Britain, Switzerland, and Australia for funding. Tamils in these countries are said to donate approximately $ 1 million US a month.[34]

LTTE's supplies, such as surface-to-air missiles, assault rifles, and grenade launchers, have been traced to Cambodian generals and the Khmer Rouge.[35] Ukraine had come onto the scene as a growing source of LTTE military equipment by providing approximately sixty tons of explosives to the rebels. The LTTE also received arms directly from Bulgarian and North Korean governments, along with dealers from Hong Kong, Singapore, Lebanon, and Cyprus.[36] Former Tamil Tigers have given account that the group had two American Stinger missile at one point, apparently acquired from Afghan Mujaheddin rebels. There have also been hints that organized crime groups in Russia, Lithuania, Bulgaria, Yugoslavia, Cambodia, Afghanistan, and Mozambique have been supporting the LTTE. Although the LTTE tends to receive most funding and arms from external sources it also had internal projects to provide for itself.

By the mid 1980s, the group had already started its own arms programme. In addition, the LTTE runs a number of small businesses such as gas stations, restaurants, and shops in Sri Lanka and elsewhere in the world to fund their cause.[37] Thus, LTTE's financial strength enabled them to have state-of-the-art technology and in later years to launch their own navy and airforce. This was an astonishing achievement, probably unique in the history of insurgency warfare.[38] It allowed the LTTE to grow from a typical extremist group to a guerilla army, albeit one that engaged in many of the activities of terrorist groups. Young recruits were indoctrinated into the ideology of dying for the cause, and the LTTE were pioneers of suicide terrorism.[39]

Jaffna and Eelam

The ultraconservative people of Jaffna supported the LTTE because they are the most nationalist of the militant groups. The LTTE literature is replete with references to the ancient glory of the Kingdom of Jaffna, Tamil tradition, culture and language, and the Tamil homeland, all of which need to be preserved and protected from the Sinhalese. In this context socialist and leftist ideas take a back seat.

Grassroots control in the LTTE and its communication with the population were and are quite close: the LTTE cooperating closely with the Citizen's Committees in Jaffna and the East who in turn were LTTE's main lines of communication with the IPKF. LTTE had organised public life in Jaffna along its own lines, running ammunition factories, nursery schools, even rudimentary military academy. This protection and organisation of daily life appealed to the people even if Prabhakaran made it clear that he does not think much of parliamentary democracy or a multi-party state. His conception of Eelam seems to be that of a benevolent dictatorship under one man.[40] The LTTE are the most tightly structured, highly disciplined and autocratically led group of the movement. The fact that all fighters carry cyanide capsules in case of capture is only one feature of this, all of which suggests that this group should be seen less as a leftist revolutionary forces than as a revival of ancient traditions of hero warriors following their chieftain into the field and into death: 'The thought of certain death is a great trial. But to whom? Certainly not to us. Because we are married to our cyanide. Yet, our death lives with us. It sleeps with us. We carry it in our shirt pockets and around our necks. That makes us clear-headed and purposeful.'[41]

The other groups had less clear ideas about the political and social structure of the future Eelam. TELO claimed that they want to establish a free socialist state and hold free elections. This makes TELO the group most amenable to maintaining a "democratic" structure of government according to the Western understanding of the term.

EPRLF, following an orthodox Marxist course, did not see the solution to the problem in an independent Eelam and a return to parliamentary democracy, but wanted a national democratic revolution in the whole of Sri Lanka. Its members would oppose any "reactionary" government. They emphasized, however, that a Marxist-Leninist programme does not mean instant and violent revolution, but that gradual change with the help of all national elements is possible.[42]

People's Liberation Organisation of Tamil Eelam's (PLOTE) visions on the shape and structure of a future Eelam are interesting, not because they are merely a repetition of EPRLF views but for the criticism they level at the LTTE for the latter's alleged mismanagement of the administration in Jaffna. PLOTE claim that LTTE have merely taken over the administrative structure from the Sri Lanka government keeping Sri Lankan civil servants and administrators and even accepting salaries from the Sri Lankan government (alluding to the fact that the LTTE allowed government pensions to be paid to former civil servants in Jaffna) while claiming not to submit to the authority of the same government.

For EROS, the fight cannot end with an independent Eelam as for its members the real struggle to establish a socialist society begins after liberation. In 1975, EROS adopted a three-point programme regarding the envisaged Eelam: (1) all Eelam Tamils must unite and live together; (2) all sides themselves to belong to Eelam; and (3) Eelam is part of the international socialist movement.[43]

To sum up: LTTE is the one group that has managed to build up any grassroots support and loyalty among the population for reasons both of ideology and organization. All other groups advocate "internationalism" and are consequently seen as less Tamil.

The Militants and the Sri Lanka State

The fact that LTTE were primarily a nationalist group shows also in their attitude towards the Sri Lankan state – the concept of a united Sri Lanka for the present being rejected. Jayawardene was depicted as not wanting a settlement, but merely leading Rajiv Gandhi up the garden path and, after the accord, getting India to do his dirty work for him. At the same time, he was seen as trying to drive a wedge between the central government and Tamil Nadu, while cooperating with India's enemies, namely Pakistan. Or he is perceived as a weak, senile old man who can no longer stand up to the hawks in his own cabinet, to the opposition parties or to the masses led by the chauvinist clergy and the Janata Vimukthi Peramuna (JVP). In either case, his sincerity in seeking a peaceful solution and his stated intention to hold elections were seriously doubted, and reference is repeatedly made to his role in abrogating the Bendarnaike-Chelvanayakam Pact of 1957 (which gave a certain amount of autonomy to the Tamil areas and even anticipated the concept of "regional and provincial councils", and which is so much talked about now) and his advocacy of "Sinhala Only" as long ago as 1943. Similarly, none of the groups have any confidence in the willingness or capability of the Sri Lanka Freedom Party (SLFP) and Mrs. Bandaranaike to reach an honourable and peaceful settlement.

However, when it comes to the smaller opposition parties and the population in general, the picture changes. The LTTE took the most extreme and intransigent stand, arguing that while the Sinhalese masses are suppressed and exploited by the Sinhalese bourgeoisie and the multi-nationals, and need liberation as much as the Tamils, the actual preconditions for such a course of action do not exist at the movement. Though the LTTE have no quarrel with the Sinhala people as such, the nationalistic and chauvinistic hatred of the Tamils generated among them by government propaganda is presently too strong to counter.

In one of their earlier publications, the LTTE discuss in detail the different leftist parties and movements, including the

JVP, that exist in south Sri Lanka and their attitudes towards the Tamil struggle. The LTTE come to the conclusion that none of them can really serve as allies because their views about the problem are confused at best and infiltrated with chauvinist ideology at works.[44] At the moment, therefore, there is no scope for any cooperation between the Sinhalese and the Tamils. Ethnicity, not capitalism, produces the primary contradiction in Sri Lanka, since the Tamils are suppressed, in the main, because of their race rather than their class.

It is quite obvious that the LTTE harbour a deep mistrust of the Sinhalese people as a whole. In one article they are called "Mlechchas", which is the Sanskrit word for impure and casteless outsiders,[45] an attitude revealing a sense of both superiority and fear.

On the other hand EROS, LTTE's mouthpiece in the South, advocates cooperation with "progressive sections" of the Sinhalese masses.[46] No information is, however, forthcoming about who these progressive sections might be and the strategy seems to be that with the help of these sections the South is to be undermined and destabilized – an intention which is demonstrated by the bombs and other attacks on so-called "economic targets". Thus, LTTE and EROS seem to be following a two-pronged strategy. LTTE reject cooperation with the Sinhalese, whereas EROS try to enlist some Sinhalese support claiming to have initiated meetings with leftist and other Sinhalese groups since 1985.[47] This strategy, however, one suspects, aims less to achieve true cooperation between the groups, which is ruled out by the LTTE, than to destabilize the South in order to ease pressure in the North and the East. EROS openly admitted that they want to create a crisis in the South to facilitate action in the North. They go on to criticize the JVP's attitude towards the Tamils and the Left's cooperation with the SLFP. If they had followed a different course, EROS argue, the 1971 insurrection might have been successful.[48]

Other groups vote for at least conditional cooperation with progressive, non-racist and amenable sections of the Sinhala population. TELO, whose aim is, as mentioned, "power-sharing", would like to talk to well-meaning Sinhalese like

Vijaya Kumaranatunga and the United Socialist Alliance (USA) founded by him. TELO argues that they are not enemies of the Sinhalese, but of Sinhalese capital, and that after the liberation of Eelam, the Prevention of Terrorism Act (PTA) and other legislation will be used against Sinhalese labour instead. In this context, the Tamil problem is seen as a way out of the economic crisis for the government and a way of keeping the Sinhalese quiet. Therefore, the members of TELO fight equally for the suppressed Sinhalese and for the suppressed Tamils, their stated aim being peace in the Indian Ocean.[49] On the other hand, members of TELO, like the LTTE, do not seem to have overmuch confidence in the willingness of the Sinhalese in general to come to a peaceful settlement and doubt that the Sinhalese will ever be prepared to recognize the nationhood of the Tamils.[50] The deep mistrust TELO has of the Sinhalese can also be seen in their rejection of the idea of a referendum on any potential settlement. Either way, a referendum is sure to go against Tamil interests. If no referendum is held, Jayawardene cannot claim to be acting in accordance with the wishes of the population, and thus his decisions will lack legitimacy and can be abrogated at any time. If, on the other hand, a referendum is held it is almost certain to go against any settlement favourable to the Tamils. Neither alternative will help the Tamils.

PLOTE and EPRLF are the two groups who explicitly favour cooperation with the Sinhalese masses for roughly the same reasons. As their struggle is seen by them not merely as a struggle for the Tamil race, on a Tamil homeland, but the struggle of a suppressed people against an imperialist, neo-colonialist or neo-fascist oppressor, the struggle is also seen to include the Sinhalese working classes, who are equally suppressed and exploited[51] with EPRLF, in particular, advocating close links with leftist and "progressive" Sinhalese organizations. Among these, EPRLF list the GP, the Nava Sama Samaja Pakshaya (NSSP) and, conditionally, the Lanka Sama Samaja Pakshaya (LSSP) who support the Tamil struggle on the side of the established left, and the NJVP on the side of the new or revolutionary left. They rule out any cooperation with JVP since this organization is seen as being "chauvinist" and "fascist". EPRLF have certainly gone farthest in cooperation with the South. In one of their pamphlets, a comrade Gamini Salvador denounces the "neo-Fascist" nature of the Sri Lankan government, charging it with violation of human, civil and democratic rights as well as onslaughts on leftist and oppositionist Sinhalese.[52]

PLOTE advocated cooperation with the Sinhalese in similar terms: this is not a fight for the Tamils alone, but for all suppressed classes, which include the Sinhalese. PLOTE refuse to divulge which groups they work with in Southern Sri Lanka. The government and informed sources claim that it is the JVP; indeed, if any one group is linked, or said to be linked, to JVP, it is consistently PLOTE. But this is hotly denied by PLOTE themselves.[53] While in recent JVP pamphlets, PLOTE are viciously attacked.[54] The suspicion remains that PLOTE do not have many contacts in the South, given their present weak position.

The claims by EPRLF, TELO and, to a lesser extent, PLOTE have been confirmed by recent events. The behaviour of these groups confirms the claim that they have always made, namely, that they have no connections with JVP, indeed, EPRLF and PLOTE joined the election coalition USA, and this is totally opposed to JVP. EPRLF have been accepted as a political party by the election commission while EROS are applying for acceptance as a party as well[55] but have been rather more circumspect in their support for the accord and the IPKF. They seem to be keeping equidistant from both factions in the conflict, but do not hesitate to protest against unfavourable IPKF actions. They led a demonstration on the anniversary of the accord to protest that the accord had not been fully implemented, and demanded the permanent merger of the North and East.[56] The LTTE have similarly, and quite literally, stuck to their guns. I do not subscribe to the view sometimes expressed that, because of a certain similarity in ideology, LTTE and JVP consciously and deliberately cooperate in trying to destabilize the South and bring about a violent Communist revolution. I would even hesitate to call either the LTTE or the JVP Communist. The fact that they have similar grievances and objectives does not necessarily mean that they cooperate: on the contrary. At the same time, I would like to emphasize that, although their rhetoric may sound similar, there are significant differences in the militant actions of LTTE and JVP. The large-scale, indiscriminate killing now indulged in by the JVP has never (with very few exceptions) been entertained or approved by the LTTE.

Besides, the LTTE have never reveled in the kind of chauvinistic, aggressive nationalism which the JVP were propagating on the Sinhalese side. To illustrate these differences we can look at the actions of both groups on 29 July 1988, the anniversary of the accord: both demanded a hartal as a means of protest. It was very successful in the North, where the IPKF declared a four-day curfew, but was far less successful in Colombo and the South.[57] The JVP saw this as a protest against the accord and a demand to scrap it since it conceded too much to the Tamils. The LTTE's protest was directed at the incomplete implementation of the accord, the actions of the IPKF and the on-going "colonization" of the Eastern province by Sinhalese.

LTTE: Resort to Suicide Terrorism

So what factors motivated the Tamil Tigers as an organization to go beyond traditional acts of terrorism to a heightened level of violence that requires the price of the terrorist's own life? Several explanations exist for why terrorist organizations, and specifically the LTTE, utilized suicide bombing, two of which have relevance here. One such theory is based on the idea that religious fundamentalism is the root cause of terrorist organnisations turning to suicide terrorism.[58] This argument holds that the LTTE turned to suicide terrorism out of zeal for Hindu beliefs. While religious differences may have been exploited by both sides during the conflict in order to justify the escalation of violence, the LTTE's nationalistic, not religious extremism shaped its strategy to achieve a Tamil homeland. Additionally, the strong Buddhist identity of the Sinhalese majority might have been one of the main sources for their discrimination against the Tamil people, but it was the dream of an ethnic Tamil nation, not a Hindu nation, that fuelled the LTTE's violence. This view is supported by examining the religion of the Tamil Tiger's victims which include not only Buddhists but also Muslims, Christians, and Hindus such as India's Rajiv Gandhi.[59]

A second theory correlates suicide terrorism and regime type, specifically democracy. Many terrorist organizations have the objective of ousting a modern democracy from their territories and will use extreme acts of violence against the occupying forces in order to incite casualty-sensitive citizens to pressure their government to leave. The LTTE case, however, does not support this theory. The Sri Lankan government may have been organized as a democracy, but it was their sanctioned discrimination against the Tamil people and the Tiger's goal of secession that proved to be the catalyst for ethnic violence, not the democratic government in and of itself. In fact, since 1948, Sri Lanka operated more on emergency laws than democratic norms in the face of civil conflict.[60] The public influence characteristic of functioning democracies could not be felt, and coercion by influencing public opinion was not possible, thus the Sri Lankan government could not be categorized as a modern democracy, and the correlation does not explain the existence of suicide terrorism.

Excluding above-mentioned religious fundamentalism and regime type theory of terrorist organizations turning to suicide terrorism, three alternative variables emerge as causal mechanism that allowed for the use of suicide terror by the LTTE between 1987 and 2001.

Alternative Variables: LTTE's Organizational Culture

The first variable that led to suicide terrorism is the LTTE's organizational culture which provided the internal conditions ripe for the use of suicide terrorism, and when combined with popular support of the Tamil community, there existed legitimate motivational factors for Black Tiger Missions.[61] Emile Durkheim's study of suicide can be used as a valuable tool to understand these underlying motivations.[62] The LTTE suicide follows most closely the form that Durkheim calls "altruistic suicide", where the individual commits the acts of suicide because he is deeply connected to a community and willing to die for this community "because it is his duty". The Black Tigers were so committed to the LTTE and the Tamil society which supports them that they were willing to die for the cause of the Tamil homeland. LTTE terrorism also fell into the category that Durkheim calls "fatalistic suicide"[63] which is caused by an individual's subjection to brainwashing by a cult-like group. Evidence for these "altruistic" suicide for the common-good and "fatalistic" suicide-for-the-group phenomenon can be found by looking at the inner workings of the LTTE and how the LTTE has successfully manipulated large segments of the Tamil population to provide support for suicide terrorism.

According to Walter Lacqueur, extremist organizations 'acquire certain mental attitude, a momentum of their own, and .... a certain cohesion, solidarity and *espirit de corps*.'[64] This is true of the LTTE, an organization characterized by extremes: extreme ethno-nationalism, militancy, moral character, and devotion to the group. It is an organization built upon and characterized by a focus on combat and violence. Its fanatical and militaristic worldview allows for members and the group itself to see everything in violent terms, including politics.[65] Within the LTTE, cadres live a regimented life of devotion and discipline, placing the organization and its goals above their own lives. This extreme devotion is essential to the functioning of the LTTE and is required by order of death, exemplified by hundred of dissenters who have been killed by LTTE authorities.[66]

The Theory of Last Resort

The second variable behind the LTTE's use of suicide terrorism was its perception of the method as one of last resort. When all other means were thought to have been exhausted to stop the Sri Lankan Government's violence against the Tamil people, the LTTE turned from conventional terrorism to suicide attacks. The theory of last resort or supreme emergency, as outlined by Michael Walzer in *Just and Unjust Wars*, states that actors resort to any means they consider necessary in order to protect the nation and its people from imminent, complete destruction.[67] Though the LTTE was known for its underhand dealings and unpredictable nature, its violence held so much power that it brought the government to its knees; it twice engaged in formal negotiations with the LTTE in order to curb the violence. By negotiating with an internationally known terrorist organization, Sri Lanka revealed its fear of the LTTE and legitimized the power of the LTTE and, by association, its method of terror.

Competition with Other Organizations

Additionally, the competition between the LTTE and other Tamil liberation organizations was a major factor in the emergence of tactical suicide bombing. For a period of time in the 1980s, more than 25 Tamil liberation groups existed.[68] In 2001, when the cease-fire brought suicide bombing to hiatus, the LTTE was the sole organization representing the Tamil people. This was due, in large part, to a war of outbidding between the groups vying for the support of the Tamil people and ultimate negotiating power with the Sri Lankan government. As Bloom states, 'when violence resonate positively with the civilian population, a variety of extremist groups might compete with one another for popularity, engage in outbidding, and use violence to mobilize and radicalize the polity.'[69] As Bloom further suggests, the Tamil community was an essential component in the Tamil Tiger's competition for dominance. The Tamil people were the backbone of the organization, providing it with human and financial resources and support, though it is unclear what the level of support would have been without active Tiger manipulation.[70]

Early on, LTTE leader realized the necessity of monopolizing Tamil popular support, and they set out to dominate the Tamil regions to get it. The LTTE joined forces with existing groups and used this to destroy them, manipulated cross-organizational power struggle to pit one liberation group against another, and murdered leaders and cadres of other groups. The result was that one by one the LTTE brought down competing organizations, killing the leaders of groups such as the Tamil Eelam Liberation Organisation (TELO), the Eelam People's Revolutionary Liberation Front (EPRLF), and the People's Liberation Organisation of Tamil Eelam (PLOTE).[71] Furthermore, as the most militaristic group in the Sri Lanka's Tamil regions, the LTTE could escape being pigeon-holed by narrowly defined ideology or having to compete for political space. Instead, it could exist with its own created space of terror without fighting for the support of one political constituency over another. Its excessive violence was hugely successful in gaining the attention of a population that believed that their very existence was being threatened and that a violent saviour was the only answer to their prayers.[72]

Indian Government's Attitude to LTTE

The July 1983, anti-Tamil riots in Sri Lanka saw strong reaction from Tamil Nadu. Exodus of refugees to India and escalation of violence subsequently, no doubt activated the local Tamil social constituency and brought together political parties, public figures and media in support of Tamils in Sri Lanka. Tamil Nadu government urged the Indian Government to take up the matter with Sri Lanka and do something or redress the wrong done to their brethren.[73] On the fall-out of July 1983 riots the members of the Tamil militant groups depended upon India's politico-military support for their survival against the Sri Lankan Army onslaught. Since 1984, India followed a two-pronged strategy of persuasion and coercion both against the Sri Lankan government and the Tamil militants on different occasions. The objective behind such a strategy was to evolve a viable political settlement through negotiations and not to weaken or strengthen one party against another.[74] In line with its objectives, India allowed the Tamil militants to undergo training and procure arms. Though India never admitted this, yet is sided with the militants with sanctuaries, arms and training.[75] In this situation, the LTTE became stronger than what the mentors (India) expected to be. However, by the beginning of 1990s, the India government's attitude to the LTTE underwent a drastic change.

Assassination of Rajiv Gandhi and Crack Down on LTTE

On May 21, 1991, while on the campaign trail in Tamil Nadu, Rajiv Gandhi was assassinated by a female suicide bomber, Dhanu. Dhanu, a young woman from Jaffna, Sri Lanka, approached Rajiv Gandhi, India's former Prime Minister, with a garland of flowers at a political rally. Dhanu smiled, dropped the garland at Gandhi's feet, and as she reached down to pick it up, she exploded. Dhanu was a member of the LTTE and one of 143 male and female Tigers to perform similar horrific acts in the last two decades. The LTTE was immediately suspected and a thorough Central Bureau of Investigation inquiry concluded that Prabhakaran had orchestrated the attack in retaliation for the Indian Peace Keeping Force (IPKF) intervention.[76] The assassination of Rajiv Gandhi alienated the popular support that the LTTE enjoyed in India. As a significant step, India dismantled its aid network, and the support for the LTTE among the Tamil politicians evaporated. And Sri Lanka definitely benefited from this change in India's policy.

The assassination of Rajiv Gandhi compelled New Delhi to declare the LTTE a terrorist outfit and the Indian government banned the LTTE in 1992 and refused to have any contacts with it. The LTTE have veered between strenuous denial and ambiguous apology in response to the above-mentioned accusations. Various conspiracy theories blamed Mossad, the CIA and the Indian mystic Chandraswami.[77] Yet, whether or not the LTTE were truly responsible – an international consensus holds that they were and the assassination virtually eradicated all support or even sympathy for the organization in India – both at the political as well as individual levels. The Indian leaders ignored the friendly overtures of the LTTE and turned down its request in 2002 for transit and medical facilities for its theoretician Anton Balasingham in Tamil Nadu on humanitarian ground.[78] In the same year the government refused to share platform with the LTTE at the donor conferences organized by Norway, the US and Japan.

LTTE: Ceasefire and Negotiations

The LTTE continued to commit various terrorist acts throughout the 1990s. The government would then retaliate against Tamil citizens, and the cycle would go on. The millennium saw failed attempts at ceasefires and negotiation. Finally in 2002, a final ceasefire was declared between the LTTE and the Sri Lankan government, moderated by the Norwegian government.[79] However, in 2003 the Tigers again quit the negotiations table in disagreement with the government on the provisional administrative structure for the development of North East. The ceasefire was maintained, but communication came to a standstill. This was an unfortunate turn of events, but nothing new to the negotiators, the government or the LTTE.[80]

In March 2004, the Tamil Tigers launched a new offensive in the eastern regions with the hope of regaining total control over claimed homeland. This was followed, two months later, by a suicide bomb in the capital city of Colombo, which was the first terrorist-style attack since 2001.[81] In the meantime, in 2004 itself, the LTTE suffered a major setback with the defection of Colonel Karuna. Karuna took with him the majority of the LTTE forces in the East, which now meant that the Tigers were fighting not one enemy, but two. This both drained LTTE resources as well as severely hurt their ability to fight the army in future wars, as they had lost several thousand troops.[82]

In 2006, the situation became even worse: the violence between the Tamil groups and the government re-escalated to the levels before the 2002 cease-fire agreements. The government was able to drive the LTTE out of the eastern areas, which had been home to the LTTE. Once again, the Norwegians, the LTTE and the Sri Lankan government went back to the drawing board; this time in Geneva, Switzerland. Unfortunately the Geneva talks failed and, more bloodshed ensued. In 2007 Colombo's Police Force evicted hundreds of Tamils from the capital and at the end of 2007, the government officially pulled out of the ceasefire agreements.[83]

After the Sri Lankan government effectively obliterated the resistance of the LTTE in the eastern region, it turned its attention to the North where the LTTE would make its last stand. In December 2008, both sides were engaged in heavy fighting in the northern regions; the civilian casualties were astronomical. In January 2009, the government sacked the city of Kilinochchi, the administrative headquarters of Tamil operations. They gained control over the Elephant Pass, which was a defensive position of the LTTE; and also besieged the entire district of Mullaitivu.[84]

The Tigers were accused of using civilians as human shields and those who fled the war testified the LTTE commanders had fired on them to stop them from escaping. The government was accused of causing substantial civilian casualties and large-scale displacement of people. The international community called on Sri Lanka to embrace a temporary cease-fire and to allow innocent civilians to leave under the auspices of various aid groups.[85] This offer was rejected by the government possibly because it did not want to lose its military advantages. In May 2009, the Sri Lankan government launched its final campaign against the LTTE and the Tamil strongholds and killed many of its senior leaders including LTTE founder Velupillai Prabhakaran. The net result is that the civil war is now over and Sri Lanka has entered a post-war stage. There are several policy decisions that will have to be implemented to reconstruct and rebuild the country, and to reunify the people of Sri Lanka.

To conclude, the Liberation Tigers of Tamil Eelam (LTTE), also known as the Tamil Tigers, has evolved into a widely known extremist group since its formation in 1976. The Sri Lankan Government's violence against the Tamil population had escalated since Sri Lankan independence was granted in 1948. Besides the disenfranchisement of Tamils in the arenas of employment and education, there were widespread accounts of government-sponsored massacres, gang rapes, and torture of the Tamil people. As time went on, and violence escalated on the Island, the LTTE and the Tamil people began to see government policy as one of genocide. This genocide was not only physical but included the destruction of Tamil culture, religion and language, the foundations of the Tamil community. To the LTTE, this threat to their existence justified the demand for absolute separation from the Sinhalese and gave means for a war with no limits.

Early on, LTTE leaders realized the necessity of monopolizing Tamil popular support, and they set out to dominate the Tamil regions to get it. The LTTE joined forces with existing groups and used this to destroy them, manipulated cross-organisational power struggle to pit one group against another, and outright secured dominance among these groups through massive violence and coercion. The LTTE had ensured a constant supply of manpower to sustain its armed campaigns through its tactics of strategic targeting of certain groups and harnessing the Tamil national sentiment of the youth to its goal of national liberation. Conscription of Tamil youth was also pursued as a popular strategy in order to maintain the required force level for operational purposes.

In fact, it took Prabhakran two decades to rebuild the LTTE after the mauling he received at the hands of the Indian Peace Keeping Force from 1987 to 1990. He took it to a peak position of power and territorial dominance in 2002 when he agreed to participate in the Norwegian peace process. For the first time Sri Lanka recognised the LTTE as the sole representative of the Tamils, just as Prabhakaran agreed to find a solution to the Tamil issue within a federal Sri Lanka. Prabhakaran could have consolidated his gains as the LTTE controlled most of the Tamil Eelam – Tamil areas of the Northern Province. But he did not. His faith in a military solution, rather than a political one, prevented him from taking the easy way out. He continued to procure modern weapons and arms even as he spoke of peace. He did everything to scuttle the peace process and took advantage of the weaknesses of Sri Lanka's polity to bring it to an end.

The peace condition that prevailed from 2002 to 2005 probably softened the LTTE cadres. They were weary; many of them had been fighting for over a decade. This became evident when they could not stop the onslaught of the rejuvenated armed forces which fought with a high morale, aided by superior firepower and number. The Tamils paid dearly for 26 years of the LTTE's armed struggle that came to naught on May 18, 2009. Sri Lanka as a whole is moving back to regain its strength after nearly three decades of intermittent war.

References

1. C. Christine Fair, "The Sri Lankan Tamil Diaspora: Sustaining, Conflict and pushing for Peace" in Hazel Smith and Paul Stares (ed.) *Diaspora in Conflict: Peace-makers or Peace Wreckers?,* United Nations University Press, New York, 2007), p. 172.
2. There was one very notable exception: India provided substantial military and political support to various factions of Tamil militants/ extremists throughout the 1970s and 1980s. This policy was mostly an effort to mollify the demands of its own Tamil population. By the late 1980s, India had reversed this policy. It has been argued that the military support was the most significant military training that the Tamil militants received and did much to enhance their battle effectiveness. Also see Alan J. Bulion, *India, Sri Lanka and Tamil Crisis 1976-1994: An International Perspective,* Pinter, London, 1995, p. 212.
3. Sarah Wayland (2004), "Ethnonationalist Networks and Transnational opportunities: The Sri Lankan Tamil Diaspora" *Review of International Studies,* London, pp. 414-415.
4. Ibid.
5. Chris Smith, "South Asia's Enduring War", in Creating Peace in Sri Lanka, ed. Robert I Rotberg (Brookings Institutions Press, Washington, D. C. 1999), p. 36.
6. For detailed discussion see Neil Devotta, Blowback: *Linguistic Nationalism, Institutional Decay, and Ethnic Conflict in Sri Lanka,* Standford University Press Standford, 2004. pp. 108-123.
7. Nigel Harris, National Liberation, (I. B. Tauris, London, 1990), p. 221.
8. Rohan Gunaratna, "Sri Lanka: Feeding the Tamil Tigers" in Karen Ballentine and Jake Sherman, eds., *Political Economy of Armed Conflict: Beyond Greed and Grievances*, Boulder, Co. Lynne Rienner, 2003, p. 198.
9. Alfred Jeyaratnam Wilson, *Sri Lankan Tamil Nationalism,* C. Hurst, London, 2000, pp. 8-12.

10. Ibid.
11. Broken Palmyra (University Teachers for Human Rights, Jaffna, 1992), Chapter – I: "Missed opportunities and the loss of Democracy".
12. Ramchandra Guha, *India After Gandhi: The History of World's Largest Democracy,* Macmillan, London, 2007. pp. 590-607.
13. Affred Jayaratnam Wilson, 1988, *The Break-up of Sri Lanka: The Sinhalese- Tamil Conflict,* Honolulu:University of Hawai Press. p. 80.
14. Ibid., pp. 90-96.
15. Ibid.
16. Patrick Peebles, *The History of Sri Lanka,* Greanwood Press, Westport, 2006, pp. 110-122.
17. Ibid.
18. V. Suryanarayan "Prospects for Reconciliation" in B. Raman, N. S. Moorthy and K. Chittaranjan (eds.) *Sri Lanka: Peace Without Process,* 2006, Observer Research Foundation, New Delhi. p. 100.
19. David Little, *Sri Lanka: The Invention of Enmity* (1994), pp. 71-72., Also see, Patrick Peebles (2006), p. 124.
20. Nira Wickramasinghe, *Sri Lanka in the Modern Age: A History of Contested Identities,* C. Hurst, London, 2006, pp. 237-252.
21. Alfred Jeyratnam Wilson, op.cit.(2000), pp. 156-170.
22. Patrick Peebles (2006), pp. 126-127.
23. Chellamuthu Kuppuswamy, *Prabhakaran: His life and Struggle for Eelam,* Oxygen Books, Chennai, 2009, p. 16.
24. Ibid.
25. Patrick Peebles (2006), pp. 130-133.
26. Chellamuthu Kuppuswamy (2009), pp. 34-40.
27. Robert N. Kearny, "Ethnic Conflict and the Tamil Separatist Movement in Sri Lanka", *Asian Survey* 25, No. 9 (1985), pp. 906-910.
28. Shantha K. Hennayake "The Peace Accord and the Tamils in Sri Lanka" *Asian Survey* 29, No. 4 (1989), p. 402.
29. C. Christine Fair, "Military Operation in Urban Areas: The Indian Experience" *India Review* (2003), 2(1), pp. 49-76.
30. Ramchandra Guha (2007), p. 612.
31. Challamuthu Kuppuswamy (2009), p. 92.
32. Raymond Bonner, "Tamil Guerrillas in Sri Lanka: Deadly and Armed to the Teeth; A World of Arms: The Colombo Connections", *New York Times,* March 7, 1998.
33. Robert I. Rotberg "Sri Lanka in Civil War: From Mayhem towards Diplomatic Resolution" in Robert I Rotberg (ed.) *Creating Peace*

in Sri Lanka, Brookings Institution Press, Washington D. C. 1999, p. 9.

34. Raymond Bonner "Tamil Guerrillas in Sri Lanka" *New York Times*, March 7, 1998.
35. Ibid.
36. Ibid.
37. Rotberg (1999), p. 9.
38. Chris Smith "South Asia's Enduring Civil War" in Robert Rotberg, ed. *Creating Peace in Sri Lanka: Civil War and Reconciliation*, Brookings, Washington D.C. 1999, pp. 9-17.
39. Robert Rotbert (1999), see "Introduction".
40. Virakecari (Brave Lion), Colombo, April-May 1986, p. 3.
41. Kalattil (On the battlefield) (LTTE: Madras), no. 9, 1986 (September-October), p. 8.
42. Gunasekeram, (Spokesman, EPRLF: London), quoted in *The Hindu*, 28 February 1987, p. 3.
43. Haporali, November-December 1986, p. 3.
44. Cociyalicat Tamil Hattai nokhi (Towards a socialist Tamil Eelam) Madras, 1980, p. 35.
45. Virakecari, January-February, 1986, p. 7.
46. EFOS Documentation Unit, 28 October 1986, pp. 3-4.
47. Ibid., p. 4.
48. S. L. Gunasekera, A Tragedy of errors (2001), Colombo: Sinhala Jathika Sangamaya, p. 56.
49. Michael Walzer, *Just and Unjust Wars* (1977), Columbia University Press, New York. pp. 201-205.
50. Mia Bloom, *Dying to Kill: The Allure of Suicide Terror*, Columbia University Press, New York. (2005), p. 56.
51. Ibid, p. 57.
52. Robert A., Pape Dying to Win (2005), p. 113.
53. Ramchandra Guha, p. 26.
54. Ibid.
55. E. Sadhadevan, *Politics of Conflict and Peace in Sri Lanka* (2006), Konark, New Delhi. p. 313.
56. Ibid., p. 314.
57. Ramchandra Guha, op. cit. p. 612.
58. Robert A. Pape, *Dying to Win: The Strategic logic of Suicide Terrorism*, Random House, New York, 2005. p. 226.
59. Ibid.
60. Kenneth D. Bush, *The Intra-Group Dimensions of Ethnic Conflict in Sri Lanka*, Palgrave Macmillan, New York, 2003. pp. 1719.
61. The LTTE used a variety of techniques but mainly relied on suicide bombers from their Black Tigers Wing.

62. Emile Durkheim, *Suicide: A Study in Sociology*, trans. John A. Spaulding and George Simson (*Free Press*, New York, 1951), p. 219.
63. Ibid.
64. Walter Laqueur, *The Age of Terrorism*, Little Brown and Co., Boston 1987. p. 95.
65. A.S. Balasingham, *Liberation Tigers and Tamil Eelam Freedom Struggle*, LTTE Publication, Sri Lanka 1983. p. 27.
66. S.L. Gunasekera, *A Tragedy of Errors* (Sinhala Jathika Sangamaya, Colombo, 2001), p. 38.
67. Michael Walzer, *Just and Unjust Wars*, Basic Books, New York, 1977. p. 252.
68. Mia Bloom, *Dying to Kill: The Allure of Suicide Terror*, Columbia University Press, New York, 2005. p. 58.
69. Ibid., p. 45.
70. Robert A. Pape, Dying to Win (2005), p. 145.
71. S. L. Gunasekara, Tigers 'Moderates' and Pandora's Package (Sinhala Jathika Sangamaya, Colombo, 1996), p. 26.
72. Dayan Jayatilleka, Sri Lanka: The Travails of a Democracy, Unfinished War, Protracted Crisis (International Centre for Ethnic Studies, New Delhi, 1995), p. 69.
73. P. Sahadevan and Neil Devotta, *Politics of Conflict and Peace in Sri Lanka* (2006), Manak, New Delhi. p. 359.
74. Mohan Ram, *Sri Lanka: The fractured Island*, Penguin, New Delhi, 1989. p. 136.
75. Ramchandra Guha (2007), P. 613.
76. Kuppuswamuy (2009), p. 138.
77. P. Sahadevan and Neil Devotta (2006), p. 368.
78. John Thornhill, "Talks Begins with Tamil Tigers", *Financial Times*, London, 5 January, 2002.
79. Patrick Peables (2006), pp. 180-185.
80. Ibid.
81. Kuppuswamy (2009), pp. 169-185.
82. Ibid.
83. Peace and Conflict Timeline, May 2009, It can be found here: http:/pactik/2009/03/03/march 2009.
84. Ibid.
85. South Asia Terrorism Portal, Sri Lanka, 2009, http.//www.satp.org/satporgtp/countries/srilanka/timeline.

CHAPTER 7

Prospects of Tamils in Sri Lanka after LTTE

The Tamils are a minority with deep roots in the north of the island nation of Sri Lanka and kinship ties to the Indian state of Tamil Nadu, which lies across a narrow sea channel. A separate group of Tamils arrived later from India as labourers during British rule and are known as Indian Tamils. Together they make up around 18 per cent of Sri Lanka's 20 million people, with the Sinhalese majority making up 74 per cent. Largely Hindu, the Tamils live mostly in the North and East, the area which was being claimed by the Liberation Tigers of Tamil Eelam (LTTE), though large numbers live in Colombo, the capital. After Sri Lanka's independence in 1948, Tamil elites excelled in English Language education and government service. Sinhalese felt excluded, and their political leaders sought to redress the balance, only to sow the seeds of civil war. The 1956 "Sinhala Only" law that promoted the majority tongue was a turning point. Ethnic relations soured, and Tamils began agitating for a federal state. By the 1970s, this demand had shifted to calls for a separate homeland and armed groups emerged in Jaffna.[1]

The story of the emergence, spread and collapse of the Tamil secessionist insurgency encapsulates some of the key contradictions in post-colonial Sri Lankan polity in general, and the Tamil ethnic formation in particular. The insurgency developed in the late 1970s against the backdrop of repeated refusals by the political elite of the majority Sinhalese community to pay heed to the Tamil demand for regional autonomy.[2] The secessionist slogan first emerged in 1975-1976 as a part of the mainstream, parliamentary politics of Tamil nationalism.

What Role did the Tigers Play?

A year later, during the parliamentary election of 1977, the campaign for self-determination for Tamils entered a period of mass mobilization. In that process, several radical Tamil youth groups sprang up, advocating armed rebellion and challenging the parliamentary strategy of the traditional Tamil leadership. The LTTE was one among a number of these radical youth groups that took up arms to carry forward the struggle for a separate state. Even when the insurgency began to take shape, the Sinhalese political leadership failed to realize that the Tamil campaign for autonomy was a serious political challenge. Instead, they treated it as a law and order problem and responded, typically by relying on the police and military. The anti-Tamil riots of 1983 in which a section of the ruling party took an active part, eventually altered the political equation in favour of a full-blown civil war between the Sri Lankan state and a host of Tamil militant groups.[3]

Among the Tamil nationalist groups, the LTTE had the strongest, and most uncompromising, commitment to the goal of a separate Tamil state called Eelam. Almost all the others gave up the path of armed struggle as well as the goal of secession by the mid-1980s, in the aftermath of the Indian government's engagement in Sri Lanka for a political solution. The Indo-Lanka Accord of July 1987, initiated by the then Indian Prime Minister Rajiv Gandhi, promised devolution to Tamils in a merged North East Province as the basis of regional autonomy for Tamils. While all other Tamil parties and groups accepted, some openly and some tacitly, the Indian mediated settlement, the LTTE stood by its secessionist agenda, eventually creating conditions for a war between itself and the Indian peace keeping forces. The LTTE survived that war by cleverly manipulating contradictions between the Sri Lankan and the Indian governments.[4]

The Indian attempt to force a settlement on "Sri Lanka's conflict in the mid-1980s only worked partially. With its failure to either defeat the LTTE militarily, or force it to accept a political deal well short of secession, the Indian government withdrew from an active role in Sri Lanka. Between 1989 and 2001, the attempts at a negotiated settlement were made essentially between the LTTE and Sri Lanka's government of the day. When those attempts failed, the parties returned to war. In 2001-2002, an internationally mediated peace attempt was made by the newly elected United National Front (UNF) government, but that too failed to produce a settlement agreement. The return to full-scale war in 2007, which led to the LTTE's defeat in May 2009, was the culmination of a prolonged process of civil war interspersed by cycles of negotiations, temporary ceasefires, and proposals for a political solution, international engagement and a relapse into war.[5]

The total military defeat of the LTTE in mid-May is without doubt the most dramatic political event to have occurred in South Asia in the year 2009. After resisting the Sri Lankan state's multi-pronged military offensive for over two years, and then being cornered to a small coastal area of Mulaithivu, the LTTE's military structure collapsed within a few days after 15 May 2009 when the top military and political leadership of the LTTE died within a space of twenty-four hours. The circumstances under which they met their death are not publicly known and will remain controversial for many years to come. Some third level leaders may have surrendered to the army, but little is known about the fate of many of them. With this unexpected collapse of the LTTE, Sri Lanka's protracted ethnic insurgency has come to a halt. But will it mark the end of the ethnic conflict as well? Many, for obvious reasons, are quite skeptical.

However, before coming down to the question of the prospects of Tamils in Sri Lanka after LTTE, it seems urgent to answer a few questions. Why did the LTTE refuse a political compromise a number of times, but particularly in 2002-2003? Why did the LTTE continue its war strategy even at the risk of being annihilated? Answers to these two questions are crucially important to understand the prospects of Tamils in Sri Lanka in the Post-LTTE era. Concerning the first question, the LTTE all along remained steadfast in its commitment to secession by military means. The LTTE seems to have translated that commitment into a long-term strategy of sustaining itself as a formidable military entity, until regional or global conditions favoured the establishment of a separate ethnic state in Sri Lanka. That was a fairly long drawn out agenda, and the LTTE seemed to have made its political calculations to cover a period of at least three to five decades of armed struggle. A political compromise to accept devolution, which LTTE saw as minimalist regional autonomy, would have diluted the commitment to that goal. Repeated reproduction of the war, after brief periods of negotiations and relative peace, seems to have been an integral part of this long-term strategy of the LTTE. And that eventually turned out to be counter-productive. Ultimately, the LTTE fell victim to its own commitment to long-term war when the global and regional conditions ruled out the legitimacy of a separatist goal by means of war and violence.[6]

For more than three decades, the Liberation Tigers of Tamil Eelam (LTTE) has been endeavouring to weaken the democratically elected government in Sri Lanka. They have primarily used adroit terror and propaganda campaigns interspersed with political negotiation. During the history of its campaign, the LTTE has not displayed any keen, sincere interest in settling the conflict through political negotiations. The apparent reason behind this could be their firm belief in carving an independent state for the Tamils in Sri Lanka through military means. It used the negotiation table mostly to buy time, regroup, and rearm. Yet, its failure or rejection to sit at the negotiation table with firm commitments and sincerity is the gravest mistake the LTTE has ever made.[7] Consequently, it had to pay the price for its failed militaristic approach towards the conflict.

The LTTE, which started its campaign as a small vanguard movement of the Tamil insurgency, later developed into a powerful and highly structured terrorist organization with international offices. Over the years, it secured support for its activities from the Tamil community and others. One of the compelling reasons behind the persistence of support for and the attraction of international Tamils towards the LTTE has been the ability of its leader to ensure absolute authority over every aspect of the organization with high discipline and strict control over cadres. Some contend that the support for the activities of the LTTE is a function of pervasive unhappiness with some aspects of the policies of the Sri Lankan government toward genuine grievances of the Tamil community.[8] According to others, a combination of social, political, and economic ills afflicting the Tamils could be the main reasons.

The most significant dynamic in shaping the affairs of the LTTE was the adoption of one-man rule, which may also be the reason for the LTTE's dramatic failure. Interestingly, the dictatorship of Vellupillai Prabhakaran had prevented the LTTE from transforming itself into a more practical organization that could correspond effectively with the rapidly changing local and global environment. Today, the LTTE is experiencing the gradual loss of everything it achieved previously in the face of its defeat by military campaign of the Sri Lankan government's security forces. During the last three decades of its struggle, the LTTE had been able to secure substantial support from certain sections of the international and Tamil communities to wage a prolonged war. It had emerged for a while as a powerful terrorist organization with the ability to present its demands convincingly in any forum. More importantly, it controlled a significant segment of lands in the north of Sri Lanka before the commencement of the 2009 Sri Lankan military actions.

LTTE: Commitment to Maximalist Option

Despite all the illusions about the inviolability of the LTTE and amidst international and domestic pressure, the Sri Lankan government was compelled to respond to the LTTE's terror campaign in order to maintain law and order in the country and to combat terrorism. However, the Sri Lankan government periodically adopted other political measures, as required. These measures include constitutional changes providing more political space for the Tamils, the introduction of political mechanisms including Provincial Councils, and engagement with the LTTE. Often during this latter process, the Sri Lankan government tolerated the intervention of third parties and respected the opinion of the international community.[9] Unfortunately, in response to the government's gestures to peacefully settle the conflict, the LTTE pounced, misinterpreting the government's peaceful intentions as weakness. In the recent past, after signing the Cease Fire Agreement with the Sri Lankan government in 2002, the LTTE continued to strengthen its military capacity and violated the agreement more than 2000 times in addition to killing politicians, security personnel, and government officials.[10] Finally, it withdrew unilaterally from the peace negotiations conducted with the backing of Norway and other international actors. Subsequently, the government abrogated the Cease Fire Agreement to look for other alternatives.

During and after the 2002 peace negotiations, the LTTE's commitment to a separatist goal turned into a huge liability, and even a trap from which the LTTE could not extricate itself. Peace talks and the ceasefire agreement actually favoured the LTTE in terms of restoring its political legitimacy and its being recognized as an equal partner not only to the ethnic problem, but also a political solution. In their liberal peace-building efforts, major global actors led by the US, EU and Japan were ready to assist both the government and LTTE with significant development assistance to lay economic foundations for peace-building. The LTTE could not have bargained for a better deal with any government in Colombo.

But after five rounds of talks, the LTTE became impatient with the peace process, probably because of the possibility of a federal solution being imposed by the Sri Lankan government, backed by a formidable international coalition. Even if the LTTE was willing to accept an interim settlement, that settlement could not have been a federal solution. The LTTE's conception of an interim solution became clear when, in October 2002, it unveiled its own proposals for a transitional arrangement in the form of an interim self-governing authority. This proposal envisaged an interim framework of regional autonomy which exceeded any known form of federalism anywhere in the world. It was in fact a confederal proposal.[11]

If the interim solution was a confederal one, the LTTE's concept of a final settlement would have been independence. A negotiated separation on the basis of military balance of power on the ground probably lay at the core of the LTTE's strategy, which turned out to be both naive and illusionary. It became quite clear that in both military and political terms the LTTE continued to show a commitment to maximalist options; and that ultimately backfired on the LTTE. "Secession or death" should have been a mere rhetorical slogan for mobilization, but not a programme of self-destruction.

To a great extent, the LTTE was also caught up in a quasi-state trap. In some parts of the northern and eastern province where the LTTE managed to establish a firm military presence, it had also set up institutions and practices of a regional mini-state with its own structures of coercion, administration and military control. The LTTE maintained a separate judiciary, a police force, an apparatus for internal taxation and machinery for education and economic development. These were primitive institutions of state power backed by an equally primitive conception of the state which essentially focused on military capacity. However, the LTTE leaders probably thought that those were tangible achievements of the armed struggle for statehood. But the trouble with these "achievements" was that they prevented the LTTE from thinking of a political compromise of devolution or federalism that would incorporate them into the terms of settlement.[12]

One crucial outcome of the LTTE's intransigent behaviour during 2002-2004 was the total loss of international sympathy. The LTTE's stubborn refusal to return to the negotiation table in response to repeated appeals by the leading global actors perhaps led to the realization in Europe, the USA and Japan that the LTTE was the key obstacle to peace in Sri Lanka. When the present Mahinda Rajapaksa administration launched its massive military assault on the LTTE, the global actors were not enthusiastic to force the government to explore the option of a negotiated peace. They appeared to have come to terms with a particular reality, that is, the pragmatic necessity to remove the LTTE from being a party to the conflict and to a possible solution as well.[13] The Rajapaksa government was exceedingly committed to make that reality actually happen.

Why the LTTE Opted for War?

The real puzzle remains why the LTTE opted for war, knowing well that its chances of winning were exceedingly remote. The same puzzle applies to the Sri Lankan government too. Why did the Rajapaksa regime opt for war, taking the risk of being forced into a costly military stalemate by the LTTE? There are a number of explanations to this puzzle. One is that both sides were pushed into a new phase of war by the logic of circumstances. For the Rajapaksa government, which was a coalition of hardline Sinhalese nationalist parties and ideological forces, a genuine attempt at defeating the LTTE militarily was an irresistible political compulsion. For the LTTE too, returning to war was absolutely necessary, particularly after its bid for an interim regional government failed. The LTTE also needed the war to maintain its permanent state of emergency over the Sri Lankan Tamil society. When the space and options for political engagement became unavailable, the logic was for each side to happily resume the war on their own terms.[14]

The second explanation is about military objectives. The LTTE's intention was perhaps to engage the Sri Lankan state in war until the Indian parliamentary elections were concluded.

The LTTE appears to have calculated on a possible BJP electoral victory and a BJP-led coalition government being formed in New Delhi. That scenario, the LTTE may have thought, would have enabled them to force a military stalemate on the Sri Lankan government, with political backing from a BJP government in New Delhi.[15]

What the LTTE wanted to achieve through this scenario in concrete terms is not clear. What is somewhat clear, however, is the fact that the LTTE probably wanted the re-entry of India into Sri Lanka's conflict in a context of a war-induced humanitarian crisis of massive magnitude. Thus, external humanitarian intervention seems to have been one key outcome the LTTE probably anticipated. As it turned out, this scenario did not work out. The BJP lost the parliamentary election and the Congress-led government re-established its authority on a firmer footing. The LTTE did manage to create a massive humanitarian crisis with the support of the adversary, but there was no significant international response to prevent or manage it.[16]

Clearly, the LTTE seems to have totally misunderstood the behaviour and agenda of the international and regional powers in relation to Sri Lanka's conflict. It also underestimated the will and commitment of the Sri Lankan political and military victory, disregarding any political or humanitarian cost it was to incur. The calculated military gamble of the Sri Lankan state prevailed over a politically isolated LTTE.

Significance of the Victory

Given the LTTE defeat, it appears to be unlikely that an LTTE resurgence in Sri Lanka remains possible. 'We have destroyed the LTTE leadership's first, second and third rungs. The LTTE is over. They may do a bit of hit-and-run tactics, but they are militarily over,' stated General Sarath Fonseka, the Sri Lanka Army's Chief of Defense Staff and former commander.[17] The LTTE lost over 22,000 combatants killed in action; over 9,100 have surrendered; all its bases and 15,000 square kilometres of territory have been overrun.[18] Among insurgent groups worldwide, the LTTE was considered the trend setter in military innovation and development at the organisational and tactical level; it was also the only insurgent-terrorist organisation to field an army, maritime force and air capability. Moreover, according to the US Federal Bureau of Investigations (FBI) website, the LTTE:

'Perfected the use of suicide bombers, invented the suicide belt, pioneered the use of women in suicide attacks, murdered some 4,000 people in past two years alone; and assassinated two world leaders (Indian Prime Minister Rajiv Gandhi and Sri Lankan President Ranasinghe Premadasa) — the only terrorist organisation to do so.'[19]

What the FBI does not mention is that the LTTE pioneered and refined the use of suicide terrorism — on land, sea and air — feats that even al-Quaeda has not achieved. In fact prior to the Second Gulf War, the LTTE led the world in the most number of suicide attacks.[20]

According to the Sri Lankan Ministry of Defense, the LTTE participated in a sustained campaign of ethnic cleansing against ethnic Sinhalese and Muslim populations in northern and eastern Sri Lanka, which from 1984 to 2009 saw at least 257 attacks that killed 4,485 civilians, wounded 5,897 and displaced around 150,000-200,000 Sinhalese and Muslims. Additionally, the LTTE insisted that it was the sole representative of the Sri Lankan Tamils and ruthlessly suppressed dissident Tamil voices. According to Sri Dharan, the dissident Tamil leader of the Eelam People's Revolutionary Liberation Front-Naba faction (EPRLF-Naba), the LTTE allegedly eliminated somewhere between 13,000-18,000 rival Tamils from 1986-2006 (EPRLF claims to have lost over 1,400 members). In direct terms, the military defeat of the LTTE translates as a victory of a democratic state over an extremist anti-democratic movement inspired by radical Tamil nationalism, or what some commentators have referred to as Tamil fascism. The defeat of a formidable terrorist organisation has also sent a strong message to aspiring insurgent groups in the South Asian region, a point emphasised by Narayan Swamy, an Indian Tamil journalist: 'The defeat of the LTTE is a defeat of the politics of no-compromise. It also marks the defeat of arrogance. Having embraced militarism and a mindset that saw every compromise as surrender.... The LTTE's refusal to embrace politics, to compromise, to take some and give some, and its failure to understand that the world would never accept an independent Tamil Eelam led to its demise.'[21]

Crucially, the void created by the LTTE defeat has dramatically altered Sri Lanka's political landscape and extracted the country from its darkest and bloodiest era, which in turn has offered opportunities and new challenges.

Implications for Sri Lanka

In Sri Lanka the defeat of the LTTE has given vital space for previously suppressed Tamil democratic parties to engage in the democratic process without fear of assassination, as evidenced recently during the Norwegian-moderated Ceasefire Agreement (CFA) of 2002-06, where over 200 Tamils from rival political parties and groups were killed by the LTTE. Additionally, the defeat of the LTTE has removed its violent dominance over Tamil politics and has enabled the process of reconciliation to start afresh. Aptly, President Mahinda Rajapaksa after his sweeping success in the Presidential and Parliamentary elections of January and April 2010 respectively, has emerged the most powerful leader in Sri Lanka. Politically he is in an unassailable position. He can use his enormous popularity and power to work out a reasonable political package that will satisfy all communities. He has repeatedly promised to carry out structural changes to do justice to the minorities.[22] However, if one goes through the development since President Mahinda Rajapaksa embarked on his second term in office as President of Sri Lanka, it is obvious that a political settlement of the ethnic conflict under the prevailing circumstances can only be one imposed by the majority Sinhala community upon the minority Tamil community though all the formalities of presenting an equitable settlement would be present. For one thing, Rajapaksa has not even attempted to ensure that a widely accepted Tamil constituent, truly representing the vital interests of the community, becomes an equal partner in the political process that he seems to have in mind.

The President had earlier hinted that a political solution would be offered once the military operations ended. There was also the hint that when the report of the All Party Representative Committee (APRC) was finalized, it would be implemented. Later, the non-participation of TNA in the formulation of policy for reconciliation was stated to be delaying progress. The President subsequently convened the All Party Meeting for Development and Reconciliation-without any linkage between political solution (power devolution) and reconciliation. These apparently dilatory tactics generate skepticism about a real intention to evolve an equitable political solution. It should be obvious that despite insisting that its enemy was the LTTE, not the Tamil minority it claimed to represent, the government has done little to ease Tamil grievances. And far from making serious plans for the devolution of power, seen as essential to ethnic harmony, the trend is relentless centralization.[23]

After a resounding military victory over the Tamil Tigers, Mahinda Rajapaksa, Sri Lanka's President must have hoped for triumph in the first post-war polls in scarred North. In the event, low turn out and the unexpected success of a pro-tiger party jolted the government in the elections in August 2009 to the Jaffna municipal and Vavuniya urban councils. Although voter turn out was low, these local elections were seen as a necessary step to foster the culture of democracy to pave the way for the much larger Northern Provincial Council election. In both these elections, the pro-Tiger Tamil National Alliance (TNA) came second. Some Sri Lanka experts see this electoral outcome as a sign of growing anger among northern Tamils at the government's failure to resolve their longstanding grievances of a political package.[24]

Even if the government's commitments to the welfare of the Tamils is accepted at face value, the latter are clearly not able to put faith in Colombo's impartiality. Right from the beginning of his first term in the President's office, Rajapaksa has been quite candid about the inherent supremacy of the majority community in Sri Lanka, and has consistently insisted that all policies and solutions adopted to rebuild the country must first win the approval of the Sinhalas. It is not very difficult to see here that Rajapaksa only defeated Prabhakaran's LTTE, not solved the wider cause of Lankan Tamils, an integral part of the Lankan polity. But Rajapaksa did not have the wisdom to see Prabhakaran as separate from the Tamils of his country whose claims for fairplay were, and remain, legitimate.[25] It is in this context that the LTTE's overseas network, though in tatters, needs to be foreseen.

While the LTTE is critically weakened in Sri Lanka its immense supporting infrastructure overseas still remains largely intact and will continue to present a threat. 'The LTTE can be revived. They can take all their activities outside Sri Lanka and build up the diaspora. It can also encourage the few remnants of the LTTE back home,' affirmed Senaka Walgampya, Sri Lanka's High Commissioner to Australia in an interview with ABC News.[26] As such, although the LTTE has lost practically all of its experienced frontline commanders and fighters, there is still the potential for it to reignite militancy among elements of the hundreds of LTTE fighters and operatives that have fled, largely undetected, to the Indian state of Tamil Nadu, and also among the 9,100 former LTTE combatants currently interned in Sri Lanka, which could disrupt the process of reconciliation and hinder the prospect of a political solution between ethnic Sinhalese and Tamils. Hence, Sri Lanka has indicated the importance of dismantling the LTTE global network.

Ramifications for the Diaspora

Even though the defeat of the LTTE in Sri Lanka means that the achievement of a separate Tamil state is no longer plausible, LTTE supporters within the Tamil Diaspora will not easily relinquish the struggle, inculcated by decades of LTTE ideology. This was seen at the end of Sri Lanka's insurgency, where many violent incidents were perpetrated by LTTE supporters in Western countries, notably against dissident

Tamils and elements of the Sinhalese expatriate community. According to Dr. Rajasingham Narendran, a dissident Tamil activist:

'The propaganda of the LTTE abroad is so powerful. The Diaspora is suffering from a syndrome. As a result they are unable to forget the past. They are ready to swallow whatever is told to them. Any story you tell about the Sri Lankan Government or the Sinhala people, they believe. It is very difficult to bring out from their present mind set. So if we take the stance of the Diaspora, 40 per cent are fully committed [to the LTTE], another 40 per cent stand in the middle and 20 per cent are totally convinced that the LTTE is not the way forward'.[27]

Since January 2009, the LTTE faced an increasingly critical military situation in Sri Lanka and was compelled to restructure its international organisation by appointing its senior most surviving leader overseas and chief arms procurer Selvarasa Pathmanathan (alias Kumaran Pathmanathan), as the head of its self-styled Department of International Relations. After the LTTE was militarily defeated on 18 May 2009, Selvarasa Pathmanathan (also a fugitive wanted by INTERPOL and India), declared the establishment of an LTTE government in exile, entitled the "Provisional Transnational Government of Tamil Eelam" (PTG) in June 2009, which also saw him appointed as the new supreme leader of the LTTE. As such, this new body consisted of representative committees of LTTE leaders from the Tamil Diaspora largely within the western world. Such an enterprise coming from a group that is recognised as a terrorist organisation in 31 countries and viewed by the FBI as: '... the Tamil Tigers are among the most dangerous and deadly extremists in the world ... its ruthless tactics have inspired terrorist networks worldwide, including al-Qaeda in Iraq,' is another attempt at reforming its image to continue its separatist agenda. Among dissident Tamils the legitimacy of the PTG has been viewed with indignation, as seen by prominent scholar and activist, Dr. Rajan Hoole, who heads the University Teachers for Human Rights-Jaffna (UTHR-J):

'As with the LTTE, the interests and arrogance evident in the PTG's attempt to continue a politics detrimental to the Tamil people inside (Sri) Lanka, is more about attempting to sustain a bankrupt enterprise abroad through further lies, mobilisation and collection of funds.'[28]

However, the LTTE international apparatus has been plagued by serious factionalism which has manifested in the emergence of a major split between Selvarasa Pathmanathan and another faction led by Veerakulasingham Manivannan (alias Castro) who allegedly oversees finance and intelligence gathering in the Tamil Diaspora. However, Selvarasa Pathmanathan's tenure as the LTTE chief ended abruptly when he was arrested in Malaysia on 5 August 2009, in a joint sting operation with Malaysian and Sri Lankan intelligence agencies. His arrest, coupled with the large amount of intelligence gathered from surrendered LTTE commanders and overrun bases in Sri Lanka, is a major setback for the LTTE network overseas, which continues to reveal crucial high-grade intelligence and insights into its key people, assets and operations. While this is certainly a major breakthrough and will have a lasting impact on the LTTE overseas, the prospect of the organisation regenerating overseas, even on a small scale, should not be underestimated.

The Future Tamil Prospects

Eelam War IV shattered and devastated Tamils social, economical, cultural and political structural factors. These four structural factors were cornerstones of the Tamil National Struggle and were intricately interconnected to each other. These became primary targets during the war and were destroyed. After the age of "alliance building" the Tamil polity needed to analyze and consider surrounding geopolitics maneuvers and the new world order. The very existence and future of Tamil politics will be based on its present moves while reflecting upon the past. It must be shaped in a manner so that it can discourse with Southern/Sinhala politics, regional/continental and global politics. In order to establish a strong foundation for Tamil politics there should be a linkage and set of leverage mechanisms between Tamil politics in Sri Lanka, the Tamil Diaspora and Tamil Nadu.[29] Improving the effectiveness and efficiency between these dynamics will increase the chances of better influencing on geopolitics. Basically, moving towards goal based unity and avoiding factionalism will ensure the re-emergence of a future Tamil Polity. To achieve this, the support of likeminded Sinhala and Muslim is essential. Their voices should be heard and the genuine concerns of both communities should not be ignored.

The formation of a strong foundation and the creation of "smart" links with the international community would lead to the achievement of this unity based goal under the basis of the right to self-determination. The support and recognition of the international community is vital for the Tamil cause. Whether it was the military victory over the LTTE or the justification of the CFA, the success of both these attempts depended on the support of the international community to Sri Lanka. 'As long as the Sri Lankan ethno-political conflict with all its ramification remains unresolved, the GOSL will look for outside assistance, in either peace or war.'[30]

In the present stage it is challenging to define whether a solution will be based on a "united" Sri Lanka or not. However, it is clear that Sri Lanka's "unitary" state concept or its present constitution is not going to be a sustainable solution to the protracted ethno-political conflict. There is a historical basis for this argument. Prior to British colonization the Tamil kingdom was ruled separately and independently. 'There was no coherent political structure uniting the entirety of the island even during the periods of colonization under the Portuguese (beginning in 1656). Rather, there were a number of fragmented Sinhalese Buddhist kingdoms scattered throughout the Island, centered in Kotte in the Southwest and in Kandy in the central highlands; and a predominantly Hindu Tamil Kingdom in the North of the island, centered in Jaffna;'[31] The British merged all three kingdoms together due to administrative purposes.[32]

The implications of separation or unification (or something in between), devolution and self-determination must be understood by all stakeholders prior to an agreement being reached. In turn, parties must understand the reasons of the "other" in the thought framework of seeking one potential solution and rejecting others.[33] It must be stated here that an independent separate state for the Tamil people is also not an achievable task, under the current circumstances and strategic importance of Sri Lanka's location in geopolitical interests. A "United Sri Lanka" may be possible for at least an initial solution, if it accepts Tamils self-autonomy based on the right to self-determination. The right to self-determination of ethnic minorities emerged as a universally recognized prerogative that ethnic minorities in Europe and the former Soviet Union used to demand political concessions and regional autonomy from ethnic majorities. In the "Charter of Paris for New Europe" 1991: the ethnic, cultural, linguistic and religious identities of national minorities have the right freely to express, preserve and develop that identity without any discrimination and in full equality before the law.... unless the Sinhalese-majority is willing to accept the right to self-determination of Tamils, it is doubtful that any peace initiative will succeed.[34]

Depending on political outcomes, the Sinhala people can think whether they want a unitary Sri Lanka or a united Sri Lanka and the Tamil people can decide whether they want to remain or understanding the potential for external self-determination. However, self-determination should be the final goal. Leader of the Tamil National Alliance, R. Sampanthan observes: 'Whether Tamil people will eventually accept the devolution package will depend on vital aspects of the final package that are contained in the proposed new constitutions, as the nature of Government, the actual power devolved relating particularly to Law and Order, State Land, Finance etc.; in the unit of devolution whether the scheme of devolution can survive the vagaries of political adventurism, whether the scheme will actually endure, and so on. If the final package is one that can provide the Tamil people a peace with honour, it is bound to have a healthy impact on all shades of Tamil political thinking."[35] Before the final package the Tamil community's basic needs of short and mid-term goals should be fulfilled. Vigorous linkage between Tamils in Sri Lanka and the Tamil Diaspora is crucial to conduct integrated macro brainstorming sessions of all different perspectives and diverse opinions, in order to achieve this goal.

Tamil National Politics in Sri Lanka

In the aftermath of the LTTE the Tamil political vision in Sri Lanka has lost its activism and identity. Tamil politics in Sri Lanka manifests itself at different levels. Actors such as the LTTE and their proxies, anti-LTTE groups, government loyalists and leftists all contain elements that are representative of these manifestations. A major Tamil political alliance known as the Tamil National Alliance – TNA became the LTTE's political proxy. The TNA is a coalition of four prominent political parties as follows: All Ceylon Tamil Congress (ACTC), Eelam People's Revolutionary Liberation Front (EPRLF), Tamil Eelam Liberation Organization (TELO) and the Tamil United Liberation Front (TULF). Conversely, there are also former militant movements which are partly used politically and but more seriously used as paramilitaries by the government as tools against the LTTE's political ideology and action. Each actor tried their utmost to make weak their adversary. Sadly, anti-LTTE politics weakened the Tamil cause. In addition, it justified government atrocities and human rights violations. On the other hand, the LTTE also failed to recognize genuine alternative voices. However, there are other political actors and voices such as politically leftist groups.

The TNA was formed just before the 2001 parliamentary election. It follows the Thimpu Principle. Furthermore its election manifesto accepted the LTTE as the sole representative of Tamils in Sri Lanka. Democratically elected, the victory of the TNA was ensured through an overwhelming Tamil vote. Senior member of the TNA, MP Suresh Premachandran said, 'The Tamil people in this country and the Tamil Diaspora all over the world wanted a peaceful settlement to this issue. They also wanted a settlement that could ensure equal rights with the Sinhalese in all spheres of life. They believe in shared rule over the Island as equal stake holders. They gave us a mandate to work for a sustainable peaceful solution.'[36] The TNA captured fifteen seats in 2001 and twenty-two in 2004 general elections.

Outside of Northeast, Ceylon Workers Congress (CWC), Up-Country People's Front (UPF) and Democratic People's Front (DPF) are prominent Tamil political parties. Apart from above-mentioned political parties, there are leftist's parties and very few alternative voices which support the Tamil cause. They are between the government and LTTE. However, they are powerless and not influential factors in Tamil or Sri Lankan politics.

Until the LTTE power existed, TNA, CWC, UPF and DPF had robust relationship with the LTTE. At least they had Memorandum of Understanding (MoU) with the LTTE. At some level and after some time CWC and then UPF links with the LTTE reduced. The DPF leader Hon. Mano Ganeshan continuously criticized the government for their human rights violations against Tamil people. Until the LTTE's military defeat, they showed their support to the LTTE and strongly opposed the government's mass atrocities and human rights violations.

The TNA did not participate in 2008 April eastern provincial council election, but when they contested without any big propaganda in the northern elections in 2009 August, even after the LTTE's military defeat the Tamil people again showed their support to the TNA. It was a big achievement for TNA and strong message to the Sinhala state and international community.

The destruction of the LTTE's establishment has started to weaken the TNA. The current ruling government plans to impose a law to get the names of "Tamil" and "Eelam" illegal to be used in the names of political parties. Since 1949, the word Tamil is in practice as a name for political parties.[37] Anti-LTTE groups who are with the government also started to feel as politically orphaned. Now it is very clear to everyone that the Southern Sinhala polity or Sinhala state used Tamils as a tool for their self-interest and their own purposes against the Tamil cause. This realization is not enough, now those Tamil political parties are re-thinking their activities and reacting real politically. It is essential that these parties join with the TNA and form a common political party whose goal must be to restore Tamil rights.

Meanwhile, it is noteworthy that not only Tamil politics weakened but the winners of the war were also divided into two. Those were President Rajapaksa and retired General Fonseka, who was the army commander who led the military operation to defeat the LTTE. Few months after the military victory over the LTTE, the war heroes got separated and formerly same regiment heroes confronted each other in the January 2010 Presidential election. It was mainly a contest between Rajapaksa and Fonseka. Actually Rajapaksa had not anticipated the rise of Fonseka as the rallying point for all his political foes, including Pro-LTTE Tamil National Alliance (TNA). The opposition parties, though they hold diametrically opposite views on virtually every contentious subject, saw the politically ambitious commander as their best bet to oust Rajapaksa. The hype and hyperbole created by the political foes of Rajapaksa had convinced everyone that the general-turned-politician would unseat the incumbent President.[38] However, President Rajapaksa trounced former Army Chief and the common opposition candidate, General Fonseka by a margin of nearly 18 percentage points. President Rajapaksa's main rival in the Presidential race, Fonseka faces a court-martial and poses no threat.[39]

Unfortunately the opposition, which had come together and put up Fonseka as its consensus candidate for the Presidential election, has no common approach to some of the key issues, including the resolution of the ethnic problem. The Pro-LTTE Tamil National Alliance (TNA) is in disarray and had not made clear the position it will take. Now the question raised towards all TNA members will be whether they will stand with their policy to work towards restoring Tamil rights or will they factionalize thus weakening the Tamil cause furthermore. However, an upper hand bargaining deal might strengthen the Tamil cause, but the issue is how it would be possible under present circumstances. One thing is clear that doing independent Tamil national politics in Sri Lanka is a big challenge. The TNA should re-strategies its activities.

Internally from now the TNA should empower itself. The Tamil Diaspora should back the TNA. The Tamil people in Sri Lanka have already shown their support to the TNA. The TNA should consider bringing all Tamil political parties together, including anti-LTTE groups, who are with the GoSL and other former militant movements, who stated that they are "mixed in mainstream democratic politics". The time has come to unite all Tamil actors in one front. Goal based unity, which is restoring Tamil rights should be the priority task and the goal. As TNA is devoid of majority seats in the parliament, it will have a difficult task in coordinating all these activities. While concentrating on long term political vision, they have to give a priority for the Tamil people's short-term and mid-term priorities, especially to fulfill their basic needs, step-by-step they have to re-develop the Tamil people's social, economical, cultural and political system and structures. Trauma healing, resettlement, rehabilitation, reconstruction, reconciliation and the development of infrastructure for the Tamil People which were destroyed by the horrible war, should be deeply considered in the future project. In addition, the TNA should form a committee to work with Sinhala and Muslim communities. They can start with like-minded people from both communities. More importantly and immediately, they have to construct a special team for public and media relations. This should be given priority for smart media strategies.[40]

Now that the LTTE is not a part of Sri Lanka's political equation, what will happen in the political process? Three broad issues are at the centre of Sri Lanka's post-civil war political agenda. They can be presented as three 'D's- democratization, demilitarization and devolution. Resettlement of large numbers of internally displaced Tamil citizens, restoration of their normal life and rebuilding of the economic and social infrastructure in the war-ravaged Northern Province are immediate priorities too. The broad and immediate issues are interrelated. All these constitute a massive challenge to the government in the form of managing transition from civil war to civil peace, peacefully and democratically. Winning the war and winning the peace are equally formidable challenges. The first will not automatically lead to the second.

Meanwhile, the LTTE's role in Sri Lanka's politics is now over, although its supporters abroad do not seem to be ready to acknowledge this reality. The Sri Lankan state, particularly its defense establishment, is not likely to allow the LTTE to re-emerge even as a parliamentary political entity. The pro-LTTE Diaspora is trying to mobilize its supporters and sympathizers abroad to keep the flag flying, but their impact on the political process within Sri Lanka appears limited. Sri Lanka's Tamil politics will in the short-run be dominated by anti-LTTE Tamil groups who have been partners with the state in the counter-insurgency war against the LTTE. It will take some time before a new moderate Tamil party can emerge to champion minority rights in Sri Lanka within a democratic framework.

The question of a political solution to the ethnic conflict encapsulates the larger framework within which the nature of post-civil war ethnic relations in Sri Lanka will continue to be defined. Both India and the western powers appear to have thought that once the intransigent LTTE was removed from Sri Lanka's political equation, a political compromise with non-LTTE Tamil parties would be immediately forthcoming. But that does not seem to be happening in Sri Lanka. During the war, President Rajapaksa assured the international actors that he would implement a political solution once the war was over. That promise now appears to be easier made than put into practice for there are internal constraints limiting the political capacity of the Rajapaksa administration to move in the direction of a political solution acceptable to the Tamil and Muslim minorities.

The regime is a coalition of hardline Sinhalese nationalists who constitute the core of a broader coalition which President Rajapaksa put together earlier to back his war effort. Included in that coalition were the military, the bureaucracy, the media, nationalist intelligentsia, political elites of the anti-LTTE Tamils as well as non-Tamil minorities, Sri Lankan diaspora and the Buddhist and Catholic religious establishments. This is a broad and powerful war coalition. One key reality in the post-civil war Sri Lanka, however, is that the same coalition that was formed to fight the LTTE militarily cannot be the vehicle for a fair and just political solution that can satisfy at least some of the key Tamil political demands. President Rajapaksa's hesitation to implement any devolution framework is largely rooted in this complex problem. Thus either President Rajapaksa has to forge a new post-war coalition of moderate political and ideological forces, or continue to defer a political solution to the ethnic problem.

Post-civil war issues of democracy in Sri Lanka are closely linked to an agenda of demilitarization. During the war, Sri Lanka saw the emergence of a national security regime in which the defence establishment played a pivotal role. Under the national security regime, both cabinet ministers and parliament became secondary to the defence establishment. Prevention of terrorism law and the emergency legislation provided the legal framework for the national security regime. During the intense period of the war, media freedom got a severe beating, both literally and metaphorically. Abductions and disappearances of journalists and vocal critics of the regime were the order of the day. The regime had no hesitation to justify aggressively and assertively, at home as well as at international fora, the grave human rights violations and humanitarian problems, claiming that the war against terrorism and state sovereignty takes precedence over other considerations.

Once the war ended, there has been a relaxation of the atmosphere of fear, intimidation and reprisals that characterized political life before May 2009. However, demilitarization is not a part of the immediate agenda of either the ruling party or the opposition. In an unusual twist of fate, the opposition's candidate for the January 2010 presidential election was the former commander of the Sri Lankan Army, who actually led the counter-insurgency war for the past three years. Sri Lanka's main political actors appear to take militarization as the normal state of affairs. In a way, Sri Lanka has entered a specific phase of post-democracy. That is a key outcome of the protracted civil war.[41]

In a political cost-benefit analysis of Sri Lanka's ethnic civil war, the ultimate losers are the Sri Lankan Tamils. After nearly thirty years of armed struggle for what was understood as "National self-determination", all they have got is the status of IDPs (internally displaced/detained persons) inside open prison camps surrounded by barbed wire. The outcome of the war has thus reaffirmed the structures of ethnic hierarchy in Sri Lanka. It will require a massive effort to reintroduce to the political debate and culture the values of inter-ethnic equality, justice and trust. During the civil war, the relationship between Sri Lanka's ethnic minorities and the state has gone through an unusual transformation. Because of the destructive consequences of LTTE's military confrontation with the state, many Tamil and Muslim political leaders have come to accept the politics of coalition collaboration with the Sinhalese political leadership as the most prudent option available to them. They have also come to terms with the hegemony of hardline Sinhalese nationalism and its continuing influence on public policy, regime agendas and state-society relations. They are acutely aware of the fact that extreme polarization of politics along Sinhalese and Tamils nationalist projects continues to prevent any significant political reform in Sri Lanka.[42]

Thus, the quest for Tamils' rights on the basis of equality and regional autonomy has now been relegated to a secondary status in the politics of non-LTTE Tamil parties, and the political parties of plantation Tamil and Muslim communities. Their emphasis is now on power-sharing at the central government in the form of obtaining lucrative cabinet positions for party leaders and regional economic development.

The end of the violent civil war and the dramatic demise of the LTTE has created a significant political disequilibrium in Sri Lanka. The signs of the war-coalition disintegrating from within are an indication of how the establishment of a new post-civil war political equilibrium has come to the centre of Sri Lanka's political agenda. The January 2010 presidential election and April 2010 parliamentary elections have provided opportunities for the political actors to forge new alliance and redefine the power bloc to manage the post-civil war politics, however, it is still in the process of being formed. One has to suspend an assessment of the possible paths of Sri Lanka's future politics until the shape of the new configuration of political forces that have emerged after April 2010 Parliamentary election becomes clearer.

To conclude the key element that defined the Vadamarachchi campaign of 1987 from the humanitarian campaign of 2009 is the fact that President Rajapaksa, unlike President Jayawardene, did not succumb to international threats and order a halt to the military operations when Mr. Prabhakaran was cornered. Mr. Mahinda Rajapaksa did not buckle under international pressure, applied at critical stages of the campaign using a variety of tactics including appeals, protests, dignitary visits, and threats of international judicial action. The commanders were able to use their creativity and strategic skills to prosecute the humanitarian campaign effectively and brilliantly as political support and decision-making continued to be predictable till the very end of the humanitarian campaign.

The belief that any political solution offered to the North and East, while LTTE was militarily strong, would eventually lead to the break-up of the country, has given way to a perception, (now that the LTTE has been comprehensively beaten), that a reasonable political solution may be offered to address the national problem. The vast majority of the Sinhala people are also beginning to believe that such an approach would provide opportunities for people in the North and East, who suffered most from LTTE terrorism, to live in dignity and honour while attaining a higher standard of living. There are also other reasons for optimism. Moderate Tamil parties and their leaders as well as the transformed LTTE leaders have demonstrated their resolve to work collaboratively within the available political structure, in a constructive manner, to find solutions to problems of the Tamil people. These processes are encouraging the Sinhala majority to begin to reconcile with the people in the North and East.

The political and psychological space that is being created now in the South in support of the offer of a political solution to address the national problem (primarily due to the defeat of the LTTE and all of the above positive causes) is growing and need to be further promoted. All responsible political leaders on both sides of the divide having experienced the new perception that is evolving in the majority Sinhala population, need to act responsibly so as to strengthen the sentiment that a political solution is beneficial to all Sri Lankans, and the Tamil people in the North and East. The Tamil diaspora in industrialized countries could also invest in the North and East to help the people who have suffered for thirty odd years to attain normality and rebuild their lives. All parties should be willing to forsake the confrontational politics that held sway for thirty years or so. As described earlier, there are examples that can be emulated to chart a new collaborative model for the development of Sri Lanka.

However, two important branches of Tamil opinion-leadership, namely the diaspora, and the Tamil National Alliance seem to be unable to grasp and capitalize on the positive sentiments that is developing in the South for promoting the normalization of lives of the people in the North and East, and catalyze a reasonable political solution to the national problem. Although weakened, the diaspora still possess enough finances and international connections to either attempt to promote national reconciliation, a reasonable political solution to the national problem, and thus help normalize the lives of people in the North and East or attempt to revive the unfruitful and destructive part of separatism. It is time for the new diaspora leadership to break out of the old conundrum of confrontation and separatism and embrace a new model of cooperation where a political solution to the national problem could be evolved on the basis of one country, one nation where equal opportunities, protection of rights, non-discrimination, and enhanced participation in development and governance, for all people living in Sri Lanka irrespective of ethnicity would be ensured, while nurturing the cultural identities of all constituent ethnic groups. However, it is unfortunate that the diaspora has so far opted to continue with the same confrontational model, which has not brought the Tamil people living in Sri Lanka any benefits.

So it is clear that the diaspora is refusing to learn lessons from the past. It is not late even now for the diaspora members to impress upon their leadership the need to learn from past mistakes and adopt a conciliatory stance which would really help people in the North and East to begin to normalize their lives peacefully and in dignity.

TNA's recent history shows that it has verily been the political face of Tamil separatism. In the 2004 parliamentary elections, TNA made a declaration to the effect that LTTE is the sole representative of the Tamil people, thus exposing TNA's "peculiar brand of democracy" and its blind acceptance of LTTE. Throughout the humanitarian operation, TNA sitting in parliament, continually voted against the extension of the Emergency, which was vital to curb LTTE's terrorist activities. TNA provided moral and propaganda support to the Tamil diaspora to lobby western governments to pressure Sri Lankan government to suspend the humanitarian operation designed to release thousands of Tamil citizens oppressed by the LTTE, and to defeat LTTE militarily. A substantial part of the TNA has yet to seek out lessons from past experiences. A list of points as issues that are of importance to the group, can be described as contentious.

Some of the key points are self-governance, re-merging of the North and East, downgrading of national intelligence apparatus; withdrawing all high-security zones in the peninsula; reducing security forces in the north east; and releasing all LTTE suspects in custody including hard-core cadres (without being either rehabilitated or indicted for crimes committed). The re-floating of these issues after the defeat of LTTE terrorists would create confusion among all Sri Lankan citizens. This may also contract the political and psychological space that has been expanding in favour of an offer of a reasonable political solution to the national problem in the

South, due to suspicion that separatist sentiments could again be stirred up especially in the North and East and generally in the whole country. If this happens, this is a real dis-service perpetrated on the people in the North and East who suffered for thirty long years due to terrorism and extremist political ideologies espoused by some politicians in the North and the East.

Therefore it is the right and duty of all Sri Lankans, to nip in the bud, all attempts to revive separatism and communalism through political pathways during this critical time. In this task, let the Tamils and Sinhalese have the wisdom to analyse and decide on issues, without being influenced by parochial considerations of ethnicity and political party affiliations.

References

1. Jonathan Spencer, *Sri Lanka: History and the Roots of Conflict*, Routledge, New York, 1990. pp. 132-146.
2. Ibid.
3. Kenneth Bush (1990), op. cit., pp. 44-45.
4. R. Swaminathan, "Emerging Trends in Sri Lanka – An Indian Perspective", *Sri Lanka Guardian*, 28 August 2009.
5. On the political Vicissitudes of Sri Lanka since December 2001, see G.H. Peiris, Twilight of the Gigers (2009) *Sunday Times*, Colombo.
6. Robert N. Kearney, "Ethnic Conflict and the Tamil Separatist Movement", *Asian Survey*, 25, No. 9, (1985), p. 912.
7. Robert Rotbery (ed.): *Creating Peace in Sri Lanka: Civil War and Reconciliation*, Brookings, Washington DC, 1999. pp. 38-42.
8. Ibid.
9. Ibid.
10. Rilkoff, Nik, *Critical Analysis: Fears, Expectations, and Issues relating to the Sri Lankan Peace Process 2002*, Impact, New Delhi, 2002. p. 26.
11. Ibid.
12. Ibid.
13. Rupesinghe, Kumar (Eds.), *Negotiating peace in Sri Lanka: Efforts, failures & lessons*, International Alert of London, UK, 1998. p. 112.

14. Liyanage, Sumanasiri, Sahadevan, P., Kinra, Anisha (Eds.) Intra-State Conflicts and Inter-State Relations – Perspectives on India–Sri Lanka Relations, (South Asia Peace Institution, Colombo, 2009), p. 112.
15. Ibid.
16. Ibid.
17. Victory (http://w.w.w.sibc.ik/henews.asp.
18. See Luther Uthayakumaran's article published in Lines magazine "Sri Lanka: after War, Justice" http./linesmagazine.org/11 May 2009.
19. Sergii De Silva Ranasinghe "The End of Sri Lanka's Insurgency: Implications" Strategic Analysis Paper, 19 January 2010.
20. Ibid.
21. Quoted in Ibid.
22. R. Hariharan "Sri Lanka: need to restore trust', *The Hindu*, 18 May 2010, p. 10.
23. "Putting the raj in Rajapaksa" *The Economist*, in the *Indian Express*, New Delhi, p. 16.
24. Apratim Mukarji, "Sri Lanka at Peace, But...." *Maistream*, Vol. XLVIII, No.31, New Delhi, July 24, 2010, pp. 5-6.
25. T.J.S. George, "Sri Lankan Model is No Model", *Mainstream*, Vol. XLVIII, No. 29, New Delhi, July 10, 2010, p. 39.
26. Luther Uthayakumaran (2009), op. cit.
27. Sergii De Sliva (2010), op. cit.
28. Human Rights watch report, entitled "Final War: LTTE intimidation and Extortion in the Tamil Diaspora" (2006).
29. Mahen Tampae, From Spices to Suicide Bombers and Beyond–A Study of Power, Politics and Terrorism in Sri Lanka (Athena Press, London, 2006), p. 227.
30. Liyanage (2009), pp. 113-115.
31. Papers for the Political Studies Association (UK 50th Conference, London, 10-13 April 2000).
32. Mahen Tampae (2006).
33. Rilkoff, Nik (2002), pp. 32-39.
34. Chelvadurai Manoharan in Rupesinghe (ed), Negotiating Peace... (1998), op. cit., pp. 253-270.
35. Rupesinghe Kumar (1998), op. cit., p. 412.
36. S. I. Keethaponecalan, Jayawardana Rane; Sri Lanka: Perspectives on the Ceasefire Agreement of 2002, (South Asia Peace Institute, 2009), p. 135.
37. See Sergie De Silva (2010), for further details.

38. Editorial, *The Hindu*, January 28, 2010
39. Ibid.
40. Sergie De Silva (2010).
41. Ibid.
42. Rohan Gunaratna "Sri Lanka's Challenge: Winning the Peace" (5 May 2010), Global Geoploitics Net Sites.

CHAPTER 8

Conclusion

It is the lack of an unbiased and balanced approach to the ethnic problem in that past that has created racists and chauvinists on both side of the divide and brought Sri Lanka to the present deplorable state. This came about through a misguided interpretation of the available historic data. It should be noted that the study of history must be for history and knowledge sake. History should never be didactic, nor should it be falsified and made into tools of politics. Nothing will be gained politically by arguing whether the chick or the egg came first. It will also not be practical or justifiable to settle one's problems on the basis of "who came first". It will be best if problems are settled on the basis of natural selections and from definitely known traceable periods and facts.

Primarily it needs to be accepted that no in-depth-comparative and analytical study of Sri Lankan history has yet been undertaken by anyone. Such a study will reveal the right and whole history and also that if at all there was an original people, all traces of such people had vanished at least about two thousand five hundred years ago as they were absorbed by the Tamils and Sinhalese and sections of whom were reabsorbed by the two main streams, a process that is going on even today. One will also find that the history of both the Tamils and Sinhalese are thoroughly mixed up and intertwined. Hence it is felt that if the right and whole history of Sri Lanka is to be known, one must adopt a very strictly unbiased and balanced approach, especially in today's atmosphere, and look for external evidence also especially when the Tamils of both India and Sri Lanka had not left much permanent records of their activities. As against this it should also be noted that the Pali chronicles which deal with Sri Lanka conceal, intentionally or unintentionally — as much as they reveal — a fact accepted by all right thinking historians.

While it is a fact that the majority of the people of Sri Lanka today are Sinhalese, yet it has to be accepted that a very large number of them are descendants of South Indian Tamils who had come to the Island throughout the ages as peaceful migrants or South Indian warriors of Sinhalese pretenders to the islands throne or as warriors of Pandyan and Chola invaders who settled here and were Sinhalised during course of time. This never ending process of amalgamation which is going on even today should have originated from the earliest time, well before the coming of Vijaya. This is the only way to explain the presence of Tamil or Tamil derived words even in the Pali chronicles. Prof. K. M de Silva in his book *History of Sri Lanka* says that the island was first populated by Aryans from the North West and North East of India. Yet he also readily admits that 'we have at present no archaeological evidence with regard to the early Indo-Aryan settlers. No sites have yet yielded data which could help us identify some of the influences which had played upon the island in the period from 650 B.C. In particular we have no archaeological finds that could be traced back to either the West or East coasts of North India'.

In fact, all that we have are finds that are traceable to a civilization congruous with that of South India. The North Indian origin of the Sinhalese is based on myths, legends and traditions that crept in recently, yet the Sinhalese call themselves Aryans. The Sinhalese language, because it contains a large percentage of Pali and Sanskrit derived words introduced through the influence of Pali speaking missionaries and Buddhist chronicles, is claimed to have originated from Pali and Sanskrit, without considering the fact that a very large percentage, if not a majority of words are Tamil derived. Further Prof. K.M. de Silva also in his *History of Sri Lanka* accepted that there was considerable Tamil influence in the vocabulary, idioms and grammatical structure of the Sinhalese language. Prof. G.C. Mendis in his book *Our Heritage* has said that if we shared the Sinhalese language of all the borrowed words we would be left with the core language, and that the closeness of this core language to a North Indian language would enable us to trace the area from which the language and immigrants came and that our knowledge of languages prevented us from coming to any conclusions. The position remains the same today too. From this statement it is obvious that no one had considered the closeness of this core language to a South Indian Dravidian language.

So far as the questions of Mahavamsa is concerned, the term Sinhala is found in the Mahavamsa only in its first few opening chapters, where it is said that the followers of Vijaya were called Sinhala because his father killed his father – a lion – and hence was called Sinhalese but it does not mention the terms Sinhala or its derivations any further. In fact, though the Mahavamsa says that when Mahinda introduced Buddhism in circa 250 B.C. he preached in the language of the Island. It does not say whether the language was Sinhala or Tamil. A liberal use of the term Sinhala is found only in the Kulavamsa which is said to have been composed in the 12th C.A.D. Even the term Sinhaladvipa is found only in the Kulavamsa. We also find that both in the Mahavamsa and Kulvamsa, it is the term Lanka which is almost always used to denote this island. There are four or five occasions where the term Tambapanni – another pre-Vijayan term and a Pali corruption of the Tamil term Tamraparni – is also used. Tamraparni is the name of a region and a river in South India almost opposite Tambapanni of Sri Lanka, a village about 20 miles north of Puttalam. Due to the fact that Pali of that time did not have alphabets like "r", "v" etc. These alphabets in the term Tamraparni were replaced by consonants "b" and "n" respectively and thus the corruption Tambapanni. Thus it becomes obvious that the term Sinhala and its derivatives gained currency only after the 5th / 6th C.A.D. and before the 12th C.A.D. It may also be noted that the excavations at Pomparipu near Tambapanni show some resemblance of a South Indian Megalithic culture.

If we gaze our attention on South Indian literature we find references to the island even in the 11th/12th C.A.D. South Indian literature – a region with which the island has had the closest and most frequent contacts, whether on war or peace, which show that the island had been referred to as Eelam or Lanka, though there are references to "Sinhalese Kings". Yet in a Telugu copper plate of the 5th C.A.D. the term Sinhaladvipa had been used. The underdeveloped phraseology of the Sinhala language used in the cave inscriptions of the 3rd C.B.C. show the infantile stage of the Sinhala language of the period. This was at a time when the Tamil language was developed. The Sinhala language should have evolved through the amalgamation of the original pre-Vijayan language of the Island which is believed by some was Elu, with Tamil and the language of a few Kings – which is once again a Sanskritised Dravidian language – and later with a voluminous vocabulary of Pali – a Sanskritised Prakrit and Sanskrit words through the influence of Buddhist chronicles and missionaries. Indications of a well developed Sinhala language are found only after the poems of the 4th / 6th C.A.D. Regarding the term Sinhala and its derivatives, it will be far more convincing if we consider that the term Sinhala was derived from Eelam and not the other way round as some Sinhalese literati would like to have. Sri Lanka is derived from Lanka, the earliest name of the Island and a pre-Vijaya term. However, unfortunately records of early travellers do not shed much light on this subject.

Thus from above analysis it is crystal clear that the Sinhalese race and language could have evolved by circa 3rd C.B.C. through the interaction of Tamil, Pali and Sanskrit – a process that is going on even today. The Tamil race and language with sea-going capability, was certainly in existence before at least 1,000 B.C., and it is logical to conjecture that the Tamils would have settled in the Island ages before Vijaya and the Sinhalese appeared in the Island. Naturally therefore, nothing will be gained by brining history into politics and politics into history.

It was in 1815 with the conquest of the Kandyan kingdom by the British, the painful history of the Tamil plantation workers begins. It was during that time the British colonialists decided to introduce the plantation economy in the Island. Coffee plantations were set up in the early 1820s, a crop which flourished in high altitudes. Speculators and entrepreneurs from England rushed to the newly conquered mountain areas and expropriated vast tracts of land, by deceit, from the Kandyan peasantry. The Kandyan peasants refused to abandon their traditional subsistence holding to become wage earners on these new capitalist estates. The pressure exerted by the colonial state to draw the labour power from the indigenous Sinhalese peasantry did not work. The British colonial masters were thus compelled to draw on their limitless reserves of labour from India. A massive army of cheap labourers were conscripted from southern India who, partly by their own poverty and partly by coercion, moved into this Promised Land to be condemned to an appalling form of slave labour. A notorious system of labour contract was established which allowed hundreds of thousands of Tamil labourers to migrate to the plantation estates. Between the 1840s and 1850s a million people were imported. The original workers were recruited from Tamil Nadu districts of Tirunelveli, Madurai and Tanjore and were from the poor, oppressed castes. This army of recruited workers was forced to walk hundreds of miles from their villages to Rameshwaram and again from Mannar through impenetrable jungles to the central hill-lands of Ceylon. Thousands of this immigerated mass perished on their long hazardous journey, a journey chartered with disease, death and despair. Those who survived the journey were weak and exhausted and thousands of them died in the nightmarish, unhealthy conditions of the early plantations.

The coffee plantation economy collapsed in the 1870s when a leaf disease ravaged the plantations. But the economic system survived intact with the introduction of a successor crop, tea. Tea was introduced in the 1880s on a wide scale. The tea plantation economy expanded with British entrepreneurial investment, export markets and consolidated companies transforming the structure of production and effectively changing the economic foundation of the old feudal society creating a basis for the development of the capitalist economic system. Though the plantation economy effectively changed the process of production, the Tamil labourers – men, women and children – were permanently condemned to slave under the white masters and the indigenous capitalists. The British planters who brought the Indian Tamil labourers into Sri Lanka deliberately segregated them inside the plantation. Such a notorious policy of segregation condemned the Tamils permanently to these miserable ghettos, isolated them from the rest of the population and prevented them from having their own land, building their own houses and leading a free social existence. British colonial rule built up the Tamil plantation community within the heartland of the Kandyan Sinhalese and manipulated the Tamil-Sinhala antagonism to divide and rule. Introduced to conditions of slavery by colonialism, the Tamil workers toiled in utter misery. Their sweat and blood sustained the worst form of exploitative economy that fed the English masters with the surplus value and enriched the Sinhala land owning classes.

The impact of British colonial domination on the indigenous Tamil people of the northern and eastern provinces had far-reaching effects. On the political level, British colonial rule imposed a unified administration with centralized institutions, establishing a singular state structure. This forceful annexation and amalgamation of two separate kingdoms, of two nations of people, disregarding their past, historical existence, their socio-cultural distinctions and their ethnic differences are the root causes of the Tamil-Sinhala racial antagonism.

The first batch of emigrants from India to Sri Lanka (then Ceylon) came in 1837. This was followed by successive batches over the next nearly 100 years, until 1939, when the Government of India banned the movement of unskilled labour to Ceylon. In the 1920s, Franchise Rights were based on a residence of six months and certain property qualifications. Due mainly to property qualifications, the total number of registered voters in Sri Lanka in 1924 "was 204,997 or four per cent of the total population of five million" (Donoughmore Commission Report, 1928). However, at the time of emigration, until 1947, there was no dispute as to the status of persons of Indian origin, because, at that time India and Ceylon were parts of the British Empire, and, consequently, persons born and living in the territory of India and Ceylon had identical status, namely, British subjects. It was under these circumstances that the Donoughmore Commission in its report of 1928 stated that 'we have decided to recommend the adoption of manhood suffrage. On this basis according to the figures supplied to us, the possible voting strength of the electorate will be increased to 1,200,000. We desire, however, to make two reservations. In the first place we consider it very desirable that a qualification of five years residence in the Island (allowing the temporary absence not exceeding eight months in all during the five years period) should be introduced in order that the privilege of voting should be confined to those who have an abiding interest in the country or who may be regarded as permanently settled in the Island .... this condition will be of particular importance in its application to the Indian immigrant population. Secondly, we consider that the registration of voters should not be compulsory or automatic but should be restricted to those who apply for it....'

The Political leadership in Sri Lanka was very apprehensive about giving a large numbers of Indians voting rights as recommended by the Donoughmore Commission in 1928. From their point of view it would have 'meant: (a) a dilution of the electoral strength of the Kandyan Sinhalese in most of the constituencies in the Kandyan areas; (b) the possibility of the Indian Tamils being returned as representatives of Kandyan Sinhalese constituencies in the event of the splitting of Kandyan Sinhalese vote between rival candidates; (c) the likelihood ... of British planters, and/or Indian estate Kanganies (overseers) herding the Indian vote in favour of the candidate of their choice.' These misgivings were conveyed to Governor Sir Herbert Stanley, and modifications were accordingly made to the Donoughmore Commission recommendations by the Colonial Secretary. He incorporated them in the Order in Council 1931. As a result of the order in Council, 'the number of Indians registered as electors in that year (1931) was about 100,000, as compared with 12,438 registered in the Indian electorate under the old Constitution – an increase of over 70 per cent...in 1936 the figure was estimated at 145,000 and by 1938, out of a total population of 670,000 Indian estate workers and their dependents, more than 170,000 had been registered as electors, in 1939 this figure exceeded 225,000.' In 1940, the procedure on revision of the registers was altered in regard to the qualification of domicile of choice and instruction given that ... 'no one was to be registered who was not orally examined ... From 1940 onwards the figures of registration of these Indians declined and the number in 1943 amounted to about 168,000... in spite of the tightening up procedure, substantial numbers... have acquired the franchise in virtue of domicile.'

Economic pressures brought on by the depression of the 1930s exacerbated the issues relating to the presence of the Indian Tamils in Sri Lanka. Due to the gravity of the circumstances, the leadership in Sri Lanka wanted emigration restricted, to the extent of even replacing Indian labour with local labour. The colonial government on the other hand, wanted to retain them. These circumstances resulted in two conferences between Sri Lanka and India. The Indo-Ceylon Relations Exploratory Conference of November 1940 was inconclusive. This was followed by the Indo-Ceylon Relations Conference of September 1941 at which ... the two delegations reached agreement on all points, inter alia, the Immigration Bill and the question of franchise. A Joint Report was signed on 21 September 1941. The India/Ceylon Joint Report in regard to Franchise stated: 'It was agreed that those Indians who could not claim domicile of origin or of choice, or a literacy and property qualification could vote only if they possessed certificates of permanent settlement which would be granted on the following conditions.' In respect of residence the recommendation was seven years for married and 10 years for unmarried period of residence. However, although it was a Joint Report the Central Legislative Assembly of India did not ratify the Report, and in January 1943, repudiated it altogether.

The Sri Lankan attitude to the issue was greatly influenced by two factors. Firstly, the economic depression of the 1930s caused severe unemployment, and Indian labour was seen as competitors who deprived the indigenous labour of gainful employment. Secondly, the transient nature of the Indian labour between India and Sri Lanka on the question of domicile became a critical issue in order to assure an "abiding interest" in the country and a desire to settle "permanently". The Donoughmore Commission, the Soulbury Commission and even the Privy Council, all recognized that commitment to domicile was directly relevant to issues of Citizenship and Franchise.

The Soulbury Commission, appointed in 1944, was aware of the '....anxieties arising out of the likelihood of large-scale enfranchisement of the Indian immigrants, and despite strong representations from the Ceylon Tamil and Indian Tamil organizations, decided that the Indian Question was an internal matter to be disposed of by the future legislature. The Commission, therefore, left the existing basis of franchise in Sri Lanka undisturbed'. The Soulbury Commission Report also stated that '...if the qualifications of these Indian immigrants for the franchise had depended solely on the condition of five years residence in the Island, as recommended by the Donoughmore Commission, the constitution of 1931 would not have been accepted by the Legislative Council.' Sri Lanka became independent in 1948 and the first Prime Minister, D. S. Senanayake of the conservative United National Party reacting to the possibilities of losing power to leftist political parties, commenced the task of weakening the leftist parties and their associate organizations. Indian Tamil labour had overwhelmingly supported these organizations. According to opposition parties he was also influenced by segments of the majority Sinhalese population who felt their voting strength was diluted due to Indian Tamils. He introduced the Ceylon Citizenship Act of 1948, the Indian-Pakistani Citizenship Act of 1949 and amended the parliamentary elections act and disfranchised the Indian Tamils along with many persons of Indian and Pakistani ancestry. As they had no means of electing any one to the Parliament they ceased to be the concern of parliament politicians. The plantation workers were thus forgotten from 1948-1964. They were unable to profit any progressive legislation.

The Srimavo-Shastri pact of 1964 and Indira-Srimavo supplementary agreement of 1974 paved the way for the repatriation of 600,000 persons of Indian origin to India. Another 375,000 persons were to be accepted as citizens of Sri Lanka, which made them enter the polity. These repatriation agreements were the harbingers of the destruction of this community, which had evolved into a composite group with a distinct culture of its own. In the fifties and sixties this community was clamoring for education and recognition of its distinctive culture. This brought in the emergence of a community consciousness and the artesian of a distinct community. An educated middle class comprising of teachers, trade unionists and other professionals began to make its appearance. There was a vigorous campaign for social ameliorations and increased educational facilities. There was a growing spirit of resistance. People destroyed Indian passports and refused to go to India. Repatriation was resisted. The J.R. Jayawardene government that came to power in 1977 rectified the existing shortcomings of the Indian Citizenship Act and granted citizenship to all Indian Estate workers.

Indian Tamils who came to this country beginning in 1830 were brought by the British colonialists to work in plantations that earned the wealth of this country. These people have contributed so much to this country but were denied all their rights and had to struggle for 55 years to achieve the rights they had prior to 1948. This is symbolic of the ethnic divide in this country.

The legislative council of 1920 had the Indian representation with Mr. Natesa Iyer being nominated. In 1924 the legislative council provided for two members to be nominated from the Indian community. Franchise was restricted to the elite and the total electoral college was 205,000 and the Indian Tamils were 12,900. Again Natesa Iyer and I.X. Pereira entered the council. In 1931 when universal adult franchise was introduced to Sri Lanka under the Donoughmore Constitution they were treated equal to all other residents and granted franchise. Mr. S. P. Vythilingam and Mr. Peri Sundaram were elected.

In this period the role of the Indians in the labour market in Sri Lanka was under challenge. The need of the Indian origin people to unite for their political survival was noticed. Though discussions took place unity was not achieved. Two important events that took place in 1939 jolted the Indian Tamils to realise that the time had come to unite. A resolution was moved by A.E. Gunasinha (a Sinhala nationalist labour leader) in the State Council calling for the deportation of 15,000 Indians. A second resolution moved by D.S. Senanayake (independent Ceylon's first Prime Minister) to deport all Indians appointed to government service after 1934 and to discontinue the service of all those with less than ten years experience. This prompted Mahatma Gandhi to send Jawaharlal Nehru as a special emissary to sort out issues. It was in 1939 with the arrival of Jawaharlal Nehru on the advice of Mahatma Gandhi that concrete steps were taken to unite all the groups. While speaking to the government Jawaharlal Nehru separately urged the Indian origin leaders to come together under one banner and thus emerged the Ceylon Indian Congress.

The years following the inauguration of the Ceylon Indian Congress were the most challenging with calls for deportation, denial of cost of living allowances and other difficulties initiated by the State Council. The 1947 election brought great political strength to the Indian Tamils community with the election of seven out of the 95 members of Parliament. The Ceylon Indian Congress led by Savumiamoorthy Thondaman sat in the opposition. This made Prime Minister D. S. Senanayake to sense the emergence of a leftist government in the future. The Ceylon Citizenship Act was a result of this fear. The Ceylon Citizenship Act, though providing the qualifications to be a citizen, was designed to disqualify persons of Indian origin. The provision said that 'only a person born in the Ceylon prior to the date of the Act coming into force, of a father born in Ceylon could be recognized as a citizen.' This decitizenized all persons of Indian origin since proof of birth of two generations was necessary. This was following by discussions that led to the India and Pakistani (Residents) Citizenship Bill. It laid down qualifications for citizenship as registered citizens (sic). The qualifications inherent in the bill were designed to deny citizenship. The procedures too were a hindrance. The Ceylon Indian Congress opposed the bill and urged that none should apply under the Act.

The 1956 elections too proved negative to the Indian origin people since they had no strength to field candidates. In 1960 the government of Mrs. Bandaranaike created a nominated representation for the people of Indian origin and appointed Savumiamoorthy Thondaman to parliament. Similarly, in 1965 the UNP government too nominated Savumiamoorthy Thondaman to parliament to return for his support to defeat the government of Mrs. Bandaranaike in 1964. In 1964 Mrs. Bandaranaike moved to solve the citizenship problem in keeping with the Sinhala thinking that persons of Indian origin should return to India. India, then led by Lal Bahadur Shastri agreed to this move by agreeing to accept 525,000 back to India. Sri Lanka had agreed to grant citizenship to 300,000 persons leaving the future of 150,000 people to be settled latter. This whole episode was like a barter trade agreement, throwing people from one country to another without consideration of their feelings. The Ceylon Workers' Congress was angered by this incident and this soured the relationship with the SLFP.

The process of granting citizenship under this agreement was slow due to the link with repatriation of those who applied for Indian citizenship. In 1977, Savumiamoorthy Thondaman, contested the Nuwara Ellya – Maskellya multi member seat and was elected to parliament as the third member. After thirty years since 1947 a member was elected to parliament by the people of Indian origin. During the period 1978 to 1988, he (Thondaman) made several representations for the expeditious grant of citizenship under the two Indo Ceylon Agreements. He also urged that persons who were left out of the two agreements be granted Sri Lankan citizenship. Only 506,000 persons applied for Indian citizenship out of the 600,000 envisaged under the agreements.

In 1986 the CWC conducted a Satyagraha campaign. A special Provision Bill was passed to de-link the grant of citizenship to repatriation and to expedite the grant of citizenship. However, citizenship was still a problem for the people of Indian origin. In 1988 prior to the presidential election Minister Savumiamoorthy Thondaman moved to achieve his goal of citizenship for all those who opted to become citizens of Sri Lanka under the Indo-Ceylon Agreements. Prime Minister R. Premadasa who was the presidential candidate moved swiftly, supporting Thondaman and persuaded the government to agree to the granting of citizenship to all those except the 506,000 persons who had applied to be repatriated to India.

Grant of Citizenship to Stateless Persons (Special Provisions) Act. No. 39 of 1988 was thus presented to parliament by Premadasa and passed. This was opposed by the SLFP who voted against it. The people of Indian origin who were until then deprived of the rights flowing from citizenship were overwhelmed by their achieving their long dreamed goal. They had been denied the basic rights such as right to own property, right to state employment, right to hold a national identity card, right to obtain a passport and travel abroad and the right to vote. With the grant of citizenship they changed their attitude towards living in this country. The struggle of the people of Indian origin did not end with achieving citizenship. They had to struggle further to obtain the rights of citizenship envisaged and this struggle goes on but even today Tamils still have to go a long way to achieve equal status in this country.

Here, it needs reiteration that while the provincial council negotiations were ongoing, the government was fighting the LTTE. The LTTE had lost much of its support in Tamil Nadu and had concentrated its activities in Jaffna, becoming the de facto government of the Northern Province. The government blockaded the Northern Province and fought the Tigers in the East where they were less strong. On February 7, 1987, the government launched a fullscale offensive in Jaffna, but three months of fighting brought few results. One might well wonder why the government was so unsuccessful in fighting the LTTE in the late 1980s, but yet was able to destroy it in 2006-09. It must be remembered that at that time the Sri Lankan army was a poorly trained, undermanned force. One contemporary estimate suggested that the combined forces of the five largest militant groups were twice the size of the Sri Lankan army. Jayawardene faced heavy pressure from the Sinhala public to militarily annihilate the LTTE, and from Rajiv Gandhi to resume negotiations. Day by day, violence against civilians on both sides were increasing. India was air-dropping supplies to the Tamils over Jaffna. Finally, over opposition from Premadasa and Athulathmudali, Jayawardene signed a peace accord with the LTTE, India sent in 6,000 soldiers, the Indian Peace Keeping Force (IPKF) to disarm the militants and enforce the accord. The IPKF was an unqualified disaster. Despite a strength of 72,000 troops at its peak, the force was unable to defeat or even substantially damage the LTTE. Ordered not to kill civilians and to limit their own casualties, they struggled to tackle a terrorist group that committed mass suicides when captured and hid behind women and children. Worst of all, the IPKF was hampered by the distrust and hostility of Prime Minister Premadasa and the Sinhala public. India began to withdraw its troops in 1989 and had completed the withdrawal by March 1990.

In May 1991, while on the campaign trail in Tamil Nadu, Rajiv Gandhi was assassinated by a female suicide bomber. The LTTE were immediately suspected and a thorough Central Bureau of Investigation inquiry concluded that Prabhakaran had orchestrated the attack in retaliation for the IPKF intervention. The LTTE have veered between strenuous denial and ambiguous apology in response to these accusations. Various conspiracy theories blamed Mossad, the CIA and the Indian mystic Chandraswami. Yet whether or not the LTTE were truly responsible, an international consensus holds that they were. The assassination virtually eradicated all support or even sympathy for the organization in India, both at the political as well as individual levels.

In the 1994 parliamentary elections, the UNP was defeated. Amidst great hope, the SLFP came to power on a peace platform. In October 1994, the LTTE made four demands: lifting the embargo on non-military goods to Jaffna, ending the ban on sea fishing, dismantling of the army base at Pooneryn, and allowing armed LTTE cadres to move freely in the Eastern Province. The government conceded the first two and said the other two could only occur after the cessation of hostilities. The LTTE accepted a ceasefire in January 1995, but at this point, neither side was willing to risk peace for fear of losing power to their internal rivals. Both sides began preparing for war.

The LTTE broke the ceasefire on April 19, 1995. Although started as a stalemate, it took six years of another bloody fighting before a cease-fire was possible. The LTTE suffered its biggest defeat in the war in July in the Weli Oya region. Weli Oya is the largest Sinhalese colony in Eastern Province. Unlike in 1993 when the LTTE successively destroyed the army base that was without a commander, this time, the army was prepared and killed hundreds of guerillas with little loss of life. The new government then pursued a policy of "war for peace". The government troops had succeeded in bringing Jaffna under government control by December 1995 and holding the city tied down many of the government forces has weakened them elsewhere.

After March, 1997, the government pushed a campaign to open a military supply route to the Jaffna Peninsula. If successful, the offensive would have split the LTTE forces and strengthen the government's bargaining position both with the LTTE and Tamil extremists. The result was a total failure. Government troops of 20,000 were simply not capable of doing what 50,000 men from IPKF had failed to do. The campaign created a great hardship for the people of the region and left another thousand youngmen dead. Bombs were exploded numerous times in populated cities. Among the 241 suicide bombers were one who attacked the central bank in Colombo in January 1996, one who bombed Sri Lankan World Trade

Centre in October 1997, one who detonated a truck bomb in Kandy in January 1998, damaging one of the holiest Buddhist shrines in the world, and those who committed suicide assault on Sri Lanka's international airport in July 24, 2001, causing $1 billion worth of damage. Terrorism not only intimidated the Sinhalese, it provoked a military and civilian backlash against innocent Tamils, which helped drive Tamils into their hands.

In February 2000, Norway was asked to mediate by both sides. After a unilateral ceasefire from December, 2000 to April, 2001, LTTE launched another offensive. By the end of that month, the LTTE had further advanced northwards and secured the Elephant Pass military complex.

Exhaustion with the war was building. The Sri Lankan military continued to grow in number but weakened in its will to fight. Up the end of 2002, the army had 5,141 deserters. It was becoming increasingly difficult for the army and the rebels to find new recruits to fight a war that looked endless. The rebels and the government signed a cease-fire agreement in February 2002.

This time, the ceasefire not only actually worked, but also had number of other achievements. Thousands of internally displaced families have returned home, food and medical support was supplied, and buildings were reconstructed while the politicians were doing the peace talks. Through six rounds of peace talks from September 2002 to April 2003, the situation made a dramatic progress. Although the government did not agree with LTTE's demand that they become an interim administration in the North and East, they agreed to share power within the federal system in which Tamils would have autonomy in the North and East of the country. The LTTE in turn, agreed to accept regional autonomy rather than a separate state. LTTE promised to stop taking on child soldiers.

For the next few years, the Sri Lanka Monitoring Mission (SLMM) has been working to keep the cease-fire going but recorded increasing number of cease-fire violations by the LTTE, and the government did not keep their promise to withdraw troops. LTTE has lost its power since then. In March 2004, Colonel Karuna betrayed the LTTE and went under government's control. The tsunami of 2004 damaged much of their equipments but above all, it lost the international support. After a few failures of two-party meetings in 2006, ceasefire violations rose to a point of low-intensity warfare by July. On April 25, a Tamil suicide bomber detonated a bomb at Army Headquarters, and another in June that killed 64 people on a bus. The government retaliated by air strikes on LTTE territory. In the later July, there was a "declaration of war" from Colombo and the ceasefire became "null and void".

Sri Lanka's Sinhala political establishment used Sinhala symbols in both war and peace with the LTTE. They were used and are being used to consolidate power of the Sinhala political class and to alienate the non-Sinhalese, particularly the Tamils. In fact, the politicization of ethnic differences began in the 1950s. Successive Sinhalese political parties formulated policies such as Sinhalese Language only, in 1956. This made Sinhala the only official language in state and public affairs and sharply discriminated against Tamil speakers. Then an educational standardization in 1972 allowed Sinhalese students to enter Science and Medicine schools with lower scores than the Tamil students. The Constitution of 1972 conferred special status to Buddhism both in the state and public corner.

Besides, peace packages of the successive Sinhala ruling class did not provide either genuine political autonomy, in clear political science language power-sharing democracy nor they had political guts or need to seek solution beyond the current unitary state structure, which is one of the major symbols of the Sinhala nation. The regime, led by Mr. Rajapaksa who came to power in 2005 by employing Sinhala symbols such as war against the LTTE and anti-peace slogans, successfully defeated the LTTE in May 2009 with the anti-Tamil statehood campaign and with the support of the global political, economic and military aid that were represented by both liberal and illiberals.

The global actors assumed that the regime would deliver peace. But it is plain fact that the regime in Colombo is not at any rate interested in building peace, and in fact, it is difficult for the regime to commence genuine peace when the Sinhala political elites had used the symbols in its war against the Tamils. The political elite may think it can retract its symbolic promises once in power. However, recent study on Sri Lanka's political outbidding strategies points that, when they have employed religion and/or ethnicity to maximize their votes or consolidate power, politicians find it next to impossible to backtrack on their divisive promises. And the same problem befalls their successors.

War destroys all possibilities for peace when it is being used by dominant groups against the weaker section of the masses or marginalized groups. The key nature of symbols in politics is that when they were being used for war against the others, it would not permit any politicians to use the same symbols to build peace. This is the result of politicization of symbols. In Sri Lanka, the Sinhala symbols (such as language, flag, and territory) are being politicized both for politics and war. Hence, politicians would find difficulties to fight the same symbols and to give justice to the ethnic others. This explains the difficulties pertaining to win peace under the Rajapaksa regime.

Evidences do not suggest that Rajapaksa regime has political will, for that matter maturity to challenge symbols and to broker peace with the ethnic Tamil minorities. In actual fact, peace is serious business than war, and when divided and conflict-ridden societies represented by power-hunger elites who resort to symbols to cling to power, peace would face severe challenges. The fact is that ethnic reconciliation is a serious political exercise, but given Sri Lanka's current political climate and inability to seek political solution beyond the unitary state structure would effectively wane any hope for true reconciliation of evocative democratic practices.

A Select Bibliography

Documents

- Amnesty International Report, Amnesty International Publication. London, 1987, 2002, 2007
- Census of Ceylon (1891)
- Ceylon State Council Debates, 1944
- Ceylon Parliament, Sessional Papers, 1951
- Ceylon Government Administrative Report, 1871
- Ceylon Citizenship Act, 1948
- Coolebrooke Cameron Commission Report, 1833
- Crown Land Encroachment Ordinance, 1840
- Donoughmore Commission Report, 1928
- Ethnic Studies Report, 2001-2009
- Encyclopaedia Britanica, 11th Edition, Cambridge, 1911 Foreign Affairs Records (FAR), Government of India, Ministery of External Affairs, New Delhi, 1987
- Government of Ceylon: Administrative Reports of the Commissioner of Labour for 1950 to 1961-62.
- Human Rights Watch Report, 2006
- International Commission of Jurists Report on Ethnic Violence in Sri Lanka.

- Jennings, Ivor The Constitution of Ceylon, London, 1953
- Lok Sabha Debates, Government of India, New Delhi, 1964, 1966, 1968
- Liberation Tigers of Tamil Eelam Publication, Sri Lanka, 1983
- Ministry of External Affairs: Brief on India-Sri Lanka Relations 26 February 2007, New Delhi: 2007
- Memorandumm of the All Ceylon Tamil Conference, 1937
- Parliamentary Papers; Great Britain 1850.
- Political Committee, LTTE, Liberation Tigers and Tamil Eelam Freedom Struggle, Madras: 1983.
- Proceedings of International Conference on Tamil National, Ottawa, Canada (1999)
- Pieres, Paulus Edward, Ceylon and the Portuguese 1505-1668, American Ceylon Mission Press, 1920
- Report of the Sixth Parliamentary General Elections in Ceylon 22-03-1965, Colombo, Government Publication Bureau, 1966.
- Robert Knox, An Historical Relations of the Island Ceylon.
- Report on Indian Labour Emigrating to Ceylon by N.E. Majoribanks and Khan Bahadur A.K.G., 1917
- Report of the Commission on Constitutional Reform, 1955
- Report of the Presidential Commission on Development Council, Government Publication Bureau, Colombo, 1990.
- Report of the Controller of Indian Immigrant Labour (1924).
- Sinhalese and Tamil as Official Languages – Report of the Select Committee of the State Sessional Paper No XXII, December 1946.
- Sinhala only Act, 1956
- Sri Lanka: The Ethnic Conflict-A Collection of Writings edited by Committee for Rational Development, New Delhi 1984.

Books

Austin, Dennis, *Democracy and Violence in India and Sri Lanka*, London, Royal Institute of International Affairs, 1994.

Bhaduri, Shankar, and Afsir Karim, *The Sri Lankan Crisis*, Lancer Paper 1, New Delhi, Lancer International, 1990.

Bond, George. *The Buddhist Revival in Sri Lanka: The Religious Tradition, Reinterpretation and Response*, Columbia, S.C.: University of South Carolina, 1988.

Brass, Paul, (ed.) *Ethnic Groups and the State*, Tatawa, N.J., Barnes and Noble, 1985. *Ethnicity and Nationalism: Theory and Practice*, New Delhi, Sage Publications, 1991.

Bullion, Alan J. *India, Sri Lanka and the Tamil Crisis 1976-1994: An International perspective*, London, Pinter Publishers, 1995.

Chattopadhyaya, H.P., *Indians in Sri Lanka*, Calcutta: OPS Publishers, 1979.

De Silva K.M. (ed.), *History of Ceylon*, University of Peradeniya, Peradeniya, 1973

_______ (ed.), *Sri Lanka: A Survey*, London, C. Hurst, 1977.

_______ , *A History of Sri Lanka*, London, C Hurst, 1981.

_______ (ed.) *Universal Franchise, 1931-1981: The Sri Lankan Experience*, Colombo, Department of Information, 1981.

_______, *Managing Ethnic Tensions in Multi Ethnic Societies: Sri Lanka, 1880-85*, Lanham, Md.: University Press of America, 1986.

_______ (ed.), *Sri Lanka: The Problems of Governance*, New Delhi, Konark, 1993.

_______ , *Regional Powers and Small State Security, India and Sri Lanka, 1977-1990*, Washington DC, Woodrow Wilson Center Press, 1995.

_______, *The Traditional Homelands of the Tamils, Separatist Ideology in Sri Lanka. A Historical Appraisal*, Kandy, International Centre for Ethnic Studies, 2nd revised ed, 1994.

_______ , K.M. (ed.) *Ethnic Conflict in Buddhist Societies: Sri Lanka, Thailand and Burma*, London, Pinter Publishers, 1988.

De Silva, R.J. May (ed.), *Internationalization of Ethnic Conflict*, London, Pinter Publishers, 1991.

De Silva, and S.W.R. de A Samarasinghe (eds.) *Ethnic Peace Accords and Ethnic Conflicts*, London, Pinter Publishers, 1993.

Dharmadasa, K N O. *Language, Religion and Ethnic Assertiveness: The Growth of Sinhalese Nationalism in Sri Lanka*, Ann Arbor, Michigan University Press, 1992.

Dharmadasa, (ed.), *National Language Policy in Sri Lanka, 1956-1996: Three Studies in Its Implementation*, ICES, Kandy, 1996.

Dissanayaka, T.D.S.A., *The Agony of Sri Lanka: An In-depth Account of the Racial Riots of July 1983*, Colombo, Swastika (Pvt) Ltd., 1993.

Dissanayaka, *The Dilemma of Sri Lanka*, Colombo, Swastika (Pvt) Ltd., 1993.

Dutta, V.P., *India's Foreign Policy in a Changing World*, New Delhi, Vikas Publishing House, 2003.

Farmer, B.H., *Ceylon: A Divided Nation*, Delhi: 1963.

Fernando, Tissa, and Robert N Kearney (ed), *Modern Sri Lanka: A Society in Transition*, Syracuse, Maxwell School of Citizenship and Public Affairs, 1979.

Gunaratna, Rohan, *Sri Lanka: A Lost Revolution? The Inside Story of the JVP*, Colombo, Institute of Fundamental Studies, 1990.

Gunaratna, *Indian Intervention in Sri Lanka: The Role of India's Intelligence Agencies*, Colombo, South Asian Network on Conflict Research, 1993.

Gupta, Babu Lal, *Political and Civil Status of Indians in Ceylon*, Agra, 1963.

Jacob, Lucy, M., *Sri Lanka from Dominion to Republic*, Delhi, 1973.

James Manor (ed.), *Sri Lanka in Change and Crisis*, London, 1984.

Jayatilleka, Dayan. *Sri Lanka. The Travails of a Democracy: Unfinished War, Protracted Crisis*, New Delhi, Vikas, 1995.

Jeyaratnam, Wilson, A., *Politics in Sri Lanka-1947-1979*, London,: Macmillan Press, 1979.

Jayawardena, Visakha Kumari, *Ethnic and Class Conflicts in Sri Lanka*, Colombo, Navagama Printers, 1986.

Jayaweera, Neville, *Sri Lanka: Towards a Multi-Ethnic Democracy?*, (Report of a fact-finding mission), Oslo, International Peace Research Institute, 1990.

Jayewardene, J.R., *Men and Memories: Autobiographical Recollections and Reflections*, New Delhi, Vikas, 1992.

Jennings, Sir Ivor, *The Constitution of Ceylon*, (3rd ed.), London, Oxford University Press, 1953.

Jiggins, Janice, *Caste and Family in the Politics of the Sinhalese 1947-1976*, Cambridge, Cambridge University Press, 1979.

Jupp, James, *Sri Lanka, Third World Democracy*, London, Frank Cass, 1978.

Kadian, Rajesh, *India's Sri Lanka Fiasco: Peace Keepers at War*, New Delhi, Vision Books, 1990.

Kapferer, Bruce, *Legends of People, Myths of State: Violence, Intolerance and Political Culture in Sri Lanka and Australia*, Washington D.C.: Smithsonian Institution Press, 1967.

Kearney, Robert N. *Communalism and Language in the Politics of Ceylon*, Durham, N.C., Duke University Press, 1967.

———, *The Politics of Ceylon* (Sri Lanka), Ithaca, N.Y., Cornell University Press, 1973.

Kemper, Steven. *The Presence of the Past: Chronicles, Politics and Culture in Sinhala Life*, Ithaca, N.Y., Cornell University Press, 1991.

Knox, Rebert, *An Historical Relations of the Island Ceylon*, London, 1681

Kodikara, Shelton U. *External Compulsions of South Asian Politics*, New Delhi, Sage, 1993.

———, *Foreign Policy of Sri Lanka*, 2nd ed., New Delhi, Chanakya Publications, 1992.

———, (ed.), *Indo-Sri Lanka Agreement of July 1987*, Colombo, University of Colombo, 1989.

———, *Indo-Ceylon Relations since Independence*, Colombo, Ceylon Institute of World Affairs, 1965.

Kotelawala, Sir John, *An Asian Prime Minister's Story*, 1956.

Kuppuswamy, Chellamuthu, Prabhakaran: *His life and struggle for Eelam*, 2009.

Little, David. Sri Lanka: *The Invention of Enmity*, Washington, D.C., United States Institute of Peace, 1994.

Manogaran, Chelvadurai. *Ethnic Conflict and Reconciliation in Sri Lanka*, Honolulu, University of Hawaii Press, 1987.

Manor, James, (ed.) *Sri Lanka in Change and Crisis*, London, Croom Helm, 1984.

_______ , *The Expedient Utopian: Bandaranaike and Ceylon*, Cambridge, Cambridge University Press, 1989.

Mendis, G.C., *The Early History of Ceylon*, Calcutta, 1947

_______ , *Ceylon Under the British*, (2nd edition) 1946

Muni, S.D. *Pangs of Proximity: India and Sri Lanka's Ethnic Crisis*, New Delhi, Sage Publications, 1993.

Narayan Swamy, M.R. *The Tiger Vanquished-LTTE's Story*, New Delhi, Sage Publication, 2010.

Navarathnam, C.S. *Tamil's and Ceylon*, Jaffna, 1971.

Narayan Swamy, M.R. *Tigers of Lanka: From Boys to Geurrillas*, Delhi, Konark, 1994.

O'Ballance, Edgar. *The Cyanide War: Tamil Insurrection in Sri Lanka 1973-88*, London, Brassey's, 1989.

Patel, S.K., *Indians in Sri Lanka*, Bombay, 1977.

Pfaffenberger, Brian. *Caste in Tamil Culture: The Religious Foundations of Sudra Domination in Tamil Sri Lanka*, Syracuse, Syracuse University, 1982.

Phadnis, Urmila, *Religion and Politics in Sri Lanka*, New Delhi, Manohar, 1976.

Pieres, Paulus Edward, *Ceylon and the Portuguese 1505-1668*, American Ceylon Mission Press 1920.

Raghavan, M.D., *Indian in Ceylonese History, Society and Culture*, Bombay, 1964.

Ratnatunga, Sinha. *The Politics of Terrorism: The Sri Lanka Experience*, Canberra, International Fellowship for Social and Economic Development, 1988.

Roberts, Michael W. *Caste Conflict and Elite Formation. The Rise of a Karava Elite in Sri Lanka, 1500-1931*, Cambridge, Cambridge University Press, 1982.

_______ , *Exploring Confrontation. Sri Lanka: Politics, Culture and History*, Victoria, Harwood Academic Publishers, 1994.

Ross, Russell R., and Andrea Matles Savada (eds.), *Sri Lanka: A Country Study*, Washington D.C., 1991.

Roy Chaudhury, P.C., *Sri Lanka – Lands and People of the World*, New Delhi, Sterling Publishers, 1985.

Ryan, Bryce. *Caste in Modern Ceylon*, New Brunswick, Rutgers University Press, 1953.

Seevaratnam, N. (ed.), *The National Question and the Indo-Sri Lanka Accord*, New Delhi, Konark, 1989.

Tambiah, Staniey J. *Sri Lanka: Ethnic Fratricide and the Dismantling of Democracy*, Chicago, University of Chicago Press, 1986.

_______, *Buddhism Betrayed? Religion, Politics and Violence in Sri Lanka*, Chicago, University of Chicago Press, 1986.

Thondaman, S. *My Life and Times, An Autobiography*, Vol. 1, Colombo, The Ceylon Workers' Congress, 1987;

Tiranagama, R., and others, *The Broken Palmyra: The Tamil Crisis in Sri Lanka, An Inside Account*, California, The Sri Lanka Studies Institute, 1990.

Vanniasingham, Somasundaram. *Sri Lanka: The Conflict Within*, New Delhi, Vikas, 1992.

Vijayavardhana, D.C. *The Revolt in the Temple*, Colombo, Sinha Publications, 1953.

Weerakoon, Bradman. *Premadasa of Sri Lanka: A Political Biography*, New Delhi, Vikas, 1992.

Wickremaratne, L.A. *Buddhism and Ethnicity in Sri Lanka: A Historical Analysis*, New Delhi, Vikas, 1995.

Wilson, A Jeyaratna. *Electoral Politics in an Emergent State: The Ceylon General Elections of May 1970*, Cambridge, Cambridge University Press, 1975.

_______, *Politics in Sri Lanka, 1947-1979*, London, Macmillan, 1979.

_______, *The Gaullist System in Asia, The Constitution of Sri Lanka*, 1978, London, Mc million, 1980.

_______, *The Break-up of Sri Lanka: The Sinhalese-Tamil Conflict*, Honolulu, University of Hawaii Press, 1988.

Warnapala, W.A. Wiswa. *Ethnic Strife and Politics in Sri Lanka: An Investigation into Demands and Responses*, New Delhi, Navrang, 1994.

Wriggins, W. Howard, *Ceylon: Dilemmas of a New Nation*, Princeton, N.J.: Princeton University Press, 1960.

Articles in Journal

Amunugama, Sarath. "Buddhaputra and Bhumiputra? Dilemma of Modern Sinhala Buddhist Monks in Relation to Ethnic and Political Conflict", *Religion* XXI (1991).

Balachanddran, P.K., 1999. "The Buddhist Monk Feels the Heat for Theory of Hindu-Muslim Takeover of Lanka", *Hindustan Times*, August 30.

Connor, Walker, "National Building or Nation Destroying", *World Politics*, XXIV(3) 1972.

Connor, "The Politics of Ethnonationalism", *Journal of International Affairs*, Vol.27, 1973.

Connor, "Ethnonationalism in the First World" in Milton J Esman (ed.), *Ethnic Conflict in the Wester World*, Ithaca, Cornell University Press, 1977.

Connor", A Nation is a Nation, is a State, is an Ethnic Group, is a ...", *Ethnic and Racial Studies*, 1(4) 1978.

Connor, "The Impact of Homelands upon Diasporas" in Gabriel Sheffer (ed), *Modern Diasporas in International Politics*, London, 1986.

Deendayal Upadhyaya, A Nation of the Refugees, *Organiser*, 9 November 1964.

De Silva, C.R. "The Constitution of the Second Republic of Sri Lanka (1978) and its Significance", *The Journal of Commonwealth and Comparative Politics*, XVII(2).

De Silva, H.L. "The Indo-Sri Lanka Agreement (1987) in the Perspective of Inter-State Relations", *Ethnic Studies Report*, Vol. X, No.2, July 1992.

De Silva, "Multi-Culturalism in Sri Lanka-Historical Legacy and Contemporary Political Reality", *Ethnic Studies Report*, 15(1), January 1997.

De Votta, Neil, "Illiberalism and Ethnic Conflict in Sri Lanka." *Journal of Democracy* 13(1), 2002.

_______, "Demography and Communalism in India", *Journal of International Affairs* 56(1), 2002.

Gooneratne Tilak, "The Present Situation in Sri Lanka", *Asian Affairs*, London: February 1986.

Halliday, F. "The Ceylonese Insurrection" in *New Left Review*, in October 1971, reprinted in R Blackburn (ed.), Explosion in a Sub-Continent, Harmondsworth, 1975.

Juergensmeyer, Mark. "What the Bhikkhu Said: Reflections on the Rise of Militant Religious Nationalism", *Religion*, 20, 1990.

Kearney, R.N. "Ethnic Conflict and the Tamil Separatist Movement in Sri Lanka", *Asian and Comparative Politics*, XII(1).

Khobragade, Vinod F., "Ethnic Politics in Sri Lanka-Political Solution to Tamil Cause and Military Solution to LTTE", Vol. 7, No. 11, New Delhi March 2009.

Obeyesekere, Ganobeyesekere, Gananath, "Religious Symbolism and Political Change in Ceylon", *Modern Ceylon Studies*, 1: 1970.

Peiris, G.H. "An Appraisal of the Concept of a Traditional Tamil Homeland in Sri Lanka", *Ethnic Studies Report*, IX(1).

Peiris, "Irrigation, Land Distribution and Ethnic Conflict in Sri Lanka: An Evaluation of Criticisms, with Special Reference to the Mahaveli Programme", *Ethnic Studies Report*, XII(1).

Peebles, Patrick. "Colonization and Ethnic Conflict in the Dry Zone of Sri Lanka", *Journal of Asian Studies*, 49, 1990.

Peiris, Roshan. "Rahula Hits Back", *Sunday Times* (Colombo), May 5, 1996.

Petersen, William, "Ethnicity in the World Today", *International Journal of Comparative Sociology*, XX(1&2) 1979.

Pfaffenberger, Brian. "The Cultural Dimension of Tamil Separatism in Sri Lanka", *Asian Survey*, XXI(12), pp. 1145-57.

Roberts, "Ethnic Conflict in Sri Lanka and Singhalese Perspectives: Barriers to Accommodation", *Modern Asian Studies*, VII(3).

Roberts, Michael, "Nationalism, the Past and The Present: The Case of Sri Lanka", (Review Essay) *Ethnic and Racial Studies*, Vol. 16 No. 1, January 1993.

Shah, Manbendra, "Citizenship Problem in Ceylon", *Indian Foreign Affairs*, Vol. XII, No. 5, May 1964.

Tilakaratne, Asanga. "Ethnic Conflict in Sri Lanka: Search for a Middle Position", *The Buddhist* 12, 1994.

Van Dyke, Vernon. "Self-Determination and Minority Rights", *International Studies Quarterly*, 111(3) 969.

Wickremesinghe, Ranil, "The Way to Resolve Sri Lanka's Political Crisis", *The Hindu*, 06-04-2007.

White, N.R. "Ethnicity, Culture and Cultural Pluralism", *Ethnic and Racial Studies*, Vol. (2) 1978.

Wilson, A.J. "The Tamil Federal Party in Ceylon Politics", *The Journal of Commonwealth Political Studies*, IV(2).

Young, Crawford, "The Temple of Ethnicity", *World Politics*, XXXV(4) 1983.

Newspapers

The Daily Mirror (Colombo)
The Hindustan Times (New Delhi)
The Hindu (New Delhi)
The Hindu (Chennai)
The Island (Colombo)
The Indian Express (New Delhi)
The Mirror (Colombo)
The Sunday Times (Colombo)
The Sunday Leader (Colombo)
The Sunday Observer (Colombo)
The Statesman (Jaffna)
The Times (London)
The Times of India (New Delhi)
The Tribune (Chandigarh)

Journals/Periodicals

Asian Survey (Berkeley, Calif)
Asian Review (London)
Christian Worker (Colombo)
Diplomatist (London)
The Economist (London)
Economic and Political Weekly (EPW) (Mumbai)

Frontline (Chennai)
Foreign Affairs (New York)
India Quarterly (New Delhi)
India Today (New Delhi)
International Studies (New Delhi)
Journal of International Affairs (New York)
Journal of Common Wealth Political Studies (Leicester, England)
Lanka Guardian (Colombo)
Orbis (Philadelphia)
South Asia Politics (New Delhi)

Index

Variety